CRIMINAL JUSTICE, LAW ENFORCEMENT AND CORRECTIONS

PERSPECTIVES ON JUVENILE OFFENDERS

CRIMINAL JUSTICE, LAW ENFORCEMENT AND CORRECTIONS

Incarceration and the Family: Issues, Effects and Approaches to Successful Reentry
United States Department of Health and Human Services
2009. ISBN: 978-1-60692-933-9

Gun Ownership and the Second Amendment
Pjeter D. Baldrige
2009. ISBN: 978-1-60692-226-2

Homicide Investigations
Allan B. Smythe
2009. ISBN: 978-1-60692-258-3

Digital Surveillance: Laws, Security and Related Issues
Joseph G. Massingale (Editor)
2009. ISBN: 978-1-60692-312-2

Mass Incarceration and Offender Reentry in the United States
Russell D. Javitze (Editor)
2009. ISBN: 978-1-60692-657-4

Homicide: Trends, Causes and Prevention
Randal B. Toliver and Ulrich R. Coyne (Editors)
2009. ISBN: 978-1-60741-625-8

Batterer Intervention: Program Approaches and Criminal Justice Strategies
Kerry Healey, Christine Smith,and Chris O'Sullivan
2009. ISBN: 978-1-60692-934-6
2009. ISBN: 978-1-60876-537-9 (E-book)

Revisiting and Enforcing the Crime Victims' Rights Act
Jorge S. Ehrlich (Editor)
2009. ISBN: 978-1-60741-231-1

Delinquency: Causes, Reduction and Prevention
Ozan Sahin and Joseph Maier (Editor)
2009. ISBN: 978-1-60741-558-9

Violent Crime and Prisons: Population, Health Conditions and Recidivism
Aidan Renshaw and Emelina Suárez (Editors)
2009. ISBN: 978-1-60741-668-5

Policing the Police: Knowledge Management in Law Enforcement
Petter Gottschalk
2009. ISBN: 978-1-60741-765-1
2009. ISBN: 978-1-60876-653-6 (E-book)

Selective Prosecution in the Federal Criminal Justice System?
Kevin H. Mabe (Editor)
2010. ISBN: 978-1-60692-684-0

Police and Augmented Reality Technology
Matthew D. Blount (Editor)
2010. ISBN: 978-1-60692-206-4

Police Guide for Responding to People with Mental Illness
Kjell Grönberg (Editor)
2010. ISBN: 978-1-60741-479-7

Mass Marketing and Consumer Fraud: Background, Issues and Data
Martin A. Parham (Editor)
2010. ISBN: 978-1-60692-793-9

Guidelines for Domestic FBI Operations
Carlo Bianchi (Editor)
2010. ISBN: 978-1-60692-798-4

Police Management: Professional Integrity in Policing
Petter Gottschalk
2010. ISBN: 978-1-60876-903-2

Digital Evidence in the Courtroom
John D. Nilsson (Editor)
2010. ISBN: 978-1-60741-803-0

Organized Crime in the U.S.
Wesley B. Knowles (Editor)
2010. ISBN: 978-1-60741-524-4

Revisiting the Social Contract: Community Justice and Public Safety
Kathleen Auerhahn and Caitlin J. McGuire
2010. ISBN: 978-1-60876-446-4

Domestic Violence: Law Enforcement Response and Legal Perspectives
Mario R. Dewalt (Editor)
2010. ISBN: 978-1-60876-774-8

Perspectives on Juvenile Offenders
Owen B. Hahn (Editor)
2010. ISBN: 978-1-60876-819-6

Not So Nice: Girls' Delinquency Issues
Adam P. Mawer (Editor)
2010. ISBN: 978-1-60876-268-2

White-Collar Criminals: Theoretical and Managerial Perspectives of Financial Crime
Peter Gottschalk
2010. ISBN: 978-1-61668-775-5
2010. ISBN: 978-1-61728-639-1 (E-book)

The Prison System and its Effects - Wherefrom, Whereto, and Why?
Antony Taylor
2010. ISBN: 978-1-61728-035-1
2010. ISBN: 978-1-61728-324-6 (E-book)

CRIMINAL JUSTICE, LAW ENFORCEMENT AND CORRECTIONS

PERSPECTIVES ON JUVENILE OFFENDERS

OWEN B. HAHN
EDITOR

Nova Science Publishers, Inc.
New York

LIBRARY OF CONGRESS CATALOGING-IN-PUBLICATION DATA

Perspectives on juvenile offenders / editor, Owen B. Hahn.
p. cm.
Includes index.
ISBN 978-1-60876-819-6 (softcover)
1. Juvenile justice, Administration of--United States. 2. Juvenile courts--United States. 3. Juvenile delinquency--United States. I. Hahn, Owen B.
HV9104.P453 2009
364.360973--dc22

2009045954

Published by Nova Science Publishers, Inc. † New York

CONTENTS

Preface		**ix**
Chapter 1	Characteristics of Juvenile Suicide in Confinement *Lindsay M. Hayes*	**1**
Chapter 2	Co-Occurrence of Substance Use Behaviors in Youth *Carl McCurley and Howard N. Snyder*	**37**
Chapter 3	Drug Offense Cases in Juvenile Courts, 1995-2004 *Anne Stahl*	**51**
Chapter 4	Juvenile Arrests 2007 *Charles Puzzanchera*	**57**
Chapter 5	Juvenile Justice: Legislative History and Current Legislative Issues *Kristin M. Finklea*	**87**
Chapter 6	Juvenile Transfer Laws: An Effective Deterrent to Delinquency? *Richard E. Redding*	**129**
Chapter 7	Psychiatric Disorders of Youth in Detention *Linda A. Teplin, Karen M. Abram, Gary M. McClelland, Amy A. Mericle, Mina K. Dulcan and Jason J. Washburn*	**157**
Chapter Sources		**193**
Index		**195**

PREFACE

Administering justice to juvenile offenders has largely been the domain of the states, and as a result of this the laws that pertain to juvenile offenders can vary widely from state to state. This book analyzes the current federal legislation that impacts the state juvenile justice systems. It also provides an overview of research on the deterrent effects of transferring youth from juvenile to criminal courts. In addition, this book examines juvenile suicides that occurred in confinement. It describes the demographic characteristics and social history of victims and examines the characteristics of the facilities in which the suicides took place. Drawing on this data, the researchers offer recommendations to prevent suicides in juvenile facilities. Moreover, this book analyzes the prevalence and overlap of substance-related behaviors among youth, with comparisons by age group, gender and race/ethnicity. The analysis shows that a youth who engages in one substance-related behavior is much more likely to engage in another. This book presents information that can help the juvenile justice system detect youth with psychiatric disorders and respond with an integrated system of services. This book consists of public documents which have been located, gathered, combined, reformatted, and enhanced with a subject index, selectively edited and bound to provide easy access.

Chapter 1- According to the Surgeon General of the United States, youth suicide is a national tragedy and a major public health problem (Carmona, 2005; U.S. Department of Health and Human Services, 1999). The suicide rate of young people (ages 15 to 24) tripled from 2.7 per 100,000 in 1950 to 9.9 per 100,000 in 2001 (Arias et al., 2003). More teenagers die from suicide than from cancer, heart disease, AIDS, birth defects, stroke, pneumonia and influenza, and chronic lung disease combined (U.S. Department of Health and Human Services, 1999). In addition, a national survey found that more than 3 million youth are at risk for suicide each year, with 37 percent of surveyed youth reporting that they attempted suicide during the previous 12 months (Substance Abuse and Mental Health Services Administration, 2001).

Although youth suicide in the general population has been identified as a significant public health problem, juvenile suicide in confinement has received little attention. The Office of Juvenile Justice and Delinquency Prevention (OJJDP) awarded a contract to the National Center on Institutions and Alternatives to conduct the first national survey of juvenile suicides in confinement. The primary goal of this effort was to determine the extent and distribution of juvenile suicides in confinement (i.e., juvenile detention centers, reception centers, training schools, ranches, camps, and farms).

The study identified 110 juvenile suicides occurring between 1995 and 1999. Data were analyzed for the 79 cases that had complete survey information. Of these 79 suicides, 42 percent occurred in training schools and other secure facilities, 37 percent in detention centers, 15 percent in residential treatment centers, and 6 percent in reception or diagnostic centers.

The survey gathered descriptive data on the demographic characteristics and social history of each victim, the characteristics of the incident, and the features of the juvenile facility in which the suicide took place. Particular attention was paid to each facility's implementation of suicide prevention programming. This Bulletin presents findings from the survey and offers recommendations for addressing this tragic problem.

Chapter 2 - This Bulletin analyzes the prevalence and overlap of substance-related behaviors among youth, with comparisons by age group, gender, and race/ethnicity. It uses data from the first two waves of the 1997 National Longitudinal Survey of Youth (NLSY97)—self-reports gathered in 1997 and 1998 from a nationally representative sample of youth ages 12–17. The data are from questions asking about drinking alcohol during the previous 30 days, using marijuana during the previous 30 days, and ever selling or helping to sell marijuana (pot, grass), hashish (hash) or other hard drugs such as heroin, cocaine, or LSD.

The central finding of the analysis is that, given one substance-related behavior, other substance-related behaviors became much more likely. For example, 9% of all youth ages 12–17 reported marijuana use and 8% said they had sold drugs. Among youth who reported drinking alcohol (23% of all youth ages 12–17), the level of marijuana use was 32% and the level of drug selling was 23%. In contrast, among youth ages 12–17 who did not report recent alcohol use, the level of marijuana use was 2% and the level of drug selling was 3%. Other findings include:

- Of youth who reported marijuana use, 81% said they drank alcohol and 45% said they had sold drugs.
- Of youth who reported drug selling, 68% said they drank alcohol and 54% reported marijuana use. In contrast, among youth who said they had not sold drugs, 19% reported drinking alcohol and 6% reported using marijuana.
- Among those who sold drugs, both white and Hispanic youth were more likely than African Americans to also report alcohol use; white youth who sold drugs were also more likely than African Americans who sold drugs to report using marijuana.

Chapter 3 - In 2004, juvenile courts in the United States handled an estimated 193,700 delinquency cases in which a drug offense was the most serious charge. Between 1991 and 2004, the number of cases involving drug offenses that juvenile courts handled more than doubled. Drug offense cases accounted for 12% of the delinquency caseload in 2004, compared with 7% in 1985.

Chapter 4 - In 2007, law enforcement agencies in the United States made an estimated 2.18 million arrests of persons under age 18.* Overall, there were 2% fewer juvenile arrests in 2007 than in 2006, and juvenile violent crime arrests declined 3%, reversing a recent upward trend. Juvenile arrest rates, particularly Violent Crime Index rates, had increased in 2005 and again in 2006 amid fears that the Nation was on the brink of another juvenile crime wave. These latest data show increases in some offense categories but declines in most— with most changes being less than 10% in either direction.

These findings are drawn from data that local law enforcement agencies across the country report to the FBI's Uniform Crime Reporting (UCR) Program. Based on these data, the FBI prepares its annual *Crime in the United States* statistical compilation, which summarizes crimes known to the police and arrests made during the reporting calendar year. This information is used to describe the extent and nature of juvenile crime that comes to the attention of the justice system. Other recent findings from the UCR Program include the following:

- Juveniles accounted for 16% of all violent crime arrests and 26% of all property crime arrests in 2007.
- Juveniles were involved in 12% of all violent crimes cleared in 2007 and 18% of property crimes cleared.

---

* Throughout this Bulletin, youth under age 18 are referred to as juveniles. See Notes on page 12.

- In 2007, 11% (1,810) of all murder victims were under age 18. More than one-third (35%) of all juvenile murder victims were under age 5, but this proportion varied widely across demographic groups.
- The juvenile murder arrest rate in 2007 was 4.1 arrests per 100,000 juveniles ages 10 through 17. This was 24% more than the 2004 low of 3.3, but 72% less than the 1993 peak of 14.4.
- Between 1998 and 2007, juvenile arrests for aggravated assault decreased more for males than for females (22% vs. 17%). During this period, juvenile male arrests for simple assault declined 4% and female arrests increased 10%.
- In 2007, although black youth accounted for just 17% of the youth population ages 10 through 17, black juveniles were involved in 51% of juvenile Violent Crime Index arrests and 32% of juvenile Property Crime Index arrests.
- The 2007 arrest rates for Violent Crime Index offenses were substantially lower than the rates in the 1994 peak year for every age group under 40.

Chapter 5 - Juvenile justice in the United States has predominantly been the province of the states and their localities. The first juvenile court in America was founded in 1899 in Cook County, Illinois, and, by 1925, all but two states had established juvenile court systems. The mission of these early juvenile courts was to rehabilitate young delinquents instead of just punishing them for their crimes; in practice, this led to marked procedural and substantive differences between the adult and juvenile court systems in the states, including a focus on the offenders and not the offenses, and rehabilitation instead of punishment.

The federal government began to play a role in the states' juvenile justice systems in the 1960s and 1970s. In 1974, Congress passed the first comprehensive piece of juvenile justice legislation, the Juvenile Justice and Delinquency Prevention Act (JJDPA). The JJDPA had three main components: it created a set of institutions within the federal government that were dedicated to coordinating and administering federal juvenile justice efforts; it established grant programs to assist the states with setting up and running their juvenile justice systems; and it promulgated core mandates that states had to adhere to in order to be eligible to receive grant funding. Although the JJDPA has been amended several times over the past 30 years, its basic shape remains similar to that of its original conception.

As it was passed in 1974, the JJDPA focused largely on preventing juvenile delinquency and on rehabilitating juvenile offenders. Subsequent revisions to the act added sanctions and accountability measures to some existing federal grant programs, and new grant programs to the act's purview. In altering the JJDPA to include a greater emphasis on punishing juveniles for their crimes, Congress has essentially followed the lead of the states. During the 1 980s and 1 990s, most states revised their juvenile justice systems to include more punitive measures and to allow juveniles to be tried as adults in more instances. This has marked a significant change in the philosophy of the juvenile justice system, both at the state level and at the federal level, from its original conception. Juvenile justice in general has thus moved away from emphasizing the rehabilitation of juveniles and toward a greater reliance on sanctioning them for their crimes.

Authorization of the JJDPA's main provisions expired at the end of FY2007 and FY2008, but its major programs have continued to receive appropriations. Reauthorization is now an issue confronting the 111th Congress. Policy issues associated with its reauthorization include what the best federal response to juvenile violence and juvenile crime should be; whether the system should focus on the rehabilitation of juvenile offenders or on holding juvenile offenders accountable for their actions; and whether the grant programs as currently comprised represent the best way to support juvenile justice efforts in the states.

This report will be updated as circumstances warrant.

Chapter 6 - Beginning in the 1980s, many States passed legal reforms designed to get tough on juvenile crime. One important reform was the revision of transfer (also called waiver or certification) laws (Griffin, 2003) to expand the types of offenses and offenders eligible for transfer from the juvenile court for trial and sentencing in the adult criminal court.[1] These reforms lowered the minimum age for transfer, increased the number of transfer-eligible offenses, or expanded prosecutorial discretion and reduced judicial discretion in transfer decisionmaking (Fagan and Zimring, 2000; Redding, 2003, 2005). In 1979, for example, 14 States had automatic transfer statutes requiring that certain juvenile offenders be tried as adults; by 1995, 21 States had such laws, and by 2003, 31 States (Steiner and Hemmens, 2003). In addition, the age at which juvenile court jurisdiction ends was lowered to 15 or 16 years in 13 States (see Snyder and Sickmund, 2006), although very recently, some States have reduced the scope of transfer laws (Bishop, 2004), and one State has raised the age at which juvenile court jurisdiction ends from 16 to 18.

In the wake of these legislative changes, the number of youth convicted of felonies in criminal courts and incarcerated in adult correctional facilities has increased (Redding, 2003), reaching a peak in the mid-1990s and then declining somewhat (Snyder and Sickmund, 2006) due, in part, to the decrease in juvenile crime. An estimated 4,100 youth were committed to State adult prisons in 1999, representing 1 percent of new prison commitments (Snyder and Sickmund, 2006). Sixty-one percent of these youth were incarcerated for person offenses, 23 percent for property offenses, 9 percent for drug offenses, and 5 percent for public order offenses (e.g., weapons possession) (Snyder and Sickmund, 2006). Transferred juveniles, particularly those convicted of violent offenses, typically receive longer sentences than those sentenced in the juvenile court for similar crimes (Bishop, 2000; Kupchik, Fagan, and Liberman, 2003; Myers, 2005; Virginia Department of Criminal Justice Services, 1996). But, they may be released on bail for a considerable period of time while they await trial in the criminal court (Myers, 2005), and many youth incarcerated in adult facilities serve no longer than the maximum time they would have served in a juvenile facility (Bishop, 2000; Fritsch, Caeti, and Hemmens, 1996; Myers, 2001). Seventy-eight percent were released from prison before their 21st birthday, and 95 percent were released before their 25th birthday, with an average of 2 years, 8 months of time served on their sentences (Snyder and Sickmund, 2006).

Chapter 7 - The juvenile justice system faces a significant challenge in identifying and responding to the psychiatric disorders of detained youth. In 2001, more than 104,000 juvenile offenders were in custody in juvenile residential placement facilities (Sickmund, Sladky, and Kang, 2004). Understanding the psychiatric disorders of juvenile detainees is an important step toward meeting their needs. Providing such youth with psychiatric services may be critical to breaking the cycle of recidivism. Without sound data on the prevalence of psychiatric disorders, however, defining the best strategies to use and allocating the juvenile justice system's scarce mental health resources are difficult.

In: Perspectives on Juvenile Offenders
Editors: Owen B. Hahn
ISBN: 978-1-60876-819-6

Chapter 1

CHARACTERISTICS OF JUVENILE SUICIDE IN CONFINEMENT

Lindsay M. Hayes
Office of Justice Programs, U.S. Dept. of Justice

According to the Surgeon General of the United States, youth suicide is a national tragedy and a major public health problem (Carmona, 2005; U.S. Department of Health and Human Services, 1999). The suicide rate of young people (ages 15 to 24) tripled from 2.7 per 100,000 in 1950 to 9.9 per 100,000 in 2001 (Arias et al., 2003). More teenagers die from suicide than from cancer, heart disease, AIDS, birth defects, stroke, pneumonia and influenza, and chronic lung disease combined (U.S. Department of Health and Human Services, 1999). In addition, a national survey found that more than 3 million youth are at risk for suicide each year, with 37 percent of surveyed youth reporting that they attempted suicide during the previous 12 months (Substance Abuse and Mental Health Services Administration, 2001).

Although youth suicide in the general population has been identified as a significant public health problem, juvenile suicide in confinement has received little attention. The Office of Juvenile Justice and Delinquency Prevention (OJJDP) awarded a contract to the National Center on Institutions and Alternatives to conduct the first national survey of juvenile suicides in confinement. The primary goal of this effort was to determine the extent and distribution of juvenile suicides in confinement (i.e., juvenile detention centers, reception centers, training schools, ranches, camps, and farms).

The study identified 110 juvenile suicides occurring between 1995 and 1999. Data were analyzed for the 79 cases that had complete survey information. Of these 79 suicides, 42 percent occurred in training schools and other secure facilities, 37 percent in detention centers, 15 percent in residential treatment centers, and 6 percent in reception or diagnostic centers.

The survey gathered descriptive data on the demographic characteristics and social history of each victim, the characteristics of the incident, and the features of the juvenile facility in which the suicide took place. Particular attention was paid to each facility's implementation of suicide prevention programming. This Bulletin presents findings from the survey and offers recommendations for addressing this tragic problem.

Victim's Demographic Characteristics

Race, Sex, and Age

More than two-thirds of the suicide victims identified in the survey were Caucasian.

A Message from OJJDP

Suicide is always tragic, but it is particularly so when the victim is young. The tragedy of young lives cut short by suicide poses a significant public health challenge. According to data from the Centers for Disease Control and Prevention, suicide is the third leading cause of death among youth 15 to 24 years old.

While experts recognize the need to intervene on behalf of vulnerable youth, little research has been conducted on the suicides of youth held in detention. To address this deficiency, the Office of Juvenile Justice and Delinquency Prevention has sponsored the first national survey of juvenile suicides in confinement.

This Bulletin examines 110 juvenile suicides that occurred in confinement between 1995 and 1999. It describes the demographic characteristics and social history of victims and examines the characteristics of the facilities in which the suicides took place. Drawing on this data, the researchers offer recommendations to prevent suicides in juvenile facilities.

The findings reported in these pages present serious challenges for healthcare and correctional professionals who work with confined youth and for administrators charged with ensuring the security and safety of youth in detention. Preventing juvenile suicides in confinement is a critical responsibility. The information provided in this Bulletin is intended to inform such endeavors.

ABOUT THE SURVEY

In August 1999, the National Center on Institutions and Alternatives was awarded a grant from the Office of Juvenile Justice and Delinquency Prevention to conduct the first national survey on juvenile suicide in confinement.[a] The primary goal of the project was to determine the extent and distribution of juvenile suicides in confinement and to gather descriptive data on the demographic characteristics of each victim, the characteristics of the incident, and the characteristics of the juvenile facility that sustained the suicide. A report of the survey's findings would serve as a resource for juvenile justice practitioners to expand their knowledge and for juvenile correctional administrators to create and/or revise policies and training curriculums on suicide prevention. Data collection occurred in two phases.

Phase 1

During phase 1, a one-page survey instrument and cover letter was sent to directors of 1,178 public and 2,634 private juvenile facilities in the United States.[b] Each of the 3,812 facility directors was asked to complete the survey if the facility experienced a juvenile suicide between 1995 and 1999.[c] Similar to OJJDP's Conditions of Confinement study (Parent et al., 1994), the project surveyed facilities that housed juveniles in more traditional types of confinement—juvenile detention centers, reception centers, training schools, ranches, camps, and farms—operated by state and local governments and private organizations.[d] Excluded from the project were open, physically unrestricted residential programs for juveniles such as shelters, halfway houses, and group homes. Phase 1 identified 110 juvenile suicides occurring between 1995 and 1999. The suicides were distributed among 38 states.

Phase 2

Once facilities that had experienced a suicide during the 5-year study period were identified, phase 2 of the survey process was initiated. It included dissemination of a seven-page survey instrument to the directors of the facilities that sustained suicides. The survey instrument was designed to collect readily available data on three types of characteristics:

- Demographic and other victim characteristics including age, sex, race, living arrangement, current offense(s), prior offense(s), legal status (detained, committed, other), length of confinement, drug/alcohol intoxication at confinement, history of room confinement, substance abuse history, medical/mental health history, physical/sexual abuse history, and history of suicidal behavior.
- Incident characteristics including date, time, and location of suicide, and housing assignment, (e.g., single or multiple occupancy) room confine- ment status, method and instrument used, time span between last contact and finding victim, and possible precipitating factors of the suicide.
- Facility characteristics including facility type, facility ownership (e.g., state, county, private), capacity/population at time of suicide, and suicide prevention components in use (written policy, intake screening, staff training in suicide prevention and cardiopulmonary resuscitation, observation levels, safe housing, and mortality review).

The phase 2 survey instruments and cover letters were mailed to directors of the 83 facilities that sustained the 110 suicides. Respondents provided com- pleted surveys on 79 suicides.

Data Limitations

Given the epidemiological data regarding youth suicide in the community, coupled with the increased risk factors associated with confinement, the reported number of suicides in this study would appear low. However, this study identified more deaths per year than a contemporary national census of juvenile facilities (OJJDP, 2002), and many experts believe that facility self-reporting" of juvenile suicides in custody results in underestimates of the problem (Sullivan, 1995; Twedt, 2001b). Despite concerted efforts by project staff to locate all possible juvenile suicides during the 5-year study period, whether every death was identified remains uncertain.

Approximately 13 percent of the reported suicides in this study were identified through nontraditional sources (including newspaper articles and the project director's consultation with facilities sustaining the deaths). In addition, more than one-third of the reported suicides were unknown to any state agency (e.g., departments of juvenile corrections or agencies responsible for licensing and regulatory services). Most of the deaths that were unknown to state agencies occurred in either county detention centers or private residential treat- ment centers.[e] Many of the reported suicides in this study were also unknown to many child advocacy agencies. The fact that any suicide occurring within a juvenile facility throughout the United States could remain outside the purview of a regulatory agency should be cause for great concern within the juvenile justice community.

For More Information

For more information about the survey methodology, including copies of the phase 1 and phase 2 survey instruments, see the OJJDP report, Juvenile Suicide in Confinement: A National Survey (Hayes, 2006). The report is available on the OJJDP Web site www.ojp.usdoj.gov/ojjdp.

Notes

a. The National Center on Institutions and Alternatives was assisted on the project by two prominent national juvenile justice organizations (the National Juvenile Detention Association and the Council of Juvenile Correctional Administrators) and a consultant team com- posed of four prominent juvenile justice practitioners and researchers (G. David Curry, Ph.D., Robert E. DeComo, Ph.D., Barbara C. Dooley, Ph.D., and David W. Roush, Ph.D.). In addition, Cedrick Heraux, a doctoral student at Michigan State University, provided both data entry and data analysis support to the project.

b. Facilities were identified through OJJDP's Census of Juveniles in Residential Placement (OJJDP, 1999). A small percentage of facilities were either closed or could not be located, and thus presumed to be closed.

c. To encourage a high rate of response, the cover letter was co-signed by officials of both the National Juvenile Detention Association and the Council of Juvenile Correctional Administrators, and business reply envelopes were enclosed with the survey nstruments.

d. By definition, detention centers hold juveniles for short periods of time in a physically restrictive environment pending juvenile court action, or following adjudication pending disposition, placement, or transfer. Reception centers are short-term facilities that hold juveniles committed by courts and conduct screening and assessment to assign them to appropriate facilities. Training schools are long-term facili-ties in which treatment and programming are provid- ed in an environment with strict physical and staff controls. Ranches, camps, and farms are long-term residential facilities that do not require the strict confinement of a training school, often allowing offenders greater contact with the community. This last category includes "residential treatment centers" and "boot camps."

e. Although the study found that 27 percent of the total number of suicides (N=110) occurred in private facilities, many of which were residential treatment centers, two-thirds (67 percent) of private facilities did not respond to survey requests.

This finding is consistent with suicides that occur each year in the general population (Arias et al., 2003). One previous study found that Caucasian youth held in detention attempted suicide at a rate approximately 3.5 times that of African American youth (Kempton and Forehand, 1992). Although African American and Hispanic youth comprised approximately 39 percent and 18 percent, respectively, of the confined juvenile population through-out the country (Sickmund and Wan, 2001),[1] they represented only 11 percent and 6 percent of the victims in this study. Caucasian and American Indian youth, on the other hand, comprised approximately 38 percent and 2 percent, respectively, of the confined juvenile population throughout the country, but 68 percent and 11 percent of the victims in this study. The causes of these disproportionate relationships are outside the purview of this analysis.

A substantial majority (80 percent) of the victims were male. Given the fact that more than 80 percent of all juveniles confined in the United States are male (Sickmund and Wan, 2001), these findings are not surprising.

More than 70 percent of the victims were between the ages of 15 and 17 (figure 1). The average (mean) age was 15.7, with one victim as young as 12 and another as old as 20. These findings are consistent with data from the Census of Juveniles in Residential Placement (Sickmund and Wan, 2001).

Living Arrangement before Confinement

More than a third (38 percent) of suicide victims were living with one parent at the time of their confinement. Slightly less than one quarter (23 percent) of the victims were living with both parents. Other living arrangements included community placement (11 percent), other relative (9 percent), foster parent or guardian (8 percent), or adoptive parents (5 percent). Two victims were living on their own (3 percent), and the living arrangements of the other three victims were unknown (4 percent).

Victim's Offense and Confinement Status

Most Serious Offense[2]

A significant majority (70 percent) of victims were confined for nonviolent (i.e., nonperson) offenses, with property offenses accounting for the highest percentage of victim confinement (figure 2). In addition, the status, probation violation, and public order categories combined represented more than a third (34 percent) of the offenses. Person offenses accounted for 30 percent of victim confinement; only 3 percent of victims were confined on drug offenses. Approximately 40 percent (13 of 33) of victims housed in a training school or other secure facility were confined for a person offense.

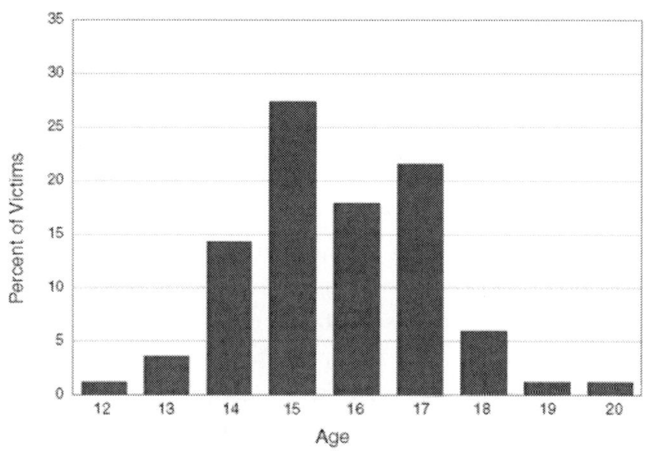

Figure 1. Suicides in Juvenile Facilities 1995–1999, by Age of Victim.

With only slight variance, these findings were consistent with data on the confined juvenile population throughout the country. For example, person offenses accounted for 35 percent and property offenses accounted for 29 percent of all confined juveniles throughout the country (Sickmund and Wan, 2001). However, whereas the status, probation violation, and public order categories combined represented 27 percent of all confined juveniles, these categories represented 34 percent of the victims in this study.

At confinement, 39 percent of victims had a second charge. Property offenses accounted for the majority (52 percent) of the additional charges, followed by person offenses (19 percent). Status, pro-bation violation, and public order offenses combined represented 29 percent of additional charges.

A substantial majority (79 percent) of suicide victims had prior offenses. Of the victims who had a history of offenses, most committed crimes of a nonviolent nature, with property offenses the most common (50 percent). Status, probation violation, and public order offenses combined represented 23 percent of the most serious prior offenses; person offenses accounted for 23 percent of victims' prior offenses.

Confinement Status

Two-thirds (67 percent) of victims were committed at the time of death (figure 3). This finding was significantly different from a national study on jail suicides that found the overwhelming majority of victims were on detention status at the time of death (Hayes, 1989). The finding was, however, somewhat consistent with national data on confined juveniles that found 74 percent of youth were committed (Sickmund and Wan, 2001). Not surprisingly, the vast majority (79 percent) of victims held in detention centers were on detention status and all training school/secure facility victims were committed at the time of death.

Less than 4 percent of juvenile suicides occurred within the first 24 hours of confinement (and all of these deaths occurred in detention centers). This finding significantly differed from a national study on jail suicides that found more than 50 percent of suicides took place within the first 24 hours, with almost a third occurring within the first 3 hours (Hayes, 1989). The deaths reported in this national survey of juvenile suicide in confinement were distributed fairly evenly during a more than 12-month period. For example, the same number of suicides (13) occurred within the first 3 days of confinement as occurred after more than 10 months of confinement.[3] Nearly a third (32 percent) of suicides occurred within 1 to 4 months of confinement. However, all detention center suicides occurred within the first 4 months of confinement, with more than 40 percent occurring within the first 72 hours, while a significant majority (73 percent) of training school/secure facility suicides occurred 3 months or more following confinement.[4]

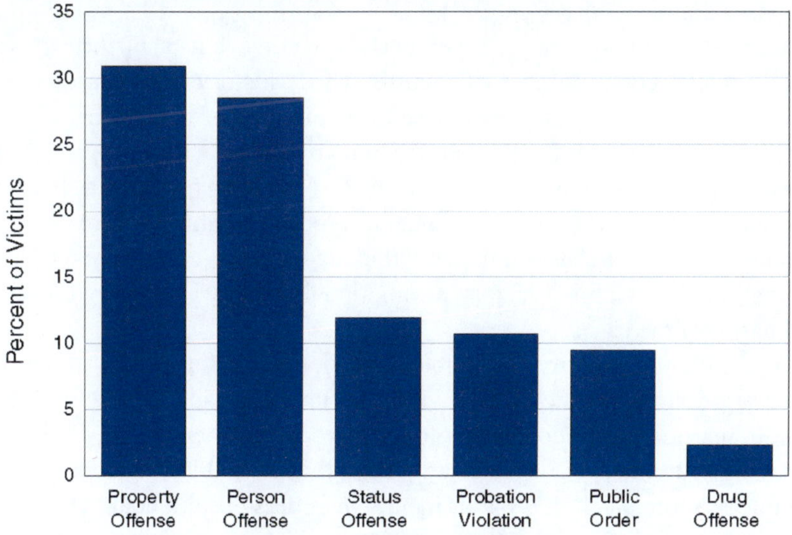

Figure 2. Suicides in Juvenile Facilities 1995–1999, by Victim's Most Serious Offense.

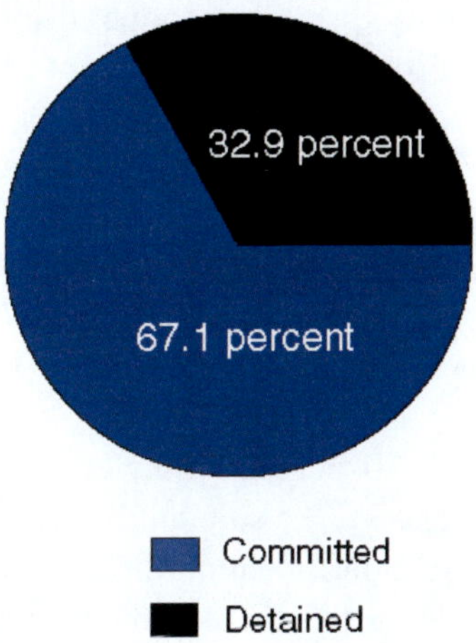

Figure 3. Suicides in Juvenile Facilities 1995–1999, by Victim's Confinement Status.

Victim's History

Slightly more than one-third of victims had a history of physical abuse (figure 4), with an immediate family member (e.g., father or stepfather) as the perpetrator in the majority of cases (20 of 27). The victim's history of physical abuse was unknown in approximately 20 percent of cases (see "Unknown Responses and Detention Centers").

More than one-quarter (28 percent) of victims had a history of sexual abuse, with an equal number of victims whose history of sexual abuse was unknown. For those who were abused, an immediate family member (e.g., father or stepfather) was the perpetrator in many cases.

Somewhat less than half the victims (44 percent) had a history of emotional abuse. The most frequent types of abuse were excessive punishment, neglect/abandonment, verbal abuse, and other types of family dysfunction. The victim's history of emotional abuse was unknown in almost one-quarter of the cases.

A significant majority (73 percent) of victims had a history of substance abuse. Approximately one-third of victims with a substance abuse history used alcohol, marijuana, or cocaine before their confinement. This finding was consistent with other recent data suggesting that two- thirds of confined youth have one or more alcohol, drug, or mental disorders (Teplin et al., 2002).

Many suicide victims (66 percent) had a history of mental illness, and a majority (65 percent) of victims with a history of mental illness were suffering from depression at the time of death. Other mental illnesses reported included attention deficit/hyperactivity disorder, conduct disorder, post-traumatic stress disorder, and psychotic disorder (54 percent of victims were taking psychotropic medication at time of death).[5] Although other research also indicates that a high percentage of youth in the juvenile justice system suffer from at least one mental disorder and have higher rates of mental disorders than youth in the general population (Cocozza and Skowyra, 2000), it should be noted that, in the current study, substance abuse disorder (which accounts for a sizable percentage of psychiatric disorders) was considered separately from mental disorders.

More than two-thirds (70 percent) of victims had a history of suicidal behavior. The most frequent type of suicidal behavior was suicide attempt (46 percent), followed by suicidal ideation/threat (31 percent), and suicidal gesture/self-mutilation (24 percent). Although other research shows that between 8 percent and 52 percent of confined youth have a history of suicidal behavior (see "Self-Injurious Behavior in Juvenile Facilities," on page 7), findings from this national survey suggest that confined youth who died by suicide have a higher incidence of prior suicidal behavior than those confined youth who engage in suicidal behavior but do not die. Suicide victims in detention centers, compared with other facility types, were less likely to have a known history of suicidal behavior (52 percent versus 80 percent in all other facilities).

Few (19 percent) victims had a known history of other medical problems. Allergies and asthma were common types of medical problems found in the few victims with documented medical conditions.

SUICIDE INCIDENT CHARACTERISTICS

Date and Time

Contrary to common belief, certain seasons of the year and holidays did not correlate with a higher number of suicides. Although more than 30 percent of all deaths occurred during the months of January and May, suicides were distributed throughout the year. Further, no statistically significant difference existed regarding the day of the week on which suicides occurred.

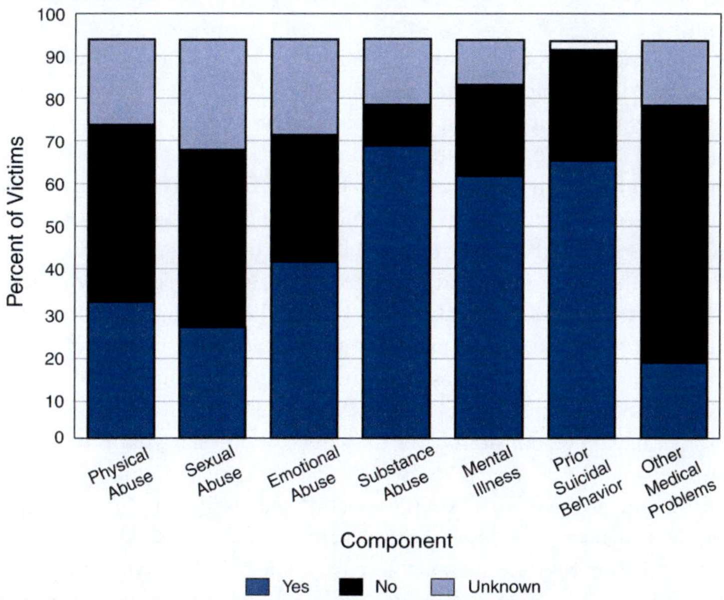

Figure 4. Suicides in Juvenile Facilities 1995–1999, by Victim's History.

Research on jail suicide has found that deaths are more prevalent when staff supervision is reduced. For example, less than 20 percent of deaths in a national study of jail suicides occurred during the 6-hour period between 9 a.m. and 3 p.m., a major portion of the day shift (Hayes, 1989). As shown in figure 5, findings from this study indicate that 71 percent of suicides occurred during traditional waking hours (6 a.m. to 9 p.m.), whereas 29 percent of suicides occurred during traditional nonwaking hours (9 p.m. to 6 a.m.). In addition, approximately half (51 percent) of suicides occurred during the 6-hour period between 6 p.m. and midnight, and almost a third (29 percent) occurred between 6 p.m. and 9 p.m.

Unknown Responses and Detention Centers

A high percentage of unknown responses to survey questions relating to several personal characteristics of the victims (including histories of substance abuse, medical problems, emotional abuse, physical abuse, sexual abuse, and mental illness) came from detention center respondents.* In addition, suicide victims housed in detention centers had a lower percentage of reported histories of suicidal behavior, suggesting that perhaps these facilities fail to inquire about such history. Finally, although the study found that many facility types lacked comprehensive suicide prevention programming at the time of the suicide, detention centers had the lowest percentage of such programming (approximately 10 percent).

According to the National Juvenile Detention Association, juvenile detention is defined as "the temporary and safe custody of juveniles who are accused of conduct subject to the jurisdiction of the court who require a restricted environment for their own and the community's protection while pending legal action" (National Juvenile Detention Association, 1990:1). Because of the lack of available community resources, and due to their unique ability to provide physical custody, detention centers often bear the responsibility for troubled youth. However, these centers are both ill-equipped and underresourced to provide anything more than basic healthcare services on a short-term basis. Although the temporary nature of the detention center experience may help to explain some of the survey findings regarding these types of facilities, such a distinction should not be viewed as a mitigating factor for suicide prevention. All juvenile facilities, regardless of size and mission, have a responsibility for the safety of all their youth, including those at risk for self-harm.

The findings from this study support the National Juvenile Detention Association's position that youth with severe mental ill ness should be provided services in "the appropriate therapeutic environment . . . when juvenile detention facilities are forced to house youth with severe mental health issues, [the

Association] promotes the provision of adequate services by appropriately trained and licensed specialists" (National Juvenile Detention Association, 2001). More importantly, the findings suggest that the significant deficiencies in intake screening and overall suicide prevention programming within detention centers experiencing suicides warrant immediate attention. Resources need to be channeled to all juvenile facilities throughout the country, particularly detention centers, to ensure that any agency housing a juvenile provides basic, yet comprehensive, suicide prevention programming.

* Communication among agencies also appeared to be a problem in many cases. Surveys were received from several detention centers in which respondents complained that they had been temporarily "holding" the victim for another jurisdiction (e.g., state correctional facility, probation office) and knew little, if anything, about the youth. As one facility director stated, "I do not know the answers to some of these questions because the child was not from our county. He was being housed here in a state-contract bed."

Method, Instrument, and Anchoring Device

The survey found that all but one victim used hanging as the method of suicide. (The sole victim of other means absconded from the facility and ran in front of a passing train.) The vast majority (72 percent) of these victims (n=78) used bedding (e.g., sheet, blanket) as the instrument to hang themselves. Clothing (13 percent), belts (5 percent), and shoelaces (5 percent) were used to a lesser degree. Other instruments included a towel and a bag. Suicide victims used a variety of anchoring devices, including door hinges/knobs, air vents, bedframes, window frames, closet rods, sprinkler heads, toilets, sinks, and television stands.

Intoxication

None of the 79 victims was under the influence of alcohol or drugs at the time of suicide. This finding is in stark contrast to a national study on jail suicides that found more than 60 percent of adult suicide victims were intoxicated at the time of their suicide (Hayes, 1989).

Room Assignment

Three-quarters (75 percent) of victims were assigned to single occupancy rooms at the time of suicide. The remainder (25 percent) were assigned to multiple occupancy rooms. No significant differences existed between room assignments and the types of facilities where the suicides occurred.

Room Confinement

For purposes of this study, room confinement was defined as a "behavioral sanction imposed on youth that restricted movement for varying amounts of time." It included, but was not limited to, isolation, segregation, time-out, or a quiet room. Room confinement did not include youth assigned to their room during traditional nonwaking hours (9 p.m. to 6 a.m.).

Most (62 percent) suicide victims had a history of room confinement. The circumstances that led to room confinement included threat or actual physical abuse of staff or peers (41 percent), verbal abuse of staff or peers (26 percent), failure to follow program rules or inappropriate behavior (26 percent), and other (7 percent), which included two cases of youth involved in gang activity and one case of a standard protocol for new intake.

Approximately half the suicide victims were on room confinement status at the time of death.[6] Compared to other facility types, a much smaller percentage (17 percent) of suicide victims housed in residential treatment centers were on room confinement status at the time of death.

In addition, 85 percent of victims who died by suicide while on room confinement status died during waking hours (6 a.m. to 9 p.m.), a percentage found to be higher than that of victims not on room confinement who died by suicide during the same hours (71 percent).

Self-Injurious Behavior in Juvenile Facilities

Although little research has been conducted regarding youth suicide in cus-tody, the information available suggests a high prevalence of self-injurious behavior in juvenile correctional facilities. For example, according to one national study, more than 11,000 juveniles are estimated to engage in more than 17,000 incidents of suicidal behavior in juvenile facilities each year (Parent et al., 1994). In another national survey, conducted in 1991, a modified version of the Centers for Disease Control's Youth Risk Behavior Surveillance System survey was administered to more than 1,800 confined youth in 39 juvenile institutions throughout the country (Morris et al., 1995). The study found that almost 22 percent of confined youth seriously considered suicide, 20 percent made a plan, 16 percent made at least one attempt, and 8 percent were injured in a suicide attempt during the previous 12 months.

Other studies found that large percentages of detained youth had histories of suicide attempts (Dembo et al., 1990) and current suicidal behavior (Robert-son and Husain, 2001; Shelton, 2000; Davis et al., 1991; Woolf and Funk, 1985). In fact, Robertson and Husain (2001) found that 31 percent of con-fined youth self-reported a suicide attempt, and 9 percent were currently suicidal with either ideation and/or a plan to act on suicidal thoughts. Finally, Chowanec et al. (1991) found higher rates of self-harm behavior among incarcerated male youth than in the general adolescent community population.

Caucasian youth appear to attempt suicide in confinement at a higher rate than African American youth (Kempton and Forehand, 1992; Alessi et al., 1984). Morris and colleagues (1995) found that American Indian and Caucasian youth reported higher rates of suicidal ideation (29 percent and 25 percent, respectively) than Hispanic, Asian, and African American youth (15 percent, 12 percent, and 8 percent, respectively). Other researchers have reported similar findings of high rates of suicidal behavior among American Indian youth confined in juvenile facilities (Duclos, LeBeau, and Elias, 1994)

Several studies consistently found that certain risk factors point to high rates of suicidal behavior for incarcerated youth. For example, researchers have reported that confined youth with either a major affective disorder or borderline personality disorder have a higher degree of suicidal ideation and more suicide attempts than adolescents in the general population (Alessi et al., 1984); incarcerated male youth whose parents had affectionless bonding styles also reported more suicidal ideation and/or attempts (McGarvey et al., 1999). Other researchers concluded that a history of sexual abuse "directly affects the development of suicidal ideation and behavior in incarcerated adolescents" (Esposito and Clum, 2002:145).

Findings from a 2002 study indicate that more than half (52 percent) of all detained youth self-reported current suicidal ideation, with 33 percent having a history of suicidal behavior (Esposito and Clum, 2002). In addition, a study of youth confined in a juvenile detention facility found that suicidal behavior in males was most significantly associated with depression, major life events (such as court involvement, death of a family member, etc.), poor social connections, and past suicide attempts, whereas suicidal behavior in females was associated with impulsivity, current depression, instability, and younger age (Mace, Rohde, and Gnau, 1997; Rohde, Seeley, and Mace, 1997). The most common correlate among both males and females was not living with a biological parent before detention. Suicidal behavior of a friend was significantly associated with past and current suicidal ideation among boys, but not girls (Rohde, Seeley, and Mace, 1997).

Finally, a recent study of confined youth referred for psychiatric assessment found that 30 percent reported suicidal ideation/behavior and 30 percent reported self-mutilative behavior while incar-cerated (Penn et al., 2003). These youth reported more depression, anxiety, and anger than nonsuicidal confined youth.

Facility Characteristics and Response

Facility Type and Population

As previously indicated, this national survey of juvenile suicides in confinement found that 42 percent of juvenile suicides took place in training schools and other secure facilities, 37 percent in detention centers, 15 percent in residential treatment centers, and 6.3 percent in reception or diagnostic centers. Almost half (48 percent) of the suicides occurred in facilities administered by state agencies, 39 percent in county facilities, and 13 percent in private programs. These percentages, however, may underestimate the actual prevalence of suicide in the types of facilities that had the highest rates of nonresponses to the survey (e.g., private programs). The 79 suicides were distributed among 70 juvenile facilities: 65 facilities sustained a single suicide, 3 facilities had 2 suicides each, 1 facility had 3 suicides, and 1 facility had 5 suicides during the survey period.

Two-thirds (67 percent) of suicides occurred in facilities with populations of 200 or fewer youth, and 42 percent in facilities with 50 or fewer youth[7] (figure 6). The study did not find any evidence to suggest that overcrowding was a contributing factor to juvenile suicide. In fact, the majority (68 percent) of suicides took place in facilities that were either at or below bed capacity; an additional 10 percent of suicides occurred in facilities that were slightly (less than 10 percent) over capacity.

Assessment by Qualified Mental Health Professional

National juvenile correctional standards and standard correctional practice indicate that confined youth should be assessed as soon as possible by a qualified mental health professional (National Commission on Correctional Health Care, 1995, 1999, 2004; Roush, 1996; Underwood and Berenson, 2001), with Performance-based Standards requiring an assessment within 7 days of entry into the facility (Council of Juvenile Correctional Administrators, 2003).[8] For the purposes of this study, and consistent with national standards, a qualified mental health professional was defined as an individual who by virtue of his or her education, credentials, and experience is permitted by law to evaluate and care for the mental health needs of patients. This definition includes, but is not limited to, psychiatrists, psychologists, clinical social workers, and psychiatric nurses. This examination by a qualified mental health professional is separate from an initial intake screening.

A large majority (70 percent) of suicide victims were assessed by a qualified mental health professional. Compared to other facility types, a significantly smaller percentage (35 percent) of suicide victims housed in detention centers received mental health assessments. However, slightly more than half (52 percent) of the detention center victims died within the first 6 days of confinement, thus reducing the opportunity for assessment.

Of those victims receiving a mental health assessment, almost half (49 percent) had a contact visit with a qualified mental health professional within 6 days of their death. However, 20 percent of assessed victims had not been assessed within 30 days of their death and slightly less than half (44 percent) of all victims either had never been assessed by a qualified mental health professional or had not been assessed within 30 days of their death.

Suicide Precaution Status

A small percentage (17 percent) of youth were on suicide precaution status at the time of death. Of these 13 victims, 10 were required to be observed at 15-minute intervals; the 3 remaining youth were to be observed at continuous, 5-minute, and 60-minute intervals, respectively. Despite their identified risk of suicide, almost half (6 of 13) of these victims were found to be last observed in excess of 15 minutes before their suicide.

Time Span

Approximately 41 percent of respondents stated that staff found the victim in less than 15 minutes following the last observation of the youth. However, slightly more than 15 percent of victims were reported to be found more than an hour following the last observation, including several victims found after 3 hours. In one case, the time span between the last observation and the suicide was not known.

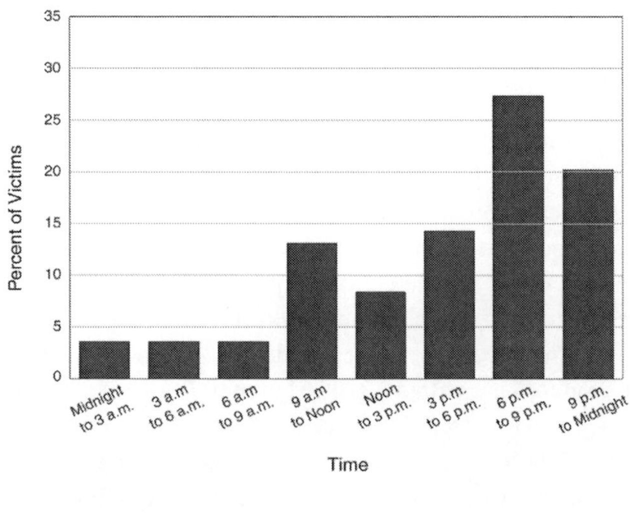

Figure 5. Suicides in Juvenile Facilities 1995–1999, by Time of Suicide.

SUICIDE PREVENTION PROGRAMMING

For this national survey of juvenile suicide in confinement, data were collected to determine whether facilities sustaining asuicide had comprehensive suicide prevention programming in place at the time of the death. Consistent with national juvenile correctional standards, comprehensive suicide prevention programming included the following seven critical components: written policy, intake screening, training, CPR certification, observation, safe housing, and mortality review (Hayes, 1999).

As indicated in figure 7, a substantial majority (90 percent) of suicides occurred in facilities that implemented one or more suicide prevention components. However, as shown in figure 8, only 20 percent of suicides occurred in facilities that implemented all seven suicide prevention components. The degree to which suicides occurred in a facility that had all seven suicide prevention components varied considerably by facility type: detention centers (10 percent), training schools and other secure facilities (24 percent), reception or diagnostic centers (40 percent), and residential treatment centers (25 percent).

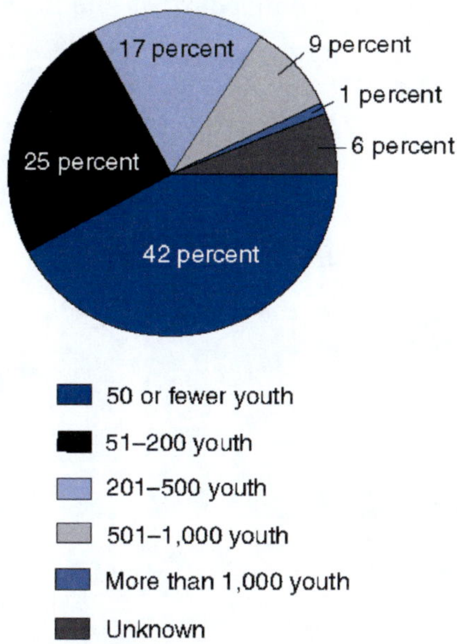

Figure 6. Suicides in Juvenile Facilities 1995–1999, by Facility Population.

Written Suicide Prevention Policy

Standard correctional practice and national juvenile correctional standards indicate that juvenile facilities should have a written suicide prevention policy that details the identification and management of suicidal youth (American Correctional Association, 1991; Council of Juvenile Correctional Administrators, 2003; Hayes, 1999; National Commission on Correctional Health Care, 1995, 1999, 2004; Roush, 1996). A significant majority (79 percent) of suicides occurred in facilities that maintained a written suicide prevention policy at the time of the suicide, although this was less true for suicides that took place in detention centers (62 percent).

Intake Screening for Suicide Risk

Most (71 percent) suicides took place in facilities that maintained an intake screening process to identify the suicide risk of youth entering the facility, although this was less true (48 percent) of suicides in detention centers. This finding is consistent with OJJDP research suggesting that approximately 70 percent of confined youth are screened for suicide risk (OJJDP, 2002).

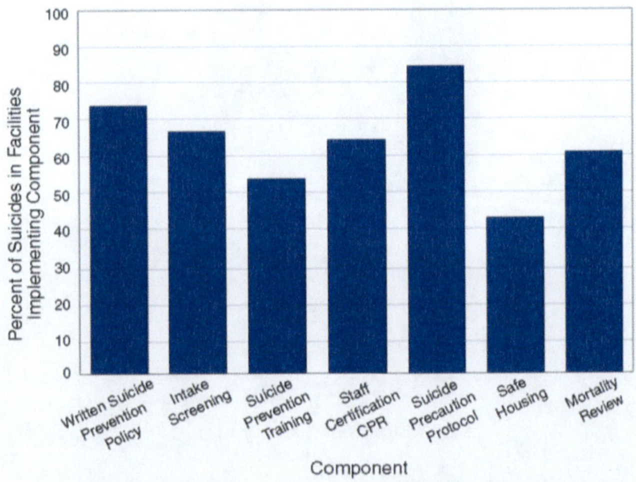

Figure 7. Suicides in Juvenile Facilities 1995–1999, by Facility's Implementation of Suicide Prevention Components.

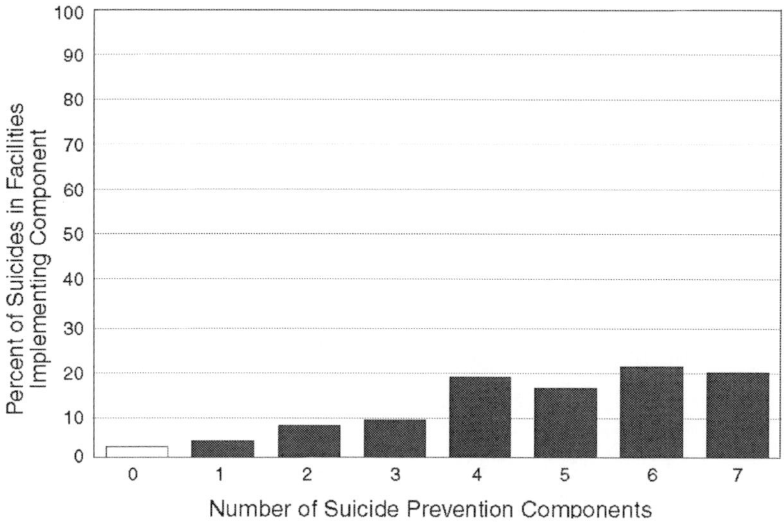

Figure 8. Suicides in Juvenile Facilities 1995–1999, by Number of Suicide Prevention Components Implemented by Facility.

Suicide Prevention Training

More than 4 in 10 juvenile suicides (43 percent) occurred in facilities that did not provide any type of suicide prevention training (pre-service, annual, and/or periodic) to their direct care staff.

Of the 45 suicides that occurred in facilities that provided suicide prevention training, two-thirds (67 percent) were in facilities that provided annual instruction, with training schools and other secure facilities providing the lowest percentage (42 percent) of annual training. Only 38 percent of juvenile suicides (30 of 79) took place in facilities that provided annual suicide prevention training to direct care staff.

Comprehensive Suicide Prevention Programming

The findings from this survey suggest that, although the rate of compliance with individual suicide prevention com-ponents was high, few juvenile facilities that sustained a suicide had all the components of a comprehensive suicide prevention program. Consistent with national correctional standards and practices, all juvenile facilities, regard-less of size and type, should have a detailed written suicide prevention poli-cy that addresses each of the following critical components (Council of Juvenile Correctional Administrators, 2003; Hayes, 1999, 2000; National Commis-sion on Correctional Health Care, 1999, 2004; Roush, 1996).

Training. All facility, medical, and mental health staff should receive 8 hours of initial suicide prevention training, followed by a minimum of 2 hours of annual refresher training. Training should provide information about predisposing factors, high-risk periods, warning signs and symptoms, identifying suicidal behavior despite the denial of risk, and components of the facility's suicide pre-vention policy.

Identification/screening. Intake screening for suicide risk should take place immediately upon confinement and prior to housing assignment, and include inquiry regarding current and past suicidal behavior, current suicidal ideation, earlier mental health treatment, recent significant loss, suicidal behavior by a family member or close friend, suicide risk during prior contact with or confinement in agency, and arresting or transporting officers' opinion regarding whether youth is currently at risk. The policy should include procedures for referral to mental health personnel for further assessment. (Several intake screening and assessment forms are available for the identification of suicide risk, including the "Intake Screening Form/Suicide Risk Assessment" [Hayes, 1999], the "Juvenile Suicide Assessment" [Galloucis and Francek, 2002], and the Massachusetts Youth Screening Instrument-MAYSI-2 [Grisso and Barnum, 2000].)

Communication. At a minimum, facility procedures should enhance communication (1) between the arresting/transporting officer(s), family members, and facility staff; (2) between and among facility staff (including medical and mental health personnel); and (3) between facility staff and the suicidal youth.

Housing. Isolation should be avoided. Whenever possible, suicidal youth should be housed in the general population, mental health unit, or infirmary, in close proximity to staff. Youth should be housed in suicide-resistant, protrusion-free rooms. Removal of clothing (excluding belts and shoelaces) and use of restraints should be avoided whenever possible, and should only be used as a last resort for short periods of time when the youth is engaging in self-destructive behavior.

Levels of supervision. Two levels are normally recommended for suicidal youth:

- Close observation—reserved for youth who are not actively suicidal, but express suicidal ideation and/or have recent histories of self-destructive behavior and are now viewed as potentially suicidal—requires supervision at staggered intervals not to exceed every 15 minutes. In addition, a youth who denies suicidal ideation or does not threaten suicide, but demonstrates other characteristics of concern (through actions, current circumstances, or recent history) indicating the potential for self-injury, should be placed on close observation.
- Constant observation—reserved for youth who are actively suicidal (threatening/engaging in the act)—requires supervision on a continuous, uninterrupted basis.

In addition, an intermediate level of supervision can be used with observation at staggered intervals not to exceed every 5 minutes. Other supervision aides (e.g., closed-circuit television, companions, or watchers) can be used as a supplement to, but not as a substitute for, these obser-vation levels.

Intervention. A facility's policy regarding intervention should be threefold:

- All staff should be trained in standard first aid and cardiopulmonary resusci-tation (CPR).
- Any staff member who discovers a youth attempting suicide should immediately respond, survey the scene to ensure the emergency is genuine, alert other staff to call for medical personnel, and begin life-saving measures.
- Staff should never presume that the youth is dead, but rather initiate and continue appropriate life-saving measures until relieved by medical personnel.

All housing units should contain a first aid kit, pocket mask or mouth shield, Ambu bag, and rescue tool (to quickly cut through fibrous material).

Reporting. In the event of an attempted or completed suicide, all appropriate facility officials should be notified through the chain of command. All staff who came in contact with the victim before the incident (or while responding to the incident) should submit a statement as to their full knowledge of the youth and the incident.

Followup/mortality review. All staff (and youth) involved in the incident should be offered critical incident stress debriefing. If resources permit, a psychological autopsy is recommended. Every completed suicide and serious suicide attempt (i.e., requiring hospitalization) should be examined by a mortality review process. Ideally, the review should be coordinated by an outside agency or facility to ensure impartiality. The mortality review—separate and apart from other formal investigations that may be required to determine the cause of death—should be multidisciplinary (i.e., involve correctional, mental health, and medical personnel) and include a critical inquiry of the following:

- The circumstances surrounding the incident.
- Facility procedures relevant to the incident.
- All relevant training received by involved staff.
- Pertinent medical and mental health services/reports involving the victim.
- Possible precipitating factors leading to the suicide.
- Recommendations, if any, for changes in policy, training, physical plant, medical or mental health services, and operational procedures.

Approximately half (51 percent) of suicides in facilities that provided suicide prevention training were in facilities that provided the training in a 1- or 2-hour block. Only three suicides took place in a facility that provided a full day (7–8 hours) of instruction.

Certification in Cardiopulmonary Resuscitation

More than two-thirds (68 percent) of suicides occurred in facilities where all direct care staff had received certification in cardiopulmonary resuscitation (CPR), although this was true to a lesser degree (55 percent) in training schools and other secure facilities.

Suicide Precaution Protocol

The overwhelming majority (90 percent) of victims were located in facilities that maintained a suicide precaution protocol for the observation (excluding closed- circuit television monitoring) of youth. Of these 71 victims, fewer than half (48 percent) were in facilities where constant observation was the highest level of suicide precaution, including only 28 percent of suicides in detention centers. More than one-third (37 percent) were in facilities that reported observation at 15- minute intervals as the highest suicide precaution level.

Safe Housing

Less than half (46 percent) the suicides occurred in a facility that had a housing process by which a suicidal youth could be assigned to a safe and protrusion-free room. Although the majority (61 percent) of suicides in training schools and other secure facilities and reception/diagnostic centers took place in a facility that provided safe and protrusion-free housing for suicidal youth, this was true for only 35 percent of suicides in detention facilities and 25 percent of suicides in residential treatment centers.

Mortality Review

National juvenile correctional standards recommend that a mortality review be conducted following each suicide (Hayes, 1999; National Commission on Correctional Health Care, 1995, 1999, 2004; Roush, 1996). For the purposes of this study, mortality review is defined as "a multidisciplinary committee process that examines the events surrounding the death to determine if the incident was preventable. The review process might include recommendations aimed at reducing the opportunity of future deaths." The process also attempts to identify any possible precipitating factors that may have caused the suicide (see "Precipitating Factors to the Suicide" above). Nearly two-thirds (65 percent) of respondents reported that a mortality review was conducted following the suicide, although deaths in detention centers were reviewed to a lesser degree (52 percent).

Recommendations

The findings from this survey reveal several key issues that merit consideration. Recommendations arising from the study are presented below:

- Consistent with national corrections standards and practices, juvenile facilities, regardless of size and type, should have a detailed written suicide prevention policy that addresses each of the following critical components: training, identification/screening, communication, housing, levels of supervision, intervention, reporting, and followup/mortality review (see "Comprehensive Suicide Prevention Programming" on page 10).
- Juvenile facility administrators should create and maintain effective training programs and ensure that direct care, medical, and mental health personnel receive both pre-service and annual instruction in suicide prevention.
- Suicide prevention training curriculums used in juvenile facilities have historically relied on information gathered about adult inmate suicide and youth suicide in the general population. Given the findings from this study, which demonstrate significant differences between adult inmate suicide and juvenile suicide, development of separate training curriculums targeted to suicide prevention within juvenile facilities is warranted.
- Significant deficiencies in intake screening and inadequate suicide prevention programming within detention centers experiencing suicides warrant immediate attention. Resources need to be channeled to juvenile facilities throughout the country, particularly detention centers, to ensure that any agency housing a juvenile provides basic, yet comprehensive, suicide prevention programming, including intake screening for suicide risk.
- More than one-third of suicides identified in this study were unknown to government agencies responsible for the care and advocacy of confined youth. The fact that any suicide occurring within a juvenile facility could remain outside the purview of regulatory agencies is disturbing. At a minimum, each death within a juvenile facility should be accounted for, comprehensively reviewed, and provisions made for appropriate corrective action.

PRECIPITATING FACTORS FOR THE SUICIDE

Of the suicides that occurred in facilities that conducted mortality reviews (*n*=51), precipitating factors were identified for more than half (59 percent). These factors included:

- Fear of waiver to adult system, transfer to a more secure juvenile facility, or pending undesirable placement (including home) (10 cases).
- Recent death of a family member (6 cases).
- Failure in the program (5 cases).
- Contagion (from another recent suicide in facility) (3 cases).
- Parent(s) threat of/failure to visit (2 cases).
- Other (i.e., loss of relationship, close proximity to birthday, suicide pact with peer, ridicule from peers) (4 cases).

In several cases, more than one precipitating factor was identified—only the perceived primary factor is listed above. However, of the 79 suicides reported in this study, possible precipitating factors for the deaths were offered by respondents in only 30 (or 38 percent) of the cases.

CONCLUSION

This study was the first attempt to collect data on the extent, characteristics, and distribution of suicides within juvenile facilities throughout the country. More research is clearly needed. For example, possible precipitating factors were identified for only slightly more than one-third of the suicides reported in this study. This indicates uncertainty of the concept of precipitants, inadequate review of the circumstances surrounding the death, limited knowledge of the victim's background, or all the preceding. Further inquiry regarding possible precipitating factors is essential to enhancing understanding of this problem.

Although approximately half the victims in this study were under room confinement at the time of death, further research is needed to explore the relationship between isolation and suicide. Despite the fact that youth were alone in their rooms between the hours of midnight and 6 a.m., with ample opportunity and privacy to engage in self-injurious behavior, few suicides took place during this 6-hour period. Instead, approximately half the deaths occurred during the 6-hour period between 6 p.m. and midnight—with almost a third occurring between 6 p.m. and 9 p.m. Perhaps most importantly, the majority of victims who died by suicide while on room confinement status died during waking hours. These are periods when youth are normally either involved in programming or back on their housing units, interacting with staff and peers— perhaps more likely to become involved in confrontations and/or behavior that results in room confinement. Further research is needed to explore this issue.

Although only a small percentage of victims died by suicide following more than 12 months of custody, the average length of confinement before suicide for these youth was quite high (approximately 22 months), suggesting that prolonged confinement might have been one of the precipitating factors in the suicides. This issue merits further study.

Findings from this study pose formidable challenges for juvenile correctional and healthcare officials and direct care staff. For example, although room confinement remains a standard procedure in most juvenile facilities, its use should be judicious and closely scrutinized. Since suicides can occur at any time during a youth's stay in a facility, with the same number of deaths occurring within the first few days of custody as after almost a year of confinement, intake screening for the identification of suicide risk should be viewed as time-limited. Because youth can be at risk at any point during confinement, the challenge for those who work in the area of juvenile detention and corrections is to establish a continuum of comprehensive suicide prevention services aimed at the collaborative identification, continued assessment, and safe management of youth at risk for self-harm.

FOR FURTHER INFORMATION

This Bulletin presents information taken from the OJJDP Report, *Juvenile Suicide in Confinement: A National Survey* (NCJ 213691). The full report is available on OJJDP's Web site (*www.ojp.usdoj.gov/* ojjdp).

References

Alessi, N., McManus, M., Brickman, A. & Grapentine, L. (1984). Suicidal behavior among serious juvenile offenders. *American Journal of Psychiatry*, *141(2)*, 286-287.

American Correctional Association. (1991). *Standards for Juvenile Detention Facilities and Standards for Juvenile Correctional Facilities.* Laurel, MD: American Correctional Association.

American Psychiatric Association. (2000). *Diagnostic and Statistical Manual of Mental Disorders (DSM-IV-TR).* Washington, DC: American Psychiatric Association.

Arias, E., Anderson, R., Kung, H., Murphy, S. & Kochanek, K. (2003). Deaths: Final data for 2001. *National Vital Statistics Report*, *52(3)*, Hyattsville, MD: National Center for Health Statistics.

Carmona, R. H. (2005). *Suicide Prevention Among Native American Youth.* Prepared Remarks of Richard H. Carmona, M.D., M.P.H., F.A.C.S., Surgeon General, U.S. Public Health Service, U.S. Department of Health and Human Services. Testimony Before the Indian Affairs Committee, U.S. Senate, June 15, 2005. AQ: Retrieved May 13, 2008 from the Web: www.surgeongeneral.gov/news/ testimony/t06152005.html.

Chowanec, G., Josephson, A., Coleman, C. & Davis, H. (1991). Self-harming behavior in incarcerated male delinquent adolescents. *Journal of the American Academy of Child and Adolescent Psychiatry*, *30(2)*, 202-207.

Cocozza, J. & Skowyra, K. (2000). Youth with mental health disorders: Issues and emerging responses. *Juvenile Justice*, *7(1)*, 3-13.

Council of Juvenile Correctional Administrators. (2003). *Performance-based Standards (PbS) for Youth Correction and Detention Facilities: PbS Goals, Standards, Outcome Measures, Expected Practices and Processes.* Braintree, MA: Council of Juvenile Correctional Administrators.

Davis, D., Bean, G., Schumacher, J. & Stringer, T. (1991). Prevalence of emotional disorders in a juvenile justice institutional population. *American Journal of Forensic Psychology*, *9,* 1-13.

Dembo, R., Williams, L., Wish, E., Berry, E., Getreu, A., Washburn, M. & Schmeidler, J. (1990). Examination of the relationships among drug use, emotional/psychological problems, and crime among youths entering a juvenile detention center. *The International Journal of the Addictions*, *25*, 1301-1340.

Duclos, C., LeBeau, W. & Elias, G. (1994). American Indian suicidal behavior in detention environments: Cause for continued basic and applied research. *Jail Suicide Update, 5(4)*, 4-9.

Esposito, C. & Clum, G. (2002). Social support and problem-solving as moderators of the relationship between childhood abuse and suicidality: Applications to a delinquent population. *Journal of Traumatic Stress, 15(2)*, 137-146.

Galloucis, M. & Francek, H. (2002). The juvenile suicide assessment: An instrument for the assessment and management of suicide risk with incarcerated juveniles. *International Journal of Emergency Mental Health, 4(3)*, 181-199.

Grisso, T. & Barnum, R. (2000). *The Massachusetts Youth Screening Instrument-2: User's Manual and Technical Report.* Worcester, MA: University of Massachusetts Medical Center.

Hayes, L. (1989). National study of jail suicides: Seven years later. *Psychiatric Quarterly, 60(1)*, 7-29.

Hayes, L. (1999). *Suicide Prevention in Juvenile Correction and Detention Facilities: A Resource Guide.* South Easton, MA: Council of Juvenile Correctional Administrators.

Hayes, L. (2000). Suicide prevention in juvenile facilities. *Juvenile Justice, 7(1)*, 24-32.

Hayes, L. (2006). *Juvenile Suicide in Confinement: A National Survey.* Report. Washington, DC: U.S. Department of Justice, Office of Justice Programs, Office of Juvenile Justice and Delinquency Prevention.

Kempton, T., & Forehand, R. (1992). Suicide attempts among juvenile delinquents: The contribution of mental health factors. *Behaviour Research and Therapy, 30(5)* , 537-54 1.

Mace, D., Rohde, P. & Gnau, V. (1997). Psychological patterns of depression and suicidal behavior of adolescents in a juvenile detention facility. *Journal for Juvenile Justice and Detention Services, 12(1)*, 18-23.

McGarvey, E., Kryzhanovskaya, L., Koopman, C., Waite, D. & Canterbury, R. (1999). Incarcerated adolescents' distress and suicidality in relation to parental bonding styles. *Crisis, 20(4)*, 164-170.

Morris, R., Harrison, E., Knox, G., Tromanhauser, E., Marquis, D. & Watts, L. L. (1995). Health Risk Behavioral Survey from 39 juvenile correctional facilities in the United States. *Journal of Adolescent Health, 17(6)*, 334-344.

National Commission on Correctional Health Care. (1995). *Standards for Health Services in Juvenile Detention and Confinement Facilities.* Chicago, IL: National Commission on Correctional Health Care.

National Commission on Correctional Health Care. (1999). *Standards for Health Services in Juvenile Detention and Confinement Facilities.* Chicago, IL: National Commission on Correctional Health Care.

National Commission on Correctional Health Care. (2004). *Standards for Health Services in Juvenile Detention and Confinement Facilities.* Chicago, IL: National Commission on Correctional Health Care.

National Juvenile Detention Association. (1990). *Position Statement: Definition of Juvenile Detention.* Richmond, KY: National Juvenile Detention Association.

National Juvenile Detention Association. (2001). *Position Statement: Use of Juvenile Detention Facilities for Youth With Severe Mental Health Issues.* Richmond, KY: National Juvenile Detention Association.

Office of Juvenile Justice and Delinquency Prevention. (1999). *Census of Juveniles in Residential Placement.* Washington, DC: U.S. Department of Justice, Office of Justice Programs, Office of Juvenile Justice and Delinquency Prevention.

Office of Juvenile Justice and Delinquency Prevention. (2002). *2000 Juvenile Residential Facility Census.* Unpublished data. Washington, DC: U.S. Department of Justice, Office of Justice Programs, Office of Juvenile Justice and Delinquency Prevention.

Parent, D., Leiter, V., Kennedy, S., Livens, L., Wentworth, D. & Wilcox, S. (1994). *Conditions of Confinement: Juvenile Detention and Corrections Facilities.* Washington, DC: U.S. Department of Justice, Office of Justice Programs, Office of Juvenile Justice and Delinquency Prevention.

Penn, J., Esposito, C., Schaeffer, L., Fritz, G. & Spirito, A. (2003). Suicide attempts and self-mutilative behavior in a juvenile correctional facility. *Journal of the American Academy of Child and Adolescent Psychiatry, 42(7)*, 762-769.

Robertson, A. & Husain, J. (2001). *Prevalence of Mental Illness and Substance Abuse Disorders Among Incarcerated Juvenile Offenders.* Jackson, MS: Mississippi Department of Public Safety and Mississippi Department of Mental Health.

Rohde, P., Seeley, J. & Mace, D. (1997). Correlates of suicidal behavior in a juvenile detention population. *Suicide and Life-Threatening Behavior, 27(2)*, 164-175.

Roush, D. (1996). *Desktop Guide to Good Juvenile Detention Practice.* Washington, DC: U.S. Department of Justice, Office of Justice Programs, Office of Juvenile Justice and Delinquency Prevention.

Shelton, D. (2000). Health status of young offenders and their families. *Journal of Nursing Scholarship*, *32(2)*, 173-178.

Sickmund, M. & Wan, T. (2001). *Census of Juveniles in Residential Placement Databook.* Washington, DC: U.S. Department of Justice, Office of Justice Programs, Office of Juvenile Justice and Delinquency Prevention.

Substance Abuse and Mental Health Services Administration. (2001). *Summary of Findings From the 2000 National Household Survey on Drug Abuse.* NHSDA Series: H-13, DHHS Publication No. SMA 01-3549. Rockville, MD: U.S. Department of Health and Human Services, Substance Abuse and Mental Health Services Administration.

Sullivan, C. (1995). Juvenile custody suicides blamed on apathy, impulse, gaps in care. *Los Angeles Times*, (March 12):A1.

Teplin, L., Abram, K., McClelland, G., Dulcan, M. & Mericle, A. (2002). Psychiatric disorders in youth in juvenile detention. *Archives in General Psychiatry*, *59*, 1133-1143.

Twedt, S. (2001b). Lack of options keeps mentally disturbed youth locked up. *Pittsburgh Post-Gazette*, (July 15):A1.

Underwood, L. & Berenson, D. (2001). *Mental Health Programming in Youth Correction and Detention Facilities: A Resource Guide.* South Easton, MA: Council of Juvenile Correctional Administrators.

U.S. Department of Health and Human Services. (1999). *The Surgeon General's Call To Action To Prevent Suicide, 1999.* Washington, DC: U.S. Department of Health and Human Services.

Woolf, A. & Funk, S. (1985). Epidemiology of trauma in a population of incarcerated youth. *Pediatrics*, *75(3)*, 463-468.

ACKNOWLEDGMENTS

Lindsay M. Hayes, M.S., is Project Director of the National Center on Institutions and Alternatives. For their support and assistance in designing the data collection instruments, analyzing the data, and reviewing the draft report, the author would like to thank G. David Curry, Ph.D., Department of Criminology, University of Missouri-St. Louis; Robert E. DeComo, Ph.D., Director of Research, National Council on Crime and Delinquency; Barbara C. Dooley, Ph.D., former Director, Madison County (TN) Juvenile

Court Services; Cedrick Heraux, Ph.D. candidate, School of Criminal Justice, Michigan State University; and David W. Roush, Ph.D., Director, Center for Research and Professional Development, Michigan State University. Thanks also to Alice Boring of the National Center on Institutions and Alternatives, who brought the report together to its final form.

In addition, two consulting agencies, the Council of Juvenile Correctional Administrators (CJCA) and the National Juvenile Detention Association (NJDA), provided invaluable assistance to the author and the team in both endorsing the project and encouraging juvenile facility directors to participate in the survey process, as well as in reviewing the draft report. Special thanks are extended to CJCA's Edward J. Loughran, Kim Godfrey, and Robert Dugan, and NJDA's Earl L. Dunlap and Michael A. Jones.

SHARE WITH YOUR COLLEAGUES

Juvenile Justice Clearinghouse
Publication Reprint/Feedback
P.O. Box 6000
Rockville, MD 20849–6000
800–851–3420
301–519–5600 (fax)
Web: tellncjrs.ncjrs.gov

This Bulletin was prepared under grant number 1999–JN–FX–0005- from the Office of Juvenile Justice and Delinquency Prevention (OJJDP), U.S. Department of Justice.

Points of view or opinions expressed in this document are those of the author(s) and do not necessarily represent the official position or policies of OJJDP or the U.S. Department of Justice.

The Office of Juvenile Justice and Delinquency Prevention is a component of the Office of Justice Programs, which also includes the Bureau of Justice Assistance; the Bureau of Justice Statistics; the Community Capacity Development Office; the National Institute of Justice; the Office for Victims of Crime; and the Office of Sex Offender Sentencing, Monitoring, Apprehending, Registering, and Tracking (SMART).

End Notes

[1] For comparative purposes, data collected from OJJDP's Census of Juveniles in Residential Placement was limited to the following: gender, age, race, placement authority, most serious offense charged, and adjudication status.

[2] For purposes of this study, offenses were broken down into six categories: property offenses included burglary, grand larceny, petty larceny, auto theft, robbery (other), receiving stolen property, shoplifting, arson, breaking and entering, entering without breaking, counterfeiting, forgery, embezzlement, vandalism, and carrying a concealed weapon; person offenses included murder, negligent manslaughter, armed robbery, rape, indecent assault, assault, battery, sexual assault, aggravated assault, and kidnapping; status offenses included running away, truancy, incorrigibility, curfew violation, and loitering; probation violation offenses included any technical violation of the terms of probation and/or parole; public order offenses included alcohol-related charges (intoxication, liquor law violation, driving under the influence), resisting arrest, disorderly conduct, prostitution, sex offenses (other), vagrancy, unauthorized use of a motor vehicle, and minor traffic offenses; and drug offenses included possession, use, and distribution of any dangerous controlled substance or narcotic.

[3] The average length of confinement prior to suicide for the 10 victims who died after more than 12 months in custody was 21.8 months.

[4] For comparative purposes, although lengths of stay within juvenile facilities throughout the country vary considerably, earlier OJJDP research has shown the average length of stay in the four facility types to be as follows: detention center (15 days), training school or other secure facility (7.5 months), reception or diagnostic center (34 days), and residential treatment center (6.5 months) (see Parent et al., 1994).

[5] For the most part, survey respondents did not report victims' mental illnesses according to the *Diagnostic and Statistical Manual (DSM) III* or *IV* editions (American Psychiatric Association, 2000).

[6] The circumstances that led to room confinement included failure to follow program rules or inappropriate behavior (47 percent), threat of or actual physical abuse of staff or peers (42 percent), and other (11 percent), which included two cases of standard procedure for new intake, one case of court-ordered confinement, and one case of group confinement during a shift change.

[7] The direction of this finding is somewhat consistent with earlier OJJDP research finding that approximately 72 percent of juveniles are housed in facilities with 250 or fewer beds,

although only 21 percent are housed in facilities with 50 or fewer beds (see Parent et al., 1994).

[8] In 1995, OJJDP contracted with the Council of Juvenile Correctional Administrators to develop, field test, and implement performance-based standards for juvenile correctional and detention facilities. The Performance-based Standards Project offers a systematic method for facilities to measure outcomes and provides guidance for facilities to review their practices and to take corrective action.

In: Perspectives on Juvenile Offenders
Editors: Owen B. Hahn
ISBN: 978-1-60876-819-6

Chapter 2

CO-OCCURRENCE OF SUBSTANCE USE BEHAVIORS IN YOUTH

Carl McCurley and Howard N. Snyder
Office of Juvenile Justice and Delinquency Prevention

This Bulletin analyzes the prevalence and overlap of substance-related behaviors among youth, with comparisons by age group, gender, and race/ethnicity. It uses data from the first two waves of the 1997 National Longitudinal Survey of Youth (NLSY97)—self-reports gathered in 1997 and 1998 from a nationally representative sample of youth ages 12–17. The data are from questions asking about drinking alcohol during the previous 30 days, using marijuana during the previous 30 days, and ever selling or helping to sell marijuana (pot, grass), hashish (hash) or other hard drugs such as heroin, cocaine, or LSD.

The central finding of the analysis is that, given one substance-related behavior, other substance-related behaviors became much more likely. For example, 9% of all youth ages 12–17 reported marijuana use and 8% said they had sold drugs. Among youth who reported drinking alcohol (23% of all youth ages 12–17), the level of marijuana use was 32% and the level of drug selling was 23%. In contrast, among youth ages 12–17 who did not report recent alcohol use, the level of marijuana use was 2% and the level of drug selling was 3%. Other findings include:

- Of youth who reported marijuana use, 81% said they drank alcohol and 45% said they had sold drugs.
- Of youth who reported drug selling, 68% said they drank alcohol and 54% reported marijuana use. In contrast, among youth who said they had not sold drugs, 19% reported drinking alcohol and 6% reported using marijuana.
- Among those who sold drugs, both white and Hispanic youth were more likely than African Americans to also report alcohol use; white youth who sold drugs were also more likely than African Americans who sold drugs to report using marijuana.

PREVALENCE OF SUBSTANCE-RELATED BEHAVIORS WAS TIED TO AGE

In general, the levels of reported substance-related behaviors climbed steadily with increasing age. From age 12 to age 17, alcohol use in the previous 30 days increased more than eightfold, from 5% to 43% of youth, as did marijuana use in the previous 30 days (from 2% to 17%). The lifetime prevalence of reported drug selling rose from 1% at age 12 to 16% at age 17.

A MESSAGE FROM OJJDP

The issue of co-occurrence of problem behaviors among juveniles is of vital importance to all who are concerned with identifying and evaluating these behaviors, making decisions about placement and treatment, and delivering services. Because substance-related behaviors such as drinking alcohol, using marijuana, and selling drugs can have such serious consequences for youth, understanding how these behaviors co-occur is especially important.

Based on self-report data from the first two waves of the 1997 National Longitudinal Survey of Youth, this Bulletin answers co-occurrence questions such as "If a youth has recently used alcohol, what is the likelihood that he has also used marijuana?" or "If a youth has sold drugs, what are the chances that she also drinks alcohol and uses marijuana?" It also compares co-occurrence findings by age group, gender, and race/ethnicity.

The analysis shows that a youth who engages in one substance-related behavior is much more likely to engage in another. For example, the percentages of youth who used marijuana or sold drugs were much greater among youth who drank alcohol than those who did not. These and other findings reported in this Bulletin contribute to our understanding of substance-related behaviors among youth and provide useful input for prevention and treatment efforts.

PREVALENCE AND FREQUENCY OF SUBSTANCE-RELATED BEHAVIORS WERE CORRELATED

Among youth ages 12–14, 11% reported drinking alcohol, 4% reported marijuana use, and 3% said they had sold drugs; the levels for those ages 15–17 were 35%, 14%, and 12%, respectively.[1] Just as the percentage of youth who reported substance-related behaviors increased with age, so did the frequency of the reported behaviors. Youth ages 12–14 who drank alcohol did so on an average of 3.4 days over a 30-day period, in contrast to 4.5 days for youth ages 15–17. Youth ages 12–14 who used marijuana did so on an average of 6.8 days across 30 days, compared to 9.3 days for youth ages 15–17. Youth ages 12–14 who sold drugs did so an average of 10.5 times in the previous year, in comparison to 16.7 times for youth ages 15–17.

NLSY97: A NEW OPPORTUNITY TO EXAMINE BEHAVIORS OF U.S. YOUTH

Analysis of data from the 1997 National Longitudinal Survey of Youth can provide criminal justice practitioners and policymakers with timely insights into delinquent careers, overlap among law-violating behaviors, the relative impact of a variety of risk and protective factors on substance use, and variation across subpopulations defined by age, gender, race/ethnicity, labor force status, and household composition. The NLSY is a large, nationally representative, continuing study of adolescents who were ages 12 through 16 as of December 31, 1996. NLSY interviewers gather responses from youth to questions about a wide array of behaviors, including undesirable or delinquent activity. Combined, the 1997 and 1998 waves include more than 15,300 observations of youth who were ages 12 through 17 at the time of the interview (the sample used in this Bulletin excludes 17-year-olds from the 1997 wave of interviews because they were disproportionately "young" 17-year-olds, with an average age of 17 years and 3 months). The NLSY97 includes oversamples of both African American (3,951 interviews) and Hispanic (3,239 interviews) youth; weighted analysis controlled for this oversampling to produce nationally representative estimates of youth behavior overall and within age, gender, and race/ethnicity groups. The sample was also weighted to produce equal proportions of youth for each year of age, ignoring minor fluctuations by year of age (among 12- to 17-year-olds) in the size of the 1997–98 U.S. population.

For more information about NLSY, refer to the Compendium of National Juvenile Justice Data Sets on OJJDP's Statistical Briefing Book Web site at http://www.ojjdp.ncjrs.gov/ojstatbb/Compendium/index.html.

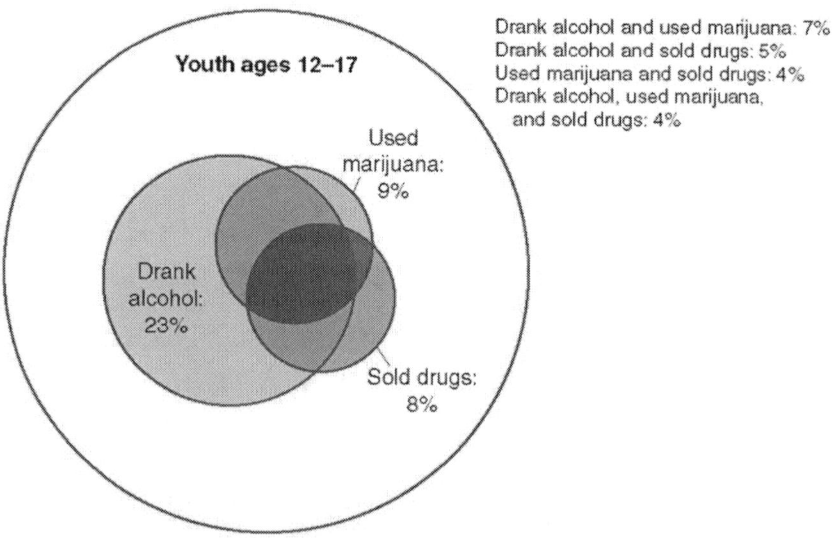

Among all youth ages 12–17, 23% said they drank alcohol during the previous 30 days, 9% said they used marijuana during the previous 30 days, and 8% said they had ever sold drugs.

Of youth ages 12–17, 27% reported drinking alcohol, using marijuana, or selling drugs

ABOUT THE DIAGRAMS IN THIS BULLETIN

The diagrams displayed throughout this Bulletin depict both the prevalence and co-occurrence of drinking alcohol, using marijuana, and selling drugs. The total area within the white circle represents all youth within the indicated category, such as "Youth ages 12–17" in the diagram on this page. The areas of the shaded circles within the white circle represent the percentage of youth within the indicated category who reported a particular behavior. For example, in the diagram on this page, among all youth ages 12–17, 23% reported that they drank alcohol within the 30 days prior to being interviewed. The area of overlap for two circles shows the percentage of youth who engaged in both behaviors; the area of overlap for three circles shows the percentage of youth who engaged in all three behaviors. For example, in the diagram on this page, among youth ages 12–17, 4% reported all three behaviors.

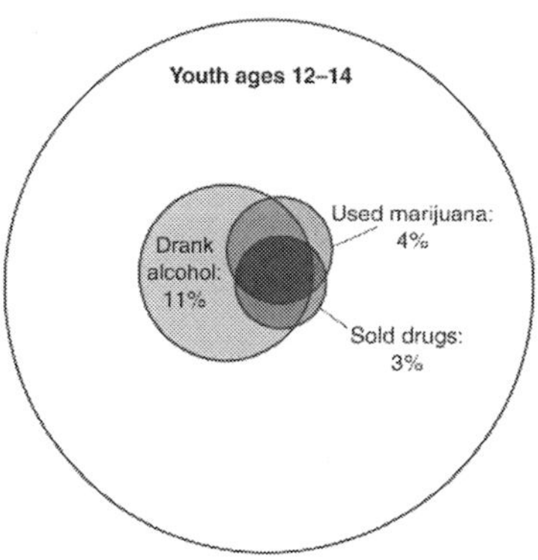

Drank alcohol and used marijuana: 3%
Drank alcohol and sold drugs: 2%
Used marijuana and sold drugs: 2%
Drank alcohol, used marijuana, and sold drugs: 1%

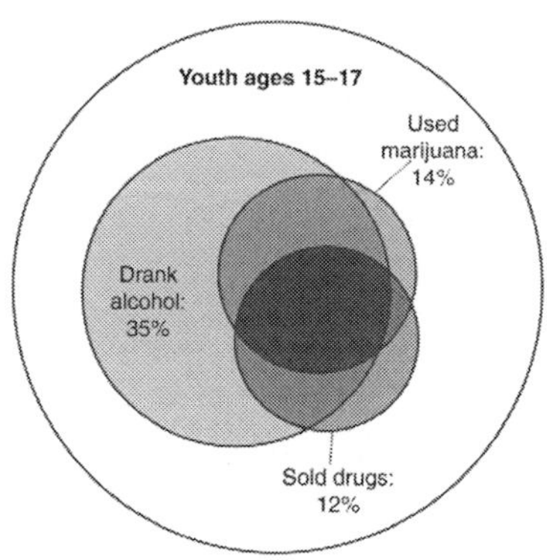

Drank alcohol and used marijuana: 12%
Drank alcohol and sold drugs: 9%
Used marijuana and sold drugs: 7%
Drank alcohol, used marijuana, and sold drugs: 6%

Youth in the older age group (15–17) were more likely than those in the younger age group (12–14) to report drinking alcohol, using marijuana, or selling drugs.

Across age groups, there was substantial overlap of drinking alcohol, using marijuana, and selling drugs.

The majority of marijuana users and drug sellers also drank alcohol, regardless of age group

SUBSTANCE-RELATED BEHAVIORS WERE CORRELATED WITH OTHER PROBLEM BEHAVIORS

NLSY97 gathered data on a number of different problem behaviors. As indicated in the accompanying table, substance use was associated with a range of other problems. Across all behaviors listed, and for both the younger and the older age groups, there were significant differences between the problem behavior levels reported by users and nonusers. For example, 31% of youth ages 12–14 who drank alcohol and 18% who did not drink alcohol reported having been suspended from school, and 21% of 15–17-year-olds who had used marijuana during the previous 30 days also said they had been arrested during the previous year, as opposed to 5% of those who had not used marijuana in the previous 30 days.

Higher Levels of Problem Behaviors and Delinquency Appeared Among Substance Users, Across Age Groups

Behavior	Drank alcohol 30 days		Used marijuana 30 days		Sold drugs ever	
	No	Yes	No	Yes	No	Yes
Youth ages 12–14						
Suspended from school	18%	31%	19%	46%	19%	55%
Vandalize property	13	37	14	50	14	56
Major theft	2	11	2	20	2	27
Attack/assault	8	28	9	36	9	53
Belong to a gang	1	7	1	16	1	18
Carry handgun	4	12	4	20	4	25
Arrested	2	8	3	15	2	22
Youth ages 15–17						
Suspended from school	27%	38%	27%	52%	27%	63%
Vandalize property	10	23	11	33	11	40
Major theft	3	10	4	17	3	23
Attack/assault	8	21	10	29	9	37
Belong to a gang	1	5	1	9	1	12
Carry handgun	4	10	5	15	5	18
Arrested	5	12	5	21	5	26

Notes: The timeframe for "Suspended from school" was ever; for the other items, it was the past 12 months. The value in the "Yes" column differs significantly ($p<.05$) from the value in the "No" column for all column pairs within substance behavior and age groups.

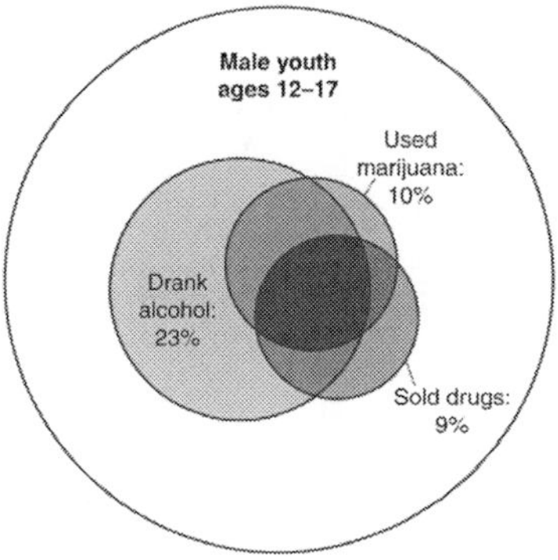

Drank alcohol and used marijuana: 8%
Drank alcohol and sold drugs: 6%
Used marijuana and sold drugs: 5%
Drank alcohol, used marijuana, and sold drugs: 4%

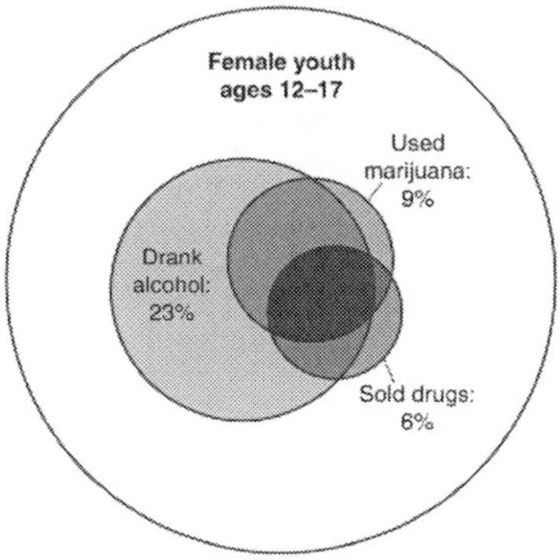

Drank alcohol and used marijuana: 7%
Drank alcohol and sold drugs: 4%
Used marijuana and sold drugs: 3%
Drank alcohol, used marijuana, and sold drugs: 3%

The patterns of substance-related behavior co-occurrence among females closely resembled those among males.

The level of drug selling among males was higher than among females, but the levels and overlap of alcohol and marijuana use were similar for males and females

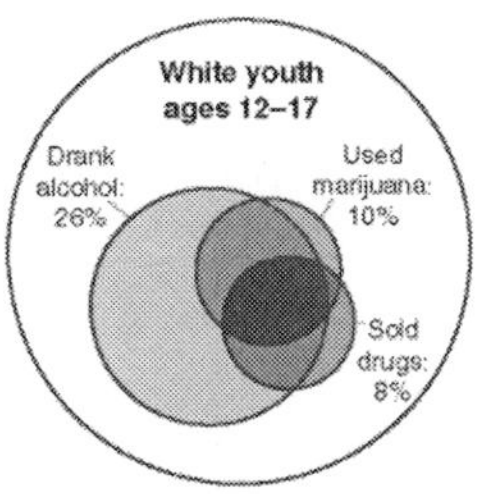

Drank alcohol and used marijuana: 8%
Drank alcohol and sold drugs: 6%
Used marijuana and sold drugs: 5%
Drank alcohol, used marijuana, and sold drugs: 4%

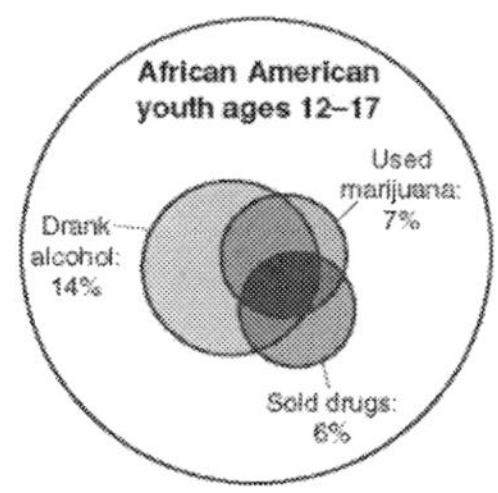

Drank alcohol and used marijuana: 5%
Drank alcohol and sold drugs: 2%
Used marijuana and sold drugs: 2%
Drank alcohol, used marijuana, and sold drugs: 2%

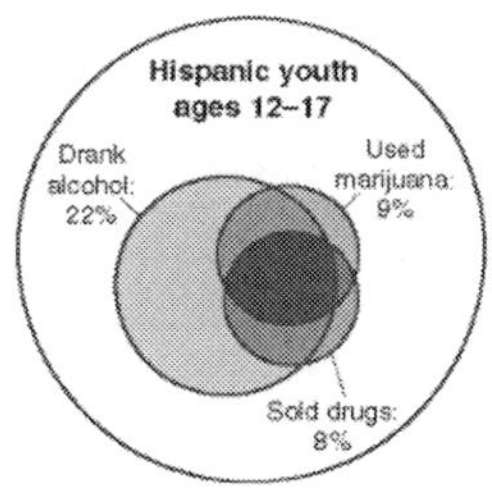

Drank alcohol and used marijuana: 7%
Drank alcohol and sold drugs: 5%
Used marijuana and sold drugs: 4%
Drank alcohol, used marijuana, and sold drugs: 4%

Both white and Hispanic youth were significantly more likely than African American youth to report any substance-related behavior (29%, 26%, and 19%, respectively); whites and Hispanics were both more likely than African Americans to report drinking alcohol; whites were more likely than African Americans to report either marijuana use or drug selling.

Note: Racial categories do not include persons of Hispanic ethnicity. Youth of Hispanic ethnicity may be of any race.

There was significantly less overlap of drug selling, alcohol use, and marijuana use among African American youth than among white or Hispanic youth

Among Youth who Drank Alcohol, 32% Also Used Marijuana, 23% Sold Drugs, and 15% Did Both

Behavior	All youth	Age group		Gender		Race/ethnicity		
	ages 12–17	12–14	15–17	Male	Female	Non-Hispanic White	Non-Hispanic African American	Hispanic
Drank alcohol	23%	11%[a]	35%[b]	23%[a]	23%[a]	26%[a]	14%[b]	22%[c]
Youth who reported drinking alcohol								
Drank alcohol only	60	69[a]	58[b]	58[a]	63[a]	60[a]	63[a]	60[a]
Used marijuana	32	27[a]	34[b]	33[a]	31[a]	32[a]	34[a]	33[a]
Sold drugs	23	17[a]	25[b]	27[a]	18[b]	24[a]	16[a]	23[a]
Used marijuana and sold drugs	15	12[a]	16[a]	18[a]	13[b]	16[a]	12[a]	16[a]
Youth who did not report drinking alcohol								
Used marijuana	2	1[a]	4[b]	3[a]	2[b]	2[a]	3[a]	2[a]
Sold drugs	3	1[a]	6[b]	4[a]	2[b]	3[a]	4[a]	4[a]
Used marijuana and sold drugs	1	<1[a]	1[b]	1[a]	<1[a]	1[a]	1[a]	1[a]

[a, b, c] Cell entries with different superscripts within age, gender, or race subsamples are significantly different at $p<.05$. For example, among youth who reported drinking alcohol, the proportion that only drank alcohol was not significantly different for males (58%) and females (63%), but the proportion that also used marijuana and sold drugs was significantly different for males (18%) and females (13%), although the difference in the percentages was the same in both examples.

Note: Racial categories do not include persons of Hispanic ethnicity. Youth of Hispanic ethnicity may be of any race.

- Most youth ages 12–17 who drank alcohol neither used marijuana nor sold drugs—32% used marijuana and 23% sold drugs.
- However, regardless of age, gender, or race/ethnicity, youth who did not drink alcohol were much less likely than those who did to report marijuana use (2% vs.

32%), drug selling (3% vs. 23%), or both marijuana use and drug selling (1% vs. 15%).

- Males were more likely than females to say they had ever sold drugs. This was true for males and females who drank alcohol (27% vs. 18%) and for males and females who did not (4% vs. 2%).
- Youth ages 15–17 were more likely than youth ages 12–14 to say they used marijuana. This general pattern was found among youth who drank alcohol (34% vs. 27%) and among those who did not drink alcohol (4% vs. 1%).
- Youth ages 15–17 were more likely than youth ages 12–14 to say they ever sold drugs. This general pattern was found among youth who drank alcohol (25% vs. 17%) and among youth who did not drink alcohol (6% vs. 1%).
- Regardless of whether youth reported drinking alcohol, the proportion who reported marijuana use was similar across the three racial/ethnic groups.
- Equal proportions of white, African American, and Hispanic youth who did not drink alcohol reported they sold drugs. This was also true among youth who drank alcohol.

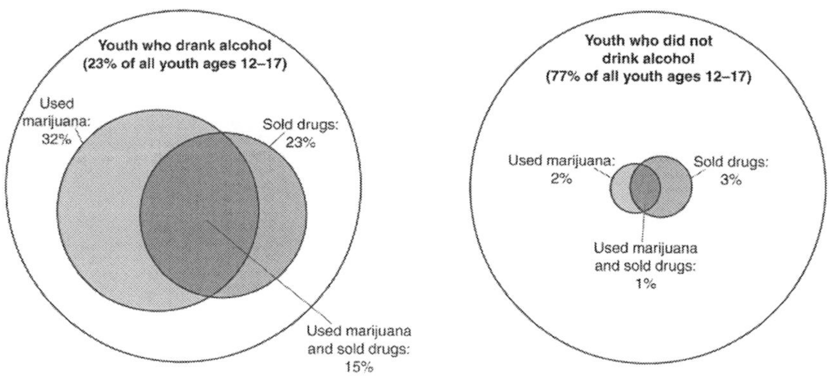

Among Marijuana Users, 81% Also Drank Alcohol, 45% Sold Drugs, and 39% Did Both

	All youth	Age group		Gender		Race/ethnicity		
Behavior	**ages 12–17**	**12–14**	**15–17**	**Male**	**Female**	**Non-Hispanic White**	**Non-Hispanic African American**	**Hispanic**
Used marijuana	9%	4%[a]	14%[b]	10%[a]	9%[a]	10%[a]	7%[b]	9%[ab]
Youth who reported marijuana use								
Marijuana only	12	20[a]	10[b]	13[a]	12[a]	10[a]	22[b]	14[ab]
Drank alcohol	81	74[a]	83[b]	79[a]	84[a]	84[a]	68[b]	80[a]
Sold drugs	45	39[a]	47[a]	51[a]	38[b]	47[a]	35[a]	47[a]
Drank alcohol and sold drugs	39	33[a]	40[a]	42[a]	34[a]	41[a]	25[b]	40[a]
Youth who did not report marijuana use								
Drank alcohol	17	9[a]	27[b]	17[a]	17[a]	20[a]	10[b]	16[c]
Sold drugs	4	2[a]	6[b]	5[a]	3[b]	4[a]	4[a]	4[a]
Drank alcohol and sold drugs	2	1[a]	3[b]	2[a]	1[a]	2[a]	1[b]	2[a]

[a, b, c] Cell entries with different superscripts within age, sex, or race subsamples are significantly different at $p<.05$.

Note: Racial categories do not include persons of Hispanic ethnicity. Youth of Hispanic ethnicity may be of any race.

- In general, a greater proportion of marijuana users than nonusers reported drinking alcohol and selling drugs. More specifically, compared with marijuana users, youth ages 12–17 who did not use marijuana were far less likely to drink alcohol (17% vs. 81%) or sell drugs (4% vs. 45%). This general distinction between marijuana users and nonusers held for youth regardless of age group, gender, or race/ethnicity.
- For marijuana nonusers, older youth (ages 15–17) were more likely than younger youth (ages 12–14) to drink alcohol or sell drugs. Similarly, for marijuana users, a greater proportion of older youth than younger youth reported drinking alcohol (83% vs. 74%). In contrast, the proportions of older and younger marijuana users who reported selling drugs (47% vs. 39%) were not statistically different.

- For youth who reported using marijuana, similar proportions of males and females reported drinking alcohol (79% vs. 84%), although males were more likely to report selling drugs (51% vs. 38%). A similar pattern held for those who said they did not use marijuana, although their levels of drinking alcohol and selling drugs were substantially lower than those of marijuana users.
- For youth who reported using marijuana, statistically equal proportions of white, African American, and Hispanic youth reported they had sold drugs (47%, 35%, and 47%, respectively). A similar pattern held for those who said they did not use marijuana, although their levels were substantially lower than those of marijuana users.

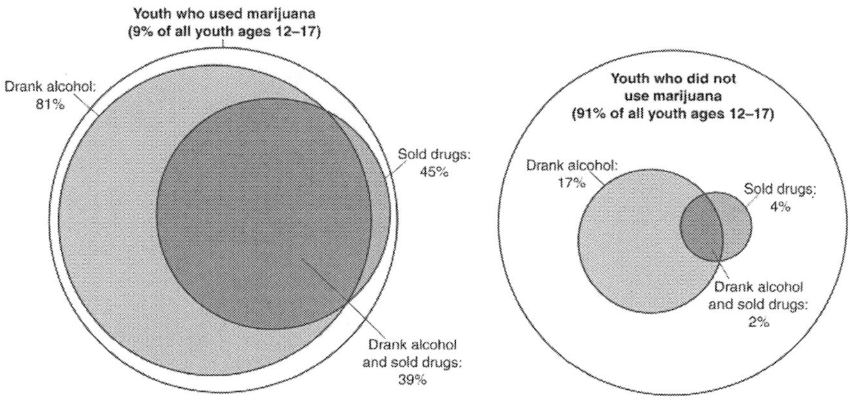

Among Youth who Sold Drugs, 68% Drank Alcohol, 54% Used Marijuana, and 46% Did Both

Behavior	All youth	Age group		Gender		Race/ethnicity		
	ages 12–17	12–14	15–17	Male	Female	Non-Hispanic White	Non-Hispanic African American	Hispanic
Sold drugs	8%	3%[a]	12%[b]	9%[a]	6%[b]	8%[a]	6%[b]	8%[ab]
Youth who reported they ever sold drugs								
Sold drugs only	24	32[a]	22[a]	25[a]	22[a]	19[a]	50[b]	28[a]
Drank alcohol	68	60[a]	70[a]	66[a]	72[a]	74[a]	38[b]	65[a]
Used marijuana	54	51[a]	55[a]	53[a]	55[a]	56[a]	41[b]	53[ab]
Drank alcohol and used marijuana	46	43[a]	47[a]	44[a]	49[a]	49[a]	30[b]	45[ab]
Youth who did not report they ever sold drugs								
Drank alcohol	19	10[a]	30[b]	19[a]	20[a]	22[a]	12[b]	18[c]
Used marijuana	6	3[a]	9[b]	5[a]	6[a]	6[a]	5[a]	5[a]
Drank alcohol and used marijuana	4	2[a]	7[b]	4[a]	5[a]	5[a]	3[b]	4[ab]

[a, b, c] Cell entries with different superscripts within age, sex, or race subsamples are significantly different at $p<.05$.

Note: Racial categories do not include persons of Hispanic ethnicity. Youth of Hispanic ethnicity may be of any race.

- Among all youth ages 12–17, those who sold drugs were much more likely than those who did not sell drugs to say they drank alcohol (68% vs. 19%), used marijuana (54% vs. 6%), or both drank alcohol and used marijuana (46% vs. 4%).
- For youth reporting they never sold drugs, greater proportions of older youth (ages 15–17) than younger youth (ages 12–14) reported they drank alcohol (30% vs. 10%) or used marijuana (9% vs. 3%). These age differences were not found among youth who reported they sold drugs.

- Among youth who sold drugs, there were no statistically significant gender differences in the proportions that reported using alcohol (66% of males and 72% of females) or the proportions that reported using marijuana (53% of males and 55% of females). This lack of gender differences was also found when focusing on youth who did not sell drugs.
- Drinking alcohol was reported by a greater proportion of white youth who sold drugs than African American youth who sold drugs (74% vs. 38%). This racial difference was also found among youth who did not sell drugs (22% vs. 12%).
- Marijuana use was also reported by a greater proportion of white youth who sold drugs than African American youth who sold drugs (56% vs. 41%). However, this racial difference was not found among youth who did not sell drugs

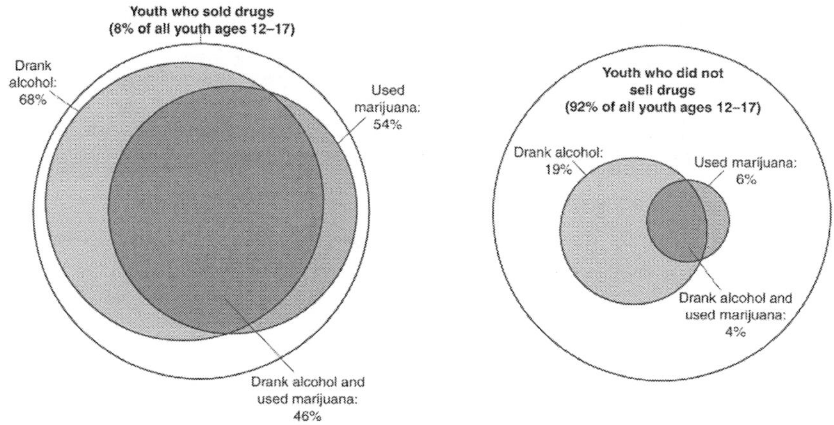

How do NLSY97 Results Compare to Other Drug Use Survey Results?

Prevalence estimates for substance use produced from NLSY97 data tend to fall between those derived from the two major, federally funded drug use surveys—the National Survey on Drug Use and Health (NSDUH, formerly the National Household Survey on Drug Abuse) and Monitoring the Future (MTF). NLSY97 estimates (for 1997 and 1998) match the 1998 NSDUH estimate of the percentage of youth ages 12–17 who used marijuana during the 30 days before the interview (30-day prevalence): 9% for NSDUH and 9% for NLSY97. Reported levels of drinking alcohol were also similar: the NSDUH 1998 estimate of 30-day alcohol prevalence was 21%, whereas the NLSY97 estimate was 23%. In contrast, MTF prevalence estimates are higher than those from the NLSY97 (or from the NSDUH). For example, the 1997 30- day marijuana prevalence estimate for 10th graders from MTF was 20%, compared with 13% for NLSY97; for 30-day alcohol prevalence, the MTF 10th grader estimate was 40% and the NLSY97 estimate was 32%.

ACKNOWLEDGMENTS

This Bulletin was written by Carl McCurley, former Research Associate, and Howard N. Snyder, former Director of Systems Research, at the National Center for Juvenile Justice, with funds provided by OJJDP to support the National Juvenile Justice Data Analysis Project.

This Bulletin was prepared under cooperative agreement number 1999–JN–FX–K002 from the Office of Juvenile Justice and Delinquency Prevention (OJJDP), U.S. Department of Justice.

Points of view or opinions expressed in this document are those of the authors and do not necessarily represent the official position or policies of OJJDP or the U.S. Department of Justice.

The Office of Juvenile Justice and Delinquency Prevention is a component of the Office of Justice Programs, which also includes the Bureau of Justice Assistance; the Bureau of Justice Statistics; the Community Capacity Development Office; the National Institute of Justice; the Office for Victims of Crime; and the Office of Sex Offender Sentencing, Monitoring, Apprehending, Registering, and Tracking (SMART).

End Notes

[1] All references to significant differences in this report imply a 95% (or greater) level of confidence.

In: Perspectives on Juvenile Offenders
Editors: Owen B. Hahn
ISBN: 978-1-60876-819-6

Chapter 3

Drug Offense Cases in Juvenile Courts, 1995-2004

Anne Stahl
Office of Juvenile Justics and Delinquency Prevention

In 2004, juvenile courts in the United States handled an estimated 193,700 delinquency cases in which a drug offense was the most serious charge. Between 1991 and 2004, the number of cases involving drug offenses that juvenile courts handled more than doubled. Drug offense cases accounted for 12% of the delinquency caseload in 2004, compared with 7% in 1985.

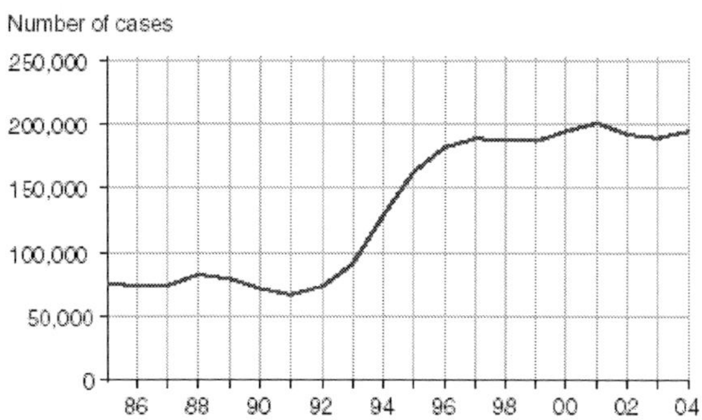

The number of drug offense cases that juvenile courts processed in 2004 was 159% greater than in 1985 and 192% greater than in 1991

Characteristics of Drug Offense Cases in Juvenile Courts

	1985	1995	2004
Gender			
Male	83%	85%	80%
Female	17	15	20
Age at Time of Referral			
15 or younger	43%	42%	43%
16	30	30	29
17 and older	27	28	29
Race/Ethnicity			
White	79%	66%	75%
Black	19	33	22
American Indian/Alaska Native	1	1	2
Asian, Native Hawaiian, and	1	1	1
other Pacific Islander			
Predisposition Detention			
Detained	22%	19%	18%
Not detained	78	81	82
Manner of Handling			
Formal	43%	59%	58%
Informal	57	41	42
Outcome of Formal Handling			
Adjudicated	67%	54%	68%
Not adjudicated	32	44	30
Waived to criminal court	1	2	1
Disposition of Adjudicated Cases			
Placed out of the home	25%	26%	18%
Probation or supervision	64	59	67
Other (fines, restitution, etc.)	11	15	15
Detail may not add up to 100% because of rounding.			

GENDER

Males have historically accounted for the majority of drug offense cases processed in juvenile courts and accounted for 80% to 88% of drug violation cases between 1985 and 2004. Males accounted for 77% to 83% of the drug offense caseload for white juveniles, 90% to 94% of the caseload for black juveniles, 70% to 79% for American Indian/Alaska Native (AI/AN) youth, and 76% to 86% for Asian, Native Hawaiian, and other Pacific Islander (Asian/ NHPI) youth. The female proportion of the juvenile drug offense caseload increased steadily from a low of 12% in 1991 to a high of NHPI) youth. The female proportion of the juvenile drug offense caseload increased steadily from a low of 12% in 1991 to a high of 20% in 2004.

RACE

From 1985 to 1991, the proportion of the drug offense caseload involving white youth decreased from 79% to 50%. This proportion increased to 75% by 2004.[1] During the same period, the proportion of cases involving black juveniles increased from 19% to 48%, then decreased to 22% in 2004.

DETENTION AND ADJUDICATION

In 2004, drug offense cases made up 10% of delinquency cases in which youth were detained; 18% of drug offense cases involved detention at some point between court referral and case disposition. Detention was more likely in drug cases involving youth age 16 and older than youth age 15 and younger (20% versus 16%), males than females (19% versus 15%), and black youth (28%) than youth of any other race (15% for white juveniles, 14% for AI/AN youth, and 22% for Asian/NHPI youth).

In 2004, juvenile courts formally processed 58% of drug offense cases. Between 1985 and 2004, the number of drug offense cases handled with the filing of a petition for adjudication increased 251% (from 31,800 to 111,500). In 2004, 1.3% of formally handled drug cases were judicially waived to criminal court, accounting for 15% of all delinquency cases waived in that year.

The majority (68%) of formally processed drug cases in 2004 resulted in the juvenile being adjudicated delinquent. Of these cases, 18% resulted in a disposition of out-of-home placement, 67% resulted in the youth being placed on probation, and 15% resulted in other sanctions.

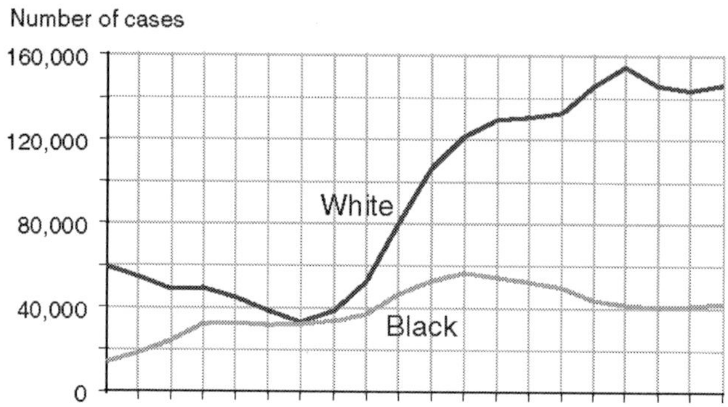

Between 1991 and 2004, the number of drug offense cases involving white juveniles increased 341% compared with 32% for black juveniles

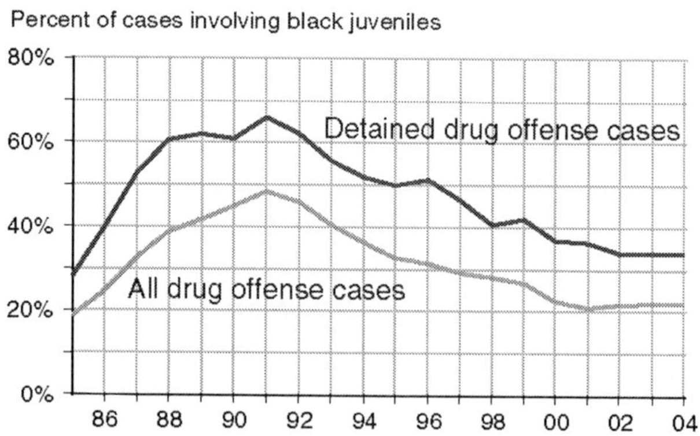

Between 1985 and 1991, the proportion of detained drug offense cases involving black youth increased from 28% to 66%. This proportion has since decreased to 34% but remains greater than the 1985 level

FOR FURTHER INFORMATION

This Fact Sheet is based on the report *Juvenile Court Statistics 2003–2004,* which is available on OJJDP's Web site (www.ojp. usdoj.gov/ojjdp).

To learn more about juvenile court cases, visit OJJDP's Statistical Briefing Book (www.ojjdp.ncjrs.gov/ojstatbb/index.html) and click on

"Juveniles in Court." From OJJDP's home page, click on "Statistics" and select "Juveniles in Court."

Anne L. Stahl is Manager of the National Juvenile Court Data Archive, which is supported by OJJDP grant 2005–JL–FX–0250.

The Office of Juvenile Justice and Delinquency Prevention is a component of the Office of Justice Programs, which also includes the Bureau of Justice Assistance; the Bureau of Justice Statistics; the Community Capacity Development Office; the National Institute of Justice; the Office for Victims of Crime; and the Office of Sex Offender Sentencing, Monitoring, Apprehending, Registering, and Tracking (SMART).

End Notes

[1] Juveniles of Hispanic ethnicity can be of any race, but most are included in the white racial category.

In: Perspectives on Juvenile Offenders
Editors: Owen B. Hahn
ISBN: 978-1-60876-819-6

Chapter 4

JUVENILE ARRESTS 2007

Charles Puzzanchera
Office of Juvenile Justice and Delinquency Prevention

In 2007, law enforcement agencies in the United States made an estimated 2.18 million arrests of persons under age 18.* Overall, there were 2% fewer juvenile arrests in 2007 than in 2006, and juvenile violent crime arrests declined 3%, reversing a recent upward trend. Juvenile arrest rates, particularly Violent Crime Index rates, had increased in 2005 and again in 2006 amid fears that the Nation was on the brink of another juvenile crime wave. These latest data show increases in some offense categories but declines in most— with most changes being less than 10% in either direction.

These findings are drawn from data that local law enforcement agencies across the country report to the FBI's Uniform Crime Reporting (UCR) Program. Based on these data, the FBI prepares its annual *Crime in the United States* statistical compilation, which summarizes crimes known to the police and arrests made during the reporting calendar year. This information is used to describe the extent and nature of juvenile crime that comes to the attention of the justice system. Other recent findings from the UCR Program include the following:

---

* Throughout this Bulletin, youth under age 18 are referred to as juveniles. See Notes on page 12.

- Juveniles accounted for 16% of all violent crime arrests and 26% of all property crime arrests in 2007.
- Juveniles were involved in 12% of all violent crimes cleared in 2007 and 18% of property crimes cleared.
- In 2007, 11% (1,810) of all murder victims were under age 18. More than one-third (35%) of all juvenile murder victims were under age 5, but this proportion varied widely across demographic groups.
- The juvenile murder arrest rate in 2007 was 4.1 arrests per 100,000 juveniles ages 10 through 17. This was 24% more than the 2004 low of 3.3, but 72% less than the 1993 peak of 14.4.
- Between 1998 and 2007, juvenile arrests for aggravated assault decreased more for males than for females (22% vs. 17%). During this period, juvenile male arrests for simple assault declined 4% and female arrests increased 10%.
- In 2007, although black youth accounted for just 17% of the youth population ages 10 through 17, black juveniles were involved in 51% of juvenile Violent Crime Index arrests and 32% of juvenile Property Crime Index arrests.
- The 2007 arrest rates for Violent Crime Index offenses were substantially lower than the rates in the 1994 peak year for every age group under 40.

A Message from OJJDP

Juvenile Arrests 2007 summarizes the juvenile data cited in the FBI report *Crime in the United States 2007*. Thus, this Bulletin serves as a baseline for comparison for juvenile justice professionals and others seeking to assess the Nation's progress in addressing juvenile crime.

The 2007 data bring some welcome news, as the recent trend of modest increases in juvenile arrests in 2005 and 2006 has been broken.

The good news is reflected not only in the 2% decline in overall juvenile arrests and the 3% decline in juvenile arrests for violent crimes from 2006 to 2007 but also in the data for most offense categories, for males and females, and for white and minority youth.

Although this general trend is indeed encouraging, it should not be misconstrued to provide a rationale for complacency.

One area that merits our continued attention is disproportionate minority contact (DMC) with the juvenile justice system. For example, the arrest rate for robbery among black juveniles was more than 10 times that for white youth in 2007. OJJDP remains committed to supporting initiatives to reduce DMC, including improved and expanded delinquency prevention efforts in minority communities.

WHAT DO ARREST STATISTICS COUNT?

To interpret the material in this Bulletin properly, the reader needs a clear understanding of what these statistics count. Arrest statistics report the number of arrests that law enforcement agencies made in a given year—not the number of individuals arrested nor the number of crimes committed. The number of arrests is not the same as the number of people arrested because an unknown number of individuals are arrested more than once during the year. Nor do arrest statistics represent counts of crimes that arrested individuals commit because a series of crimes that one person commits may culminate in a single arrest, and a single crime may result in the arrest of more than one person. This latter situation, where many arrests result from one crime, is relatively common in juvenile law-violating behavior because juveniles are more likely than adults to commit crimes in groups. For this reason, one should not use arrest statistics to indicate the relative proportions of crime that juveniles and adults commit. Arrest statistics are most appropriately a measure of flow into the justice system.

Arrest statistics also have limitations in measuring the volume of arrests for a particular offense. Under the UCR Program, the FBI requires law enforcement agencies to classify an arrest by the most serious offense charged in that arrest. For example, the arrest of a youth charged with aggravated assault and possession of a weapon would be reported to the FBI as an arrest for aggravated assault. Therefore, when arrest statistics show that law enforcement agencies made an estimated 43,900 arrests of young people for weapons law violations in 2007, it means that a weapons law violation was the most serious charge in these 43,900 arrests. An unknown number of additional arrests in 2007 included a weapons charge as a lesser offense.

What Do Clearance Statistics Count?

Clearance statistics measure the proportion of reported crimes that were cleared (or "closed") by either arrest or other, exceptional means (such as the death of the offender or unwillingness of the victim to cooperate). A single arrest may result in many clearances. For example, 1 arrest could clear 10 burglaries if the person was charged with committing all 10 crimes. Or multiple arrests may result in a single clearance if a group of offenders committed the crime. For those interested in juvenile justice issues, the FBI also reports the proportion of clearances that involved only offenders under age 18. This statistic is a better indicator of the proportion of crime that this age group commits than is the proportion of arrests, although there are some concerns that even the clearance statistic overestimates the proportion of crimes committed by juveniles.

Research has shown that juvenile offenders are more easily apprehended than adult offenders; thus, the juvenile proportion of clearances probably overestimates juveniles' responsibility for crime. To add to the difficulty in interpreting clearance statistics, the FBI's reporting guidelines require that clearances involving both juvenile and adult offenders be classified as clearances for crimes committed by adults. Because the juvenile clearance proportions include only those clearances in which no adults were involved, they underestimate juvenile involvement in crime. Although these data do not present a definitive picture of juvenile involvement in crime, they are the closest measure generally available of the proportion of crime known to law enforcement that is attributed to persons under age 18.

In 2007, about 1 in 10 (1,810) Murder Victims Were Juveniles

Each *Crime in the United States* report presents estimates of the number of crimes reported to law enforcement agencies. Although many crimes are never reported to law enforcement, murder is one crime that is nearly always reported.

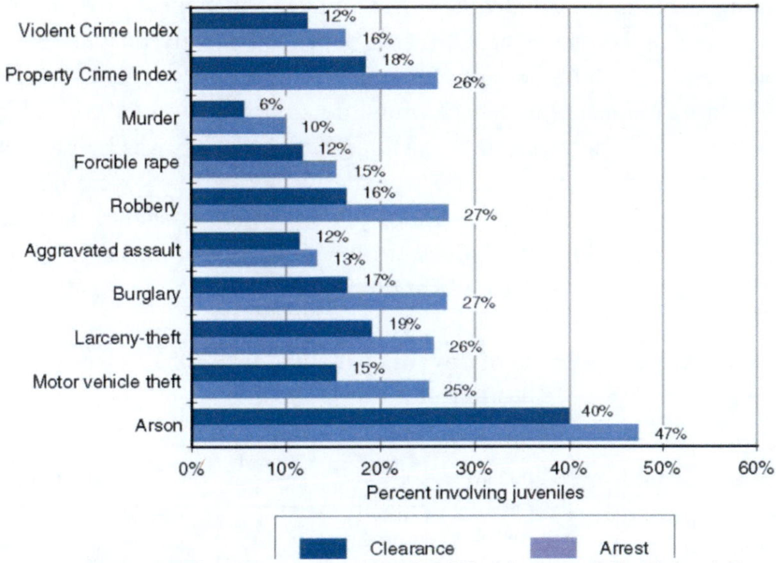

Data source: *Crime in the United States 2007* (Washington, DC: Federal Bureau of Investigation, 2008), tables 28 and 38.

The juvenile proportion of arrests exceeded the juvenile proportion of crimes cleared (or "closed") by arrest in each offense category, reflecting that juveniles are more likely than adults to commit crimes in groups and to be arrested

An estimated 16,930 murders were reported to law enforcement agencies in 2007, or 5.6 murders for every 100,000 U.S. residents. The murder rate was essentially constant between 1999 (the year with the fewest murders in the last three decades) and 2007. Prior to 1999, the last year in which the U.S. murder rate was less than 6.0 was 1966.

Of all murder victims in 2007, 89% (or 15,120 victims) were 18 years of age or older. The other 1,810 murder victims were under age 18 (i.e., juveniles). The number of juveniles murdered in 2007 was 9% more than the average number of juveniles murdered in the prior 5-year period, and 37% less than the peak year of 1993, when an estimated 2,880 juveniles were murdered. During the same prior 5-year period, the estimated number of adult murder victims fell 30%.

Of all juveniles murdered in 2007, 35% were under age 5, 69% were male, and 49% were white. Of all juveniles murdered in 2007, 26% of male victims, 53% of female victims, 41% of white victims, and 27% of black victims were under age 5.

In 2007, 68% of all murder victims were killed with a firearm. Adults were more likely to be killed with a firearm (70%) than were juveniles (52%). However, the involvement of a firearm depended greatly on the age of the juvenile victim. In 2007, 17% of murdered juveniles under age 13 were killed with a firearm, compared with 80% of murdered juveniles age 13 or older. The most common method of murdering children under age 5 was by physical assault: in 50% of these murders, the offenders' only weapons were their hands and/or feet, compared with only 2% of juvenile victims age 13 or older and 4% of adult victims. In 2007, knives or other cutting instruments were used in 8% of juvenile murders and 13% of adult murders.

The 2.18. Million Arrests of Juveniles in 2007 was 20% Fewer than the Number of Arrests in 1998

Most Serious Offense	2007 Estimated Number of Juvenile Arrests	Percent of Total Juvenile Arrests		Percent Change		
		Female	Under Age 15	1998–2007	2003–2007	2006–2007
Total	**2,180,500**	**29%**	**28%**	**–20%**	**–3%**	**–2%**
Violent Crime Index	97,100	17	28	–14	5	–3
Murder and nonnegligent manslaughter	1,350	8	10	–23	26	3
Forcible rape	3,580	2	35	–32	–13	–2
Robbery	34,490	10	21	6	35	–1
Aggravated assault	57,650	23	31	–21	–6	–4
Property Crime Index	419,000	35	31	–33	–10	4
Burglary	81,900	12	30	–30	–3	–2
Larceny-theft	300,300	43	31	–32	–9	8
Motor vehicle theft	29,600	16	22	–49	–30	–14
Arson	7,200	12	59	–19	–7	–8
Nonindex						
Other assaults	240,700	34	39	0	–1	–3
Forgery and counterfeiting	3,100	31	12	–60	–37	–11
Fraud	7,800	36	16	–26	–6	–2

(Continued)

Most Serious Offense	2007 Estimated Number of Juvenile Arrests	Percent of Total Juvenile Arrests		Percent Change		
		Female	Under Age 15	1998–2007	2003–2007	2006–2007
Embezzlement	1,700	42	4	5	43	25
Stolen property (buying, receiving, possessing)	22,400	18	24	–33	–9	–4
Vandalism	111,800	13	41	–14	4	–4
Weapons (carrying, possessing, etc.)	43,900	10	32	–8	12	–7
Prostitution and commercialized vice	1,500	78	13	6	1	–4
Sex offense (except forcible rape and prostitution)	15,500	10	48	–15	–18	–4
Drug abuse violations	195,700	16	15	–6	0	0
Gambling	2,100	2	14	–27	9	–14
Offenses against the family and children	5,800	38	29	–46	–16	11
Driving under the influence	18,200	24	3	–17	–10	–6
Liquor laws	141,000	37	9	–20	2	1
Drunkenness	16,900	25	11	–28	3	3
Disorderly conduct	201,200	33	38	3	–1	–5
Vagrancy	3,800	29	31	51	–33	–21
All other offenses (except traffic)	378,900	26	24	–22	–3	–3
Suspicion (not inclu-ded in totals)	400	24	26	–72	–25	–8
Curfew and loitering	143,000	31	26	–30	3	–5
Runaways	108,900	56	32	–36	–9	–3

- In 2007, there were an estimated 300,300 juvenile arrests for larceny-theft. Between 1998 and 2007, the number of such arrests fell by one-third (32%).

- Of the four offenses that make up the Violent Crime Index, only juvenile arrests for murder increased in 2006–2007 (up 3%).
- In 2007, females accounted for 17% of juvenile Violent Crime Index arrests, 35% of juvenile Property Crime Index arrests, and 33% of juvenile disorderly conduct arrests.
- Youth under age 15 accounted for more than one-fourth (28%) of all juvenile arrests for Violent Crime Index offenses in 2007 and nearly one-third (31%) of all Property Crime Index offenses.

Note: Detail may not add to totals because of rounding.

Data source: *Crime in the United States 2007* (Washington, DC: Federal Bureau of Investigation, 2008), tables 29, 32, 34, 36, 38, and 40. Arrest estimates were developed by the National Center for Juvenile Justice.

One in Eight Violent Crimes Were Attributed to Juveniles

The relative responsibility of juveniles and adults for crime is difficult to determine. Law enforcement agencies are more likely to clear (or "close") crimes that juveniles commit than those committed by adults. Thus, law enforcement records may overestimate juvenile responsibility for crime.

Data on crimes cleared or closed by arrest or exceptional means show that the proportion of violent crimes cleared and attributed to juveniles has been rather constant in recent years, holding between 12% and 13% from 1996 through 2007. The proportions of both forcible rapes and aggravated assaults attributed to juveniles fluctuated between 11% and 12% over this period, while the proportion of murders ranged between 5% and 6% from 1998 through 2007. In contrast, the proportion of robberies attributed to juveniles varied, falling from 18% to 14% between 1996 and 2002 and then increasing gradually to 17% by 2007.

In 2007, 18% of Property Crime Index offenses cleared by arrest or exceptional means were cleared by the arrest of a juvenile. This was one percentage point less than the level in 2006; the level in 2007 was the lowest level since at least the mid-1960s. For comparison, the proportion of Property Crime Index offenses that law enforcement attributed to juveniles was 28% in 1980 and 22% in both 1990 and 2000.

Juvenile Arrests for Violence Declined between 2006 and 2007

The FBI assesses trends in violent crimes by monitoring four offenses that are consistently reported by law enforcement agencies nationwide. These four crimes— murder and nonnegligent manslaughter, forcible rape, robbery, and aggravated assault—form the Violent Crime Index.

Following 10 years of declines between 1994 and 2004, juvenile arrests for Violent Crime Index offenses increased 11% from 2004 to 2006, then declined 4% through 2007. Given that the number of arrests in 2004 was smaller than in any year since 1987, the number of juvenile Violent Crime Index arrests in 2007 was still relatively low. In fact, the number of juvenile violent crime arrests in 2007 was less than any year in the 1990s, and just 3% greater than the average annual number of such arrests between 2001 and 2006.

The number of juvenile arrests in 2007 for forcible rape was less than in any year since at least 1980, and the number of juvenile aggravated assault arrests in 2007 was less than in any year since 1988. In contrast, after also falling to a relatively low level in 2004, juvenile arrests for murder increased each year from 2005 to 2007. To put it in perspective, if the 2004–2007 increase was to continue annually into the future, it would take another 20 years for the annual number of juvenile murder arrests to return to its peak level of the mid-1990s. However, juvenile arrests for robbery increased more than 30% since 2004. If this pace continues, the annual number of juvenile robbery arrests will return to its 1995 peak in just 4 years.

Between 1998 and 2007, the number of arrests in most offense categories declined more for juveniles than for adults:

Most Serious Offense	Percent Change in Arrests 1998–2007	
	Juvenile	Adult
Violent Crime Index	–14%	–8%
Murder	–23	–10
Forcible rape	–32	–21
Robbery	6	6
Aggravated assault	–21	–10
Property Crime Index	–33	–2
Burglary	–30	6

(Continued)

Most Serious Offense	Percent Change in Arrests 1998–2007	
	Juvenile	Adult
Larceny-theft	–42	–4
Motor vehicle theft	–53	–7
Simple assault	0	–2
Weapons law violations	–8	–2
Drug abuse violations	–6	21

Data source: *Crime in the United States 2007*, table 32.

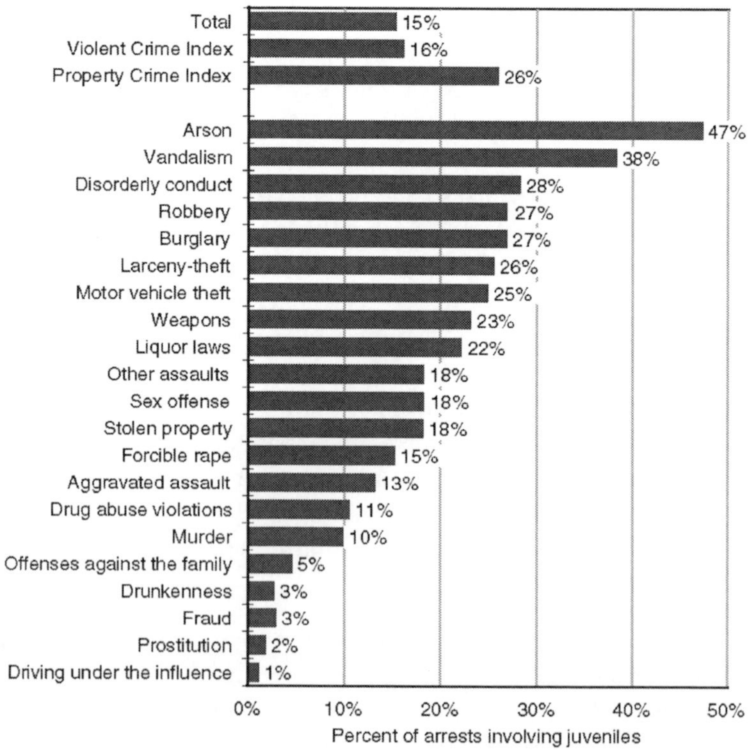

Data source: *Crime in the United States 2007* (Washington, DC: Federal Bureau of Investigation, 2008), table 38.

In 2007, juveniles were involved in 1 in 10 arrests for murder and about 1 in 4 arrests for robbery, burglary, larceny-theft, motor vehicle theft, and weapons violations

JUVENILE PROPERTY CRIME ARRESTS INCREASED IN 2007—THE FIRST TIME IN 13 YEARS

As with violent crime, the FBI assesses trends in the volume of property crimes by monitoring four offenses that are consistently reported by law enforcement agencies nationwide. These four crimes, which form the Property Crime Index, are burglary, larceny-theft, motor vehicle theft, and arson.

For the period 1980–1994, during which juvenile violent crime arrests increased substantially, juvenile property crime arrests remained relatively constant. After this long period of relative stability, juvenile property crime arrests began to fall. Between 1994 and 2006, the number of juvenile Property Crime Index arrests fell by half to their lowest level since at least the 1970s. However, between 2006 and 2007, the number of juvenile arrests for property crimes increased (up 4%)—for the first time since 1993–1994. This increase was a result of growth in the number of juvenile arrests for larceny-theft, which rose 8% from 2006 to 2007. Juvenile arrests for motor vehicle theft and arson reached historic lows in 2007, while arrests for burglary declined 2% since 2006.

MOST ARRESTED JUVENILES WERE REFERRED TO COURT

In most States, some persons younger than age 18 are, because of their age or by statutory exclusion, under the jurisdiction of the criminal justice system. For arrested persons under age 18 and under the original jurisdiction of their State's juvenile justice system, the FBI's UCR Program monitors what happens as a result of the arrest. This is the only instance in the UCR Program in which the statistics on arrests coincide with State variations in the legal definition of a juvenile.

In 2007, 19% of arrests involving youth who were eligible in their State for processing in the juvenile justice system were handled within law enforcement agencies and the youth were released, 70% were referred to juvenile court, and 9% were referred directly to criminal court. The others were referred to a welfare agency or to another police agency. In 2007, the proportion of juvenile arrests sent to juvenile court in cities with a population of more than 250,000 (68%) was similar to that in smaller cities (71%).

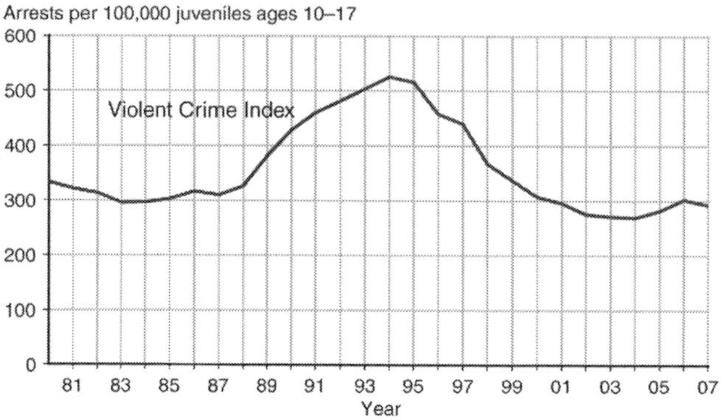

- The juvenile Violent Crime Index arrest rate reached a historic low in 2004, down 49% from its 1994 peak. This decade-long decline was followed by a 12% increase over the next 2 years, and then a 3% decline between 2006 and 2007.

Data source: Analysis of arrest data from the FBI and population data from the U.S. Census Bureau and the National Center for Health Statistics. [*See data source note on p. 12 for detail.*]

The increase in the juvenile Violent Crime Index arrest rate since 2004 was interrupted in 2007

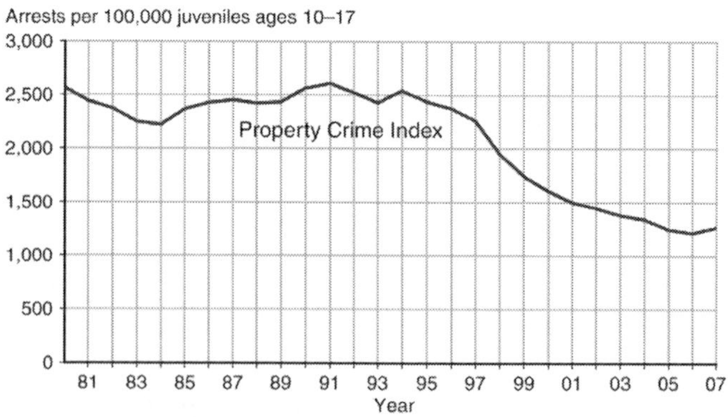

- Despite the recent increase, the 2007 juvenile Property Crime Index arrest rate was 51% less than the 1991 peak. The large declines over the last decade in the two arrest indexes that have traditionally been used to monitor juvenile crime indicate a substantial reduction in the law-violating behavior of America's youth over this period.

Data source: Analysis of arrest data from the FBI and population data from the U.S. Census Bureau and the National Center for Health Statistics. [*See data source note on p. 12 for detail.*]

The juvenile arrest rate for Property Crime Index offenses rose 4% between 2006 and 2007, the first increase since 1993–1994

Murder

- From the mid-1980s to the peak in 1993, the juvenile arrest rate for murder more than doubled.
- Then, the juvenile arrest rate for murder declined through the mid-2000s, reaching a level in 2004 that was 77% less than the 1993 peak.
- The growth in the juvenile murder arrest rate between 2004 and 2007 returned it to near its 2002 level; but even with this increase, the rate in 2007 was 72% less than its 1993 peak.

Forcible Rape

- Following the general pattern of other assaultive offenses, the juvenile arrest rate for forcible rape increased from the early 1980s through the early 1990s and then fell substantially.
- Over the 1980–2007 period, the juvenile arrest rate for forcible rape peaked in 1991, 44% more than its 1980 level.
- With few exceptions, the juvenile arrest rate for forcible rape dropped annually from 1991 through 2007. By 1999, it had returned to its 1980 level. By 2007, the rate had fallen to a point 34% less than the 1980 level and 54% less than its 1991 peak.

Robbery

- In contrast with the juvenile arrest rates for other violent crimes, the rate for robbery declined through much of the 1980s, reaching a low point in 1988. Then, like the violent crime arrest rate in general, by the mid-1990s the juvenile robbery arrest rate grew to a point greater than the 1980 level.
- The juvenile robbery arrest rate declined substantially (62%) between 1995 and 2002. Since 2002, however, the arrest rate rose again, so that by 2007 the rate was 41% greater than its low point in 2002 but still 47% less than its 1995 peak.

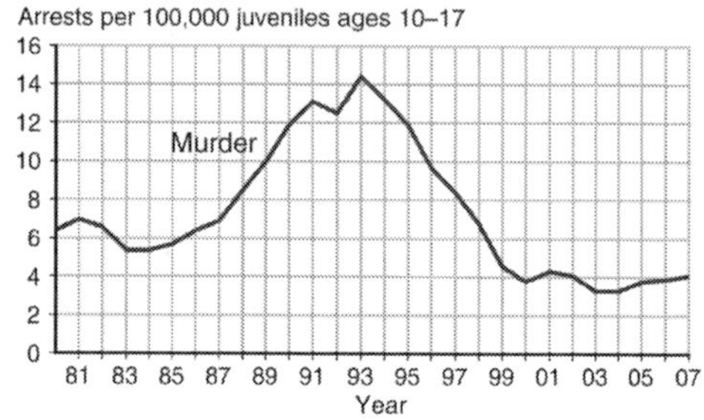

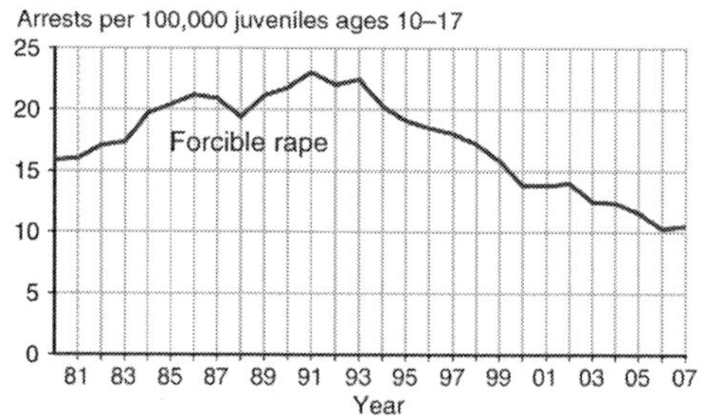

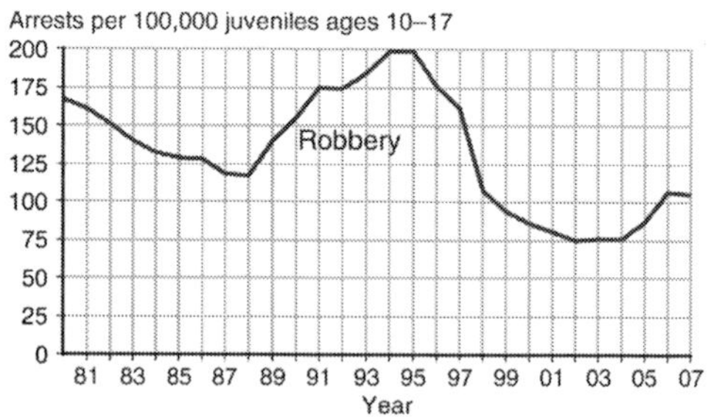

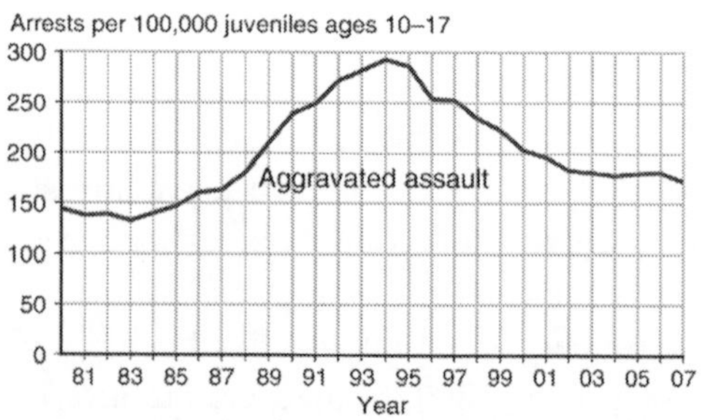

Data source: Analysis of arrest data from the FBI and population data from the U.S. Census Bureau and the National Center for Health Statistics. [*See data source note on p. 12 for detail.*]

In 2007, the juvenile arrest rates for murder, forcible rape, robbery, and aggravated assault each remained well below their peak levels of the 1990s

Aggravated Assault

- The juvenile arrest rate for aggravated assault doubled between 1980 and 1994 and then fell substantially and consistently through 2004, down 39% from its 1994 peak.
- This pattern of decline was interrupted recently, as the juvenile aggravated assault arrest rate increased 2% between 2004 and 2006. By 2007, however, the rate declined 5%, reaching its lowest point since the late 1980s.

Burglary

- Unique in the set of Property Crime Index offenses, the juvenile arrest rate for burglary declined almost consistently and fell substantially between 1980 and 2007, down 69%.
- This large fall in juvenile burglary arrests from 1980 through 2007 was not replicated in the adult statistics. For example, between 1998 and 2007, the number of juvenile burglary arrests fell 30%, while adult burglary arrests increased 6%. In 1980, 45% of all burglary arrests were arrests of a juvenile; in 2007, reflecting the greater decline in juvenile arrests, just 27% of burglary arrests were juvenile arrests.

Larceny-Theft

- The juvenile arrest rate for larceny-theft remained essentially constant between 1980 and 1997, then fell 47% between 1997 and 2006, reaching its lowest point since 1980. This decline reversed in 2007, as the juvenile arrest rate for larceny- theft increased 9%.
- In 2007, 72% of all juvenile arrests for Property Crime Index offenses were for larceny-theft. Thus, juvenile Property Crime Index arrest trends largely reflect the pattern of larceny-theft arrests (which itself is dominated by shoplifting—the most common larceny-theft offense).

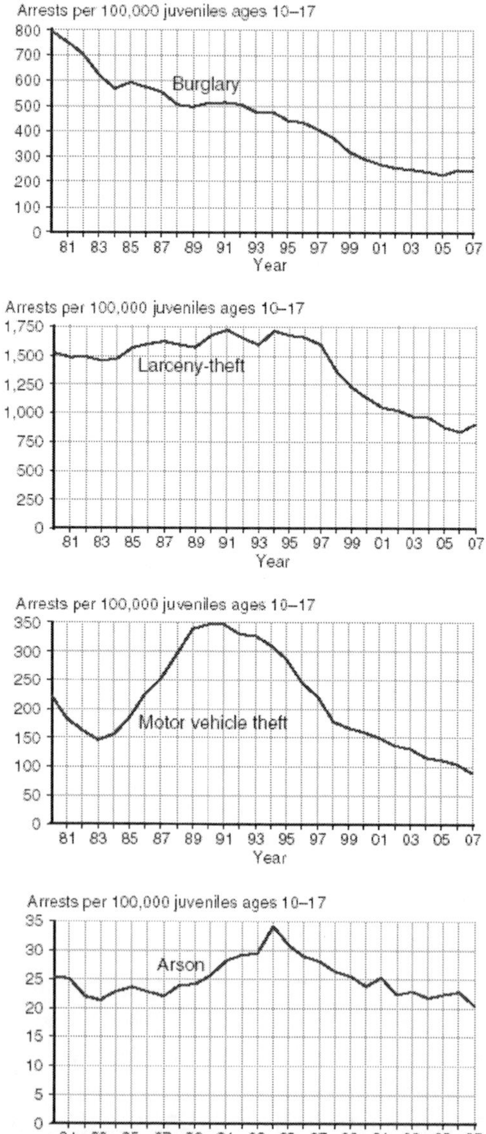

Data source: Analysis of arrest data from the FBI and population data from the U.S. Census Bureau and the National Center for Health Statistics. *[See data source note on p. 12 for detail.]*

The four offenses that make up the Property Crime Index show very different juvenile arrest rate patterns over the 1980–2007 period

Motor Vehicle Theft

- The juvenile arrest rate for motor vehicle theft more than doubled between 1983 and 1990, up 137%.
- After the peak years of 1990 and 1991, the juvenile arrest rate for motor vehicle theft declined steadily through 2007, falling 74%. In 2007, the juvenile arrest rate for motor vehicle theft was lower than in any year in the 1980–2007 period.
- This large decline in juvenile arrests was not replicated in the adult statistics. Between 1996 and 2007, the number of juvenile motor vehicle theft arrests fell more than 49%, while adult motor vehicle theft arrests decreased just 7%.

Arson

- After being relatively stable for most of the 1980s, the juvenile arrest rate for arson grew 33% between 1990 and 1994.
- The juvenile arrest rate for arson declined substantially between 1994 and 2007, falling 40%.
- Following an 11% decline between 2006 and 2007, the juvenile arrest rate for arson in 2007 reached its lowest point since 1980.

IN 2007, FEMALES ACCOUNTED FOR 29% OF JUVENILE ARRESTS

Law enforcement agencies made 641,000 arrests of females under age 18 in 2007. From 1998 through 2007, arrests of juvenile females decreased less than male arrests in most offense categories (e.g., aggravated assault, burglary, and larceny-theft); in some categories (e.g., simple assault, drug abuse violations, and DUI), female arrests increased, while male arrests decreased.

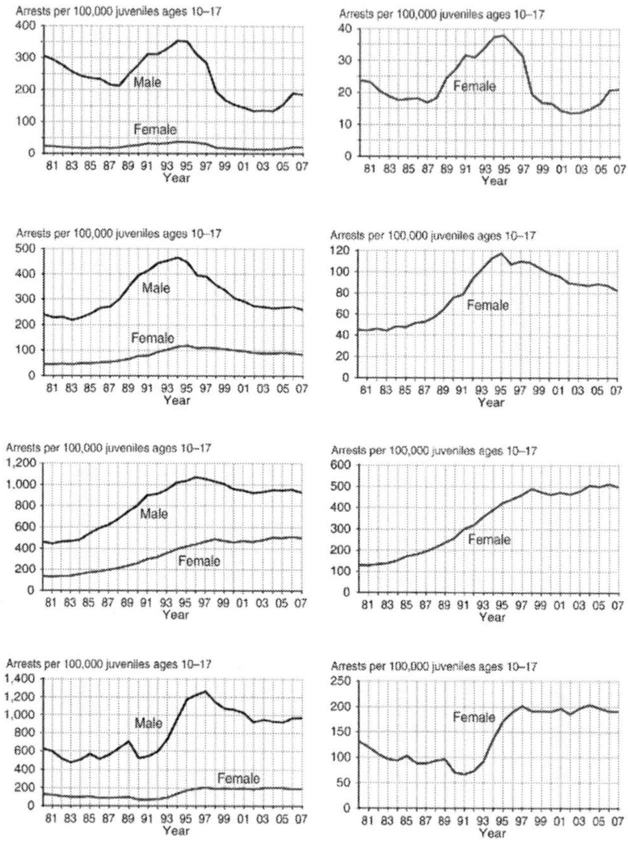

- Juvenile male and female robbery arrest rates both decreased through the late 1980s and climbed to a peak in the mid-1990s; by 2002, both had fallen to their lowest level since at least 1980. Following these declines, the rates for both groups increased through 2007 (39% for males and 55% for females).
- The juvenile female arrest rate for aggravated assault did not decline after its 1990s peak as much as did the male rate. As a result, in 2007, the juvenile male arrest rate was just 8% more than its 1980 level, while the female rate was 83% more than its 1980 rate. Similarly, while the male arrest rate for simple assault doubled between 1980 and 2007, the female rate more than tripled.

Data source: Analysis of arrest data from the FBI and population data from the U.S. Census Bureau and the National Center for Health Statistics. *[See data source note on p. 12 for detail.]*

Although arrest trends by gender were similar for robbery, recent trends showed greater declines for males in other offenses

Most Serious Offense	Percent Change in Juvenile Arrests 1998–2007	
	Female	Male
Violent Crime Index	–13%	–14%
Aggravated assault	–17	–22
Simple assault	10	–4
Property Crime Index	–18	–39
Burglary	–24	–31
Larceny-theft	–15	–41
Motor vehicle theft	–50	–49
Vandalism	–4	–15
Weapons	–1	–9
Drug abuse violations	6	–8
Liquor law violations	–2	–28
DUI	14	–24
Disorderly conduct	20	–5

Data source: *Crime in the United States 2007*, table 33.

Gender differences also occurred in the assault arrest trends for adults. Between 1998 and 2007, adult male arrests for aggravated assault fell 12%, while female arrests fell 1%. Similarly, adult male arrests for simple assault fell 6% between 1998 and 2007, while adult female arrests rose 11%. Therefore, the female proportion of arrests grew for both types of assault. It is likely that the disproportionate growth in female assault arrests over this period was related to factors that affected both juveniles and adults.

Gender differences in arrest trends also increased the proportion of arrests involving females in other offense categories for both juveniles and adults. The number of drug abuse violation arrests of juvenile females grew 6% between 1998 and 2007, while juvenile male arrests declined 8%. Drug abuse violation arrests of adult females grew more than adult male arrests (31% and 19%, respectively). The greater decline in male than in female arrests for Property Crime Index offenses seen for juveniles between 1998 and 2007 was also seen in adult arrests, with adult male arrests falling 7% and adult female arrests increasing 9%.

JUVENILE ARRESTS DISPROPORTIONATELY INVOLVED MINORITIES

The racial composition of the U.S. juvenile population ages 10–17 in 2007 was 78% white, 17% black, 5% Asian/Pacific Islander, and 1% American Indian. Most juveniles of Hispanic ethnicity were included in the white racial category. Of all juvenile arrests for violent crimes in 2007, 47% involved white youth, 51% involved black youth, 1% involved Asian youth, and 1% involved American Indian youth. For property crime arrests, the proportions were 66% white youth, 32% black youth, 1% Asian youth, and 1% American Indian youth. Black youth were overrepresented in juvenile arrests.

Most Serious Offense	**Black Proportion of Juvenile Arrests in 2007**
Murder	57%
Forcible rape	37
Robbery	68
Aggravated assault	41
Simple assault	40
Burglary	33
Larceny-theft	31
Motor vehicle theft	42
Weapons	38
Drug abuse violations	30
Vandalism	19
Liquor laws	5

Data source: *Crime in the United States 2007*, table 43.

The Violent Crime Index arrest rate (i.e., arrests per 100,000 juveniles in the racial group) in 2007 for black juveniles (903) was about 5 times the rates for white juveniles (180) and American Indian juveniles (183) and 16 times the rate for Asian juveniles (57). For Property Crime Index arrests, the rate for black juveniles (2,453) was more than double the rates for white juveniles (1,081) and American Indian juveniles (1,147) and more than 6 times the rate for Asian juveniles (371).

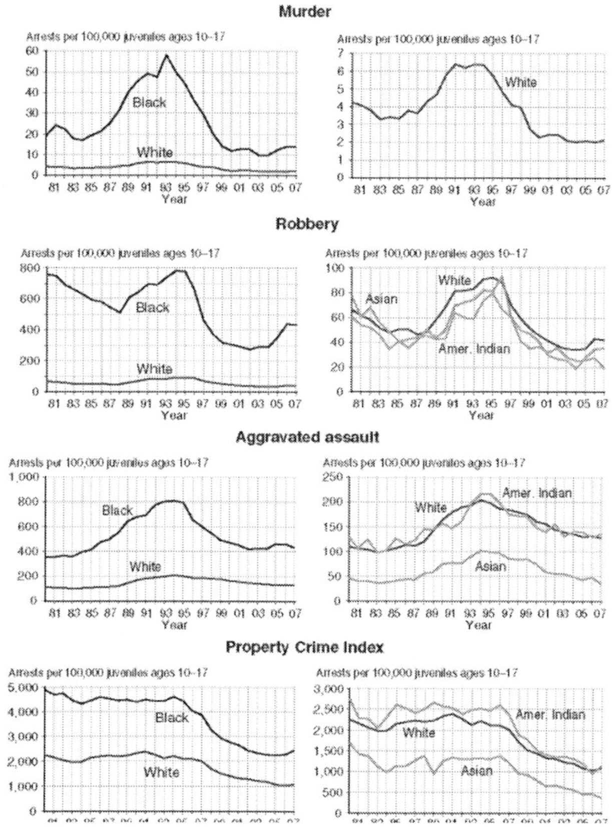

- The white juvenile murder rate in 2007 was near its lowest level since at least 1980, having fallen 67% since its 1993 peak. The black rate in 2007 was well below (76%) its 1993 peak, even though it increased since 2004.
- After peaking in the mid-1990s, robbery and aggravated assault arrest rates fell substantially for all four racial groups.
- From 1994 through 2007, the Property Crime Index arrest rates dropped dramatically for juveniles in all racial groups—declining 45% or more.

Note: Murder rates for American Indian youth and Asian youth are not presented because the small number of arrests and small population sizes produce unstable rate trends.

Data source: Analysis of arrest data from the FBI and population data from the U.S. Census Bureau and the National Center for Health Statistics. [*See data source note on p. 12 for detail.*]

Arrest rate trends from 1980 through 2007 were similar across racial groups; the differences were in the volume of arrests

In the 1980s, the Violent Crime Index arrest rate for black juveniles was between 6 and 7 times the white rate. This ratio declined during the 1990s, falling to 4-to-1 in 1999. Between 1999 and 2007, the racial disparity in the rates increased, reaching 5-to-1 in 2007. This increase resulted from an increase in the black rate (5%) and a decline in the white rate (25%). More specifically, the robbery arrest rate increased 37% for black juveniles while the white rate declined 17%, and the aggravated assault rate declined less for black (12%) than for white juveniles (27%).

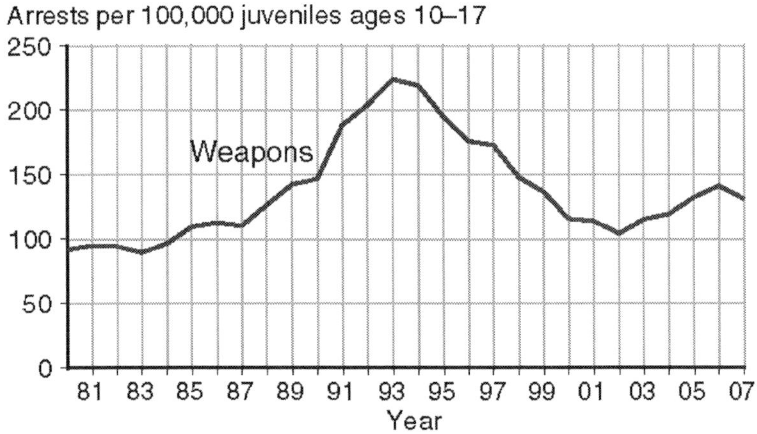

- Between 1980 and 1993, the juvenile arrest rate for weapons law violations increased more than 140%. Then the rate fell substantially, so that by 2002 the rate was just 14% more than the 1980 level.
- However, between 2002 and 2006, the juvenile weapons arrest rate grew 35%, then fell 7% through 2007. As a result, the rate in 2007 was 43% more than the 1980 level and 41% less than its 1993 peak. Between 2006 and 2007, the rate declined more for females (10%) than for males (6%), and more for whites (8%) than for blacks (5%).

The decline in the juvenile arrest rate for weapons law violations between 2006 and 2007 broke the trend of increasing rates that began in 2003

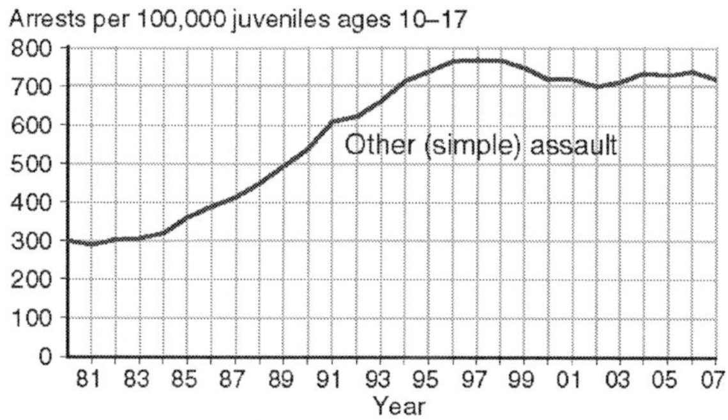

- The juvenile arrest rate for simple assault increased 156% between 1980 and 1997, declined slightly through 2002, then rose again through 2006. The rate dropped 3% in 2007 to a level 6% less than the 1997 peak.
- Unlike the trend for simple assault, the juvenile aggravated assault arrest rate declined steadily since the mid-1990s, falling 41% between 1994 and 2007.
- The 2007 juvenile arrest rate for simple assault was substantially greater than the 1980 rate for most racial groups.

The juvenile arrest rate for simple assault has changed little since 2000, fluctuating less than 4% in any given year

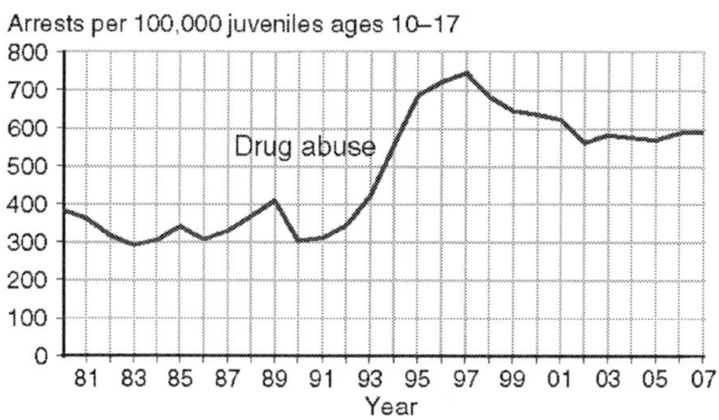

- Between 1990 and 1997, the juvenile arrest rate for drug abuse violations increased 145%. The rate declined 21% between 1997 and 2007, but the 2007 rate was still almost double the 1990 rate.
- Over the 1980–2007 period, the juvenile drug arrest rate for whites peaked in 1997 and then held relatively constant through 2007 (down 10%). In contrast, the rate for blacks peaked in 1995, then fell 49% by 2002. Despite the recent increase—23% since 2002—the rate in 2007 was 37% less than the 1995 peak.

After a period of substantial growth during the 1990s, the juvenile arrest rate for drug abuse violations declined after 1997

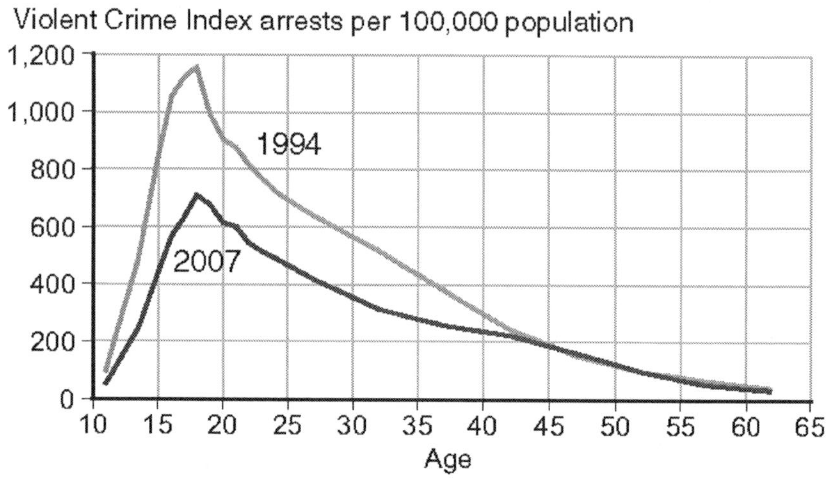

- Juveniles showed the largest decline—falling nearly 50% in each age group from 10 through 17. Between 1994 and 2007, the Violent Crime Index arrest rates for 18-year-olds fell 39%. The Violent Crime Index arrest rates for persons age 19–39 fell more than 30% for each age group.
- Over the 1994–2007 period, the Violent Crime Index arrest rates for persons age 40–54 changed little, while the arrest rates for persons age 55–64 declined.

Between the 1994 peak and 2007, arrest rates for Violent Crime Index offenses fell substantially for every age group younger than 40

Data source: Analysis of arrest data from the FBI and population data from the U.S. Census Bureau and the National Center for Health Statistics. *[See data source note on p. 12 for detail.]*

Data Source Note

Analysis of arrest data from unpublished FBI reports for 1980 through 1997, from *Crime in the United States* reports for 1998 through 2003 (Washington, DC: U.S. Government Printing Office, 1999 through 2004, respectively) and from *Crime in the United States* reports for 2004 through 2007, which are available online at www.fbi.gov/ucr/ucr.htm#cius, released September 2008; population data for 1980–1989 from the U.S. Census Bureau, *U.S. Population Estimates by Age, Sex, Race, and Hispanic Origin: 1980 to 1999* [machine-readable data files available online, released April 11, 2000]; population data for 1990–1999 from the National Center for Health Statistics (prepared by the U.S. Census Bureau with support from the National Cancer

Institute), *Bridged-race Intercensal Estimates of the July 1, 1990–July 1, 1999, United States Resident Population by County, Single-year of Age, Sex, Race, and Hispanic Origin* [machine-readable data files available online at www.cdc.gov/nchs/ about/major/dvs/popbridge/popbridge.htm, released July 26, 2004]; and population data for 2000–2007 from the National Center for Health Statistics (prepared under a collaborative arrangement with the U.S. Census Bureau), *Estimates of the July 1, 2000–July 1, 2007, United States Resident Population From the Vintage 2007 Postcensal Series by Year, County, Age, Sex, Race, and Hispanic Origin* [machine-readable data files available online at www. cdc.gov/nchs/about/major/dvs/popbridge/ popbridge.htm, released September 5, 2008].

NOTES

In this Bulletin, "juvenile" refers to persons under age 18. This definition is at odds with the legal definition of juveniles in 2007 in 13 States—10 States where all 17-year-olds are defined as adults and 3 States where all 16- and 17-year-olds are defined as adults.

FBI arrest data in this Bulletin are counts of arrests detailed by age of arrestee and offense categories from all law enforcement agencies that reported complete data for the calendar year. (See *Crime in the United States* for offense definitions.) The proportion of the U.S. population covered by these reporting agencies ranged from 63% to 94% between 1980 and 2007, with 2007 coverage of 75%.

Estimates of the number of persons in each age group in the reporting agencies' resident populations assume that the resident population age profiles are like the Nation's. Reporting agencies' total populations were multiplied by the U.S. Census Bureau's most current estimate of the proportion of the U.S. population for each age group.

State Variations in Juvenile Arrest Rates May Reflect Differences in Juvenile Law-Violating Behavior, Police Behavior, and/or Community Standards; Therefore, Comparisons Should be Made with Caution

State	Reporting Coverage	2007 Juvenile Arrest Rate[*]				State	Reporting Coverage	2007 Juvenile Arrest Rate[*]			
		Violent Crime Index	Property Crime Index	Drug Abuse	Weapons			Violent Crime Index	Property Crime Index	Drug Abuse	Weapons
United States	81%[†]	301	1,293	590	128	Missouri	85%	257	1,573	641	97
Alabama	75	180	757	249	46	Montana	84	90	1,745	378	41
Alaska	96	220	1,559	328	68	Nebraska	85	138	1,823	644	109
Arizona	94	228	1,546	784	84	Nevada	96	238	1,313	517	152
Arkansas	66	147	1,012	381	60	New Hampshire	68	86	692	540	30
California	98	410	1,074	519	202	New Jersey	97	334	864	689	185
Colorado	90	173	1,621	741	137	New Mexico	71	279	1,045	752	178
Connecticut	93	282	1,017	442	89	New York	55	270	1,002	520	66
Delaware	99	591	1,647	819	137	North Carolina	77	318	1,431	508	215
District of Columbia	0	NA	NA	NA	NA	North Dakota	88	79	1,874	436	43
Florida	100	477	1,864	763	106	Ohio	60	150	1,001	414	70
Georgia	62	294	1,342	591	223	Oklahoma	100	178	1,122	503	87
Hawaii	0	NA	NA	NA	NA	Oregon	94	230	1,855	603	94
Idaho	92	141	1,823	544	110	Pennsylvania	92	426	1,075	523	127
Illinois	23	913	1,547	2,152	294	Rhode Island	83	86	960	386	117
Indiana	71	209	1,510	486	59	South Carolina	95	294	1,120	705	168
Iowa	86	258	1,860	450	45	South Dakota	49	95	1,461	476	68

(Continued)

State	Reporting Coverage	2007 Juvenile Arrest Rate*				State	Reporting Coverage	2007 Juvenile Arrest Rate*			
		Violent Crime Index	Property Crime Index	Drug Abuse	Weapons			Violent Crime Index	Property Crime Index	Drug Abuse	Weapons
Kansas	64	168	952	533	77	Tennessee	79	332	1,249	626	144
Kentucky	20	343	2,168	1,360	127	Texas	91	188	1,087	593	64
Louisiana	61	364	1,617	623	113	Utah	88	120	1,879	506	133
Maine	100	63	1,477	417	44	Vermont	98	65	570	286	35
Maryland	99	548	1,876	1,192	221	Virginia	95	146	784	359	88
Massachusetts	91	307	521	377	46	Washington	75	267	1,897	540	144
Michigan	92	224	1,024	337	89	West Virginia	77	42	368	161	16
Minnesota	98	217	1,758	507	135	Wisconsin	98	298	2,634	806	233
Mississippi	37	138	1,227	495	120	Wyoming	99	124	1,748	994	85

* Throughout this Bulletin, juvenile arrest rates are calculated by dividing the number of arrests of persons ages 10–17 by the number of persons ages 10–17 in the population. In this table only, arrest rate is defined as the number of arrests of persons under age 18 for every 100,000 persons ages 10–17. Juvenile arrests (arrests of youth under age 18) reported at the State level in *Crime in the United States* cannot be disaggregated into more detailed age categories so that the arrest of persons under age 10 can be excluded in the rate calculation. Therefore, there is a slight inconsistency in this table between the age range for the arrests (birth through age 17) and the age range for the population (ages 10–17) that are the basis of a State's juvenile arrest rates. This inconsistency is slight because just 1% of all juvenile arrests involved youth under age 10. This inconsistency is preferable to the distortion of arrest rates that would be introduced were the population base for the arrest rate to incorporate the large volume of children under age 10 in a State's population.

† The reporting coverage for the total United States in this table (81%) includes all States reporting arrests of persons under age 18. This is greater than the coverage in the rest of the Bulletin (75%) for various reasons. For example, Florida provided arrest counts of persons under age 18 but did not provide the age detail required to support other presentations in *Crime in the United States 2007*.

NA = *Crime in the United States 2007* reported no arrest counts for the District of Columbia and Hawaii.

Interpretation cautions: Arrest rates are calculated by dividing the number of youth arrests made in the year by the number of youth living in reporting jurisdictions. While juvenile arrest rates in part reflect juvenile behavior, many other factors can affect the size of these rates. For example, jurisdictions that arrest a relatively large number of nonresident juveniles would have higher arrest rates than jurisdictions where resident youth behave in an identical manner. Therefore, jurisdictions that are vacation destinations or regional centers for economic activity may have arrest rates that reflect more than the behavior of their resident youth. Other factors that influence the magnitude of arrest rates in a given area include the attitudes of its citizens toward crime, the policies of the jurisdiction's law enforcement agencies, and the policies of other components of the justice system. **Consequently, comparisons of juvenile arrest rates across States, while informative, should be made with caution**. In most States, not all law enforcement agencies report their arrest data to the FBI. Rates for these States are necessarily based on partial information. If the reporting law enforcement agencies in these States are not representative of the entire State, then the rates will be biased. **Therefore, reported arrest rates for States with less than complete reporting coverage may not be accurate.**

Data source: Analysis of arrest data from the FBI's *Crime in the United States 2007* (Washington, DC: Federal Bureau of Investigation, 2008), tables 5 and 69, and population data from the National Center for Health Statistics' *Estimates of the July 1, 2000–July 1, 2007, United States Resident Population From the Vintage 2007 Postcensal Series by Year, County, Age, Sex, Race, and Hispanic Origin* [machine-readable data files available online at http://www.cdc.gov/nchs/about/major/dvs/popbridge/popbridge.htm, released 9/5/2008].

ACKNOWLEDGMENTS

This Bulletin was written by Charles Puzzanchera, Senior Research Associate, with assistance from Melissa Sickmund, Ph.D., Chief of Systems Research, and Ben Adams, Research Assistant, at the National Center for Juvenile Justice, with funds provided by OJJDP to support the National Juvenile Justice Data Analysis Project.

This Bulletin was prepared under cooperative agreement number 2007–JF–FX–K003 from the Office of Juvenile Justice and Delinquency Prevention (OJJDP), U.S. Department of Justice.

In: Perspectives on Juvenile Offenders
Editors: Owen B. Hahn
ISBN: 978-1-60876-819-6

Chapter 5

JUVENILE JUSTICE: LEGISLATIVE HISTORY AND CURRENT LEGISLATIVE ISSUES

Kristin M. Finklea

SUMMARY

Juvenile justice in the United States has predominantly been the province of the states and their localities. The first juvenile court in America was founded in 1899 in Cook County, Illinois, and, by 1925, all but two states had established juvenile court systems. The mission of these early juvenile courts was to rehabilitate young delinquents instead of just punishing them for their crimes; in practice, this led to marked procedural and substantive differences between the adult and juvenile court systems in the states, including a focus on the offenders and not the offenses, and rehabilitation instead of punishment.

The federal government began to play a role in the states' juvenile justice systems in the 1960s and 1970s. In 1974, Congress passed the first comprehensive piece of juvenile justice legislation, the Juvenile Justice and Delinquency Prevention Act (JJDPA). The JJDPA had three main components: it created a set of institutions within the federal government that were dedicated to coordinating and administering federal juvenile justice efforts; it established grant programs to assist the states with setting up and running their juvenile justice systems; and it promulgated core mandates that states had to adhere to in order to be eligible to receive grant funding. Although the JJDPA has been amended several times over the past 30 years, its basic shape remains similar to that of its original conception.

As it was passed in 1974, the JJDPA focused largely on preventing juvenile delinquency and on rehabilitating juvenile offenders. Subsequent revisions to the act added sanctions and accountability measures to some existing federal grant programs, and new grant programs to the act's purview. In altering the JJDPA to include a greater emphasis on punishing juveniles for their crimes, Congress has essentially followed the lead of the states. During the 1 980s and 1 990s, most states revised their juvenile justice systems to include more punitive measures and to allow juveniles to be tried as adults in more instances. This has marked a significant change in the philosophy of the juvenile justice system, both at the state level and at the federal level, from its original conception. Juvenile justice in general has thus moved away from emphasizing the rehabilitation of juveniles and toward a greater reliance on sanctioning them for their crimes.

Authorization of the JJDPA's main provisions expired at the end of FY2007 and FY2008, but its major programs have continued to receive appropriations. Reauthorization is now an issue confronting the 111th Congress. Policy issues associated with its reauthorization include what the best federal response to juvenile violence and juvenile crime should be; whether the system should focus on the rehabilitation of juvenile offenders or on holding juvenile offenders accountable for their actions; and whether the grant programs as currently comprised represent the best way to support juvenile justice efforts in the states.

This report will be updated as circumstances warrant.

INTRODUCTION

Administering justice to juvenile offenders has largely been the domain of the states, and as a result of this the laws that pertain to juvenile offenders can vary widely from state to state. There is no federal juvenile justice system. Although the federal government does not play a direct role in administering juvenile justice, in the 1960s, the federal government began establishing federal juvenile justice agencies and grant programs in order to influence the states' juvenile justice systems. The Juvenile Justice and Delinquency Prevention Act (JJDPA) of 1974 created many of the federal entities and grant programs that continue to operate today, including the Office of Juvenile Justice and Delinquency Prevention (OJJDP) and the state formula grants. Eligibility for many of these grant programs is tied to certain mandates that the states must adhere to in order to receive federal funding. Over the ensuing decades, the JJDPA has been modified a number of times, broadening the mandate of the agencies it created and adding to the grant programs it established.

This report will analyze the current federal legislation that impacts the state juvenile justice systems. Although the report provides some background information on the evolution of juvenile justice in the United States, the main focus of the report is the major federal legislation that impacts the states juvenile justice systems, including the JJDPA. As the major provisions of the JJDPA expired in FY2007 and FY2008, several issues pertaining to its reauthorization may be of concern to the 111th Congress, including, but not limited to, the following:

- Should the core mandates associated with the state formula grants be expanded or modified?
- Are the current grant programs effective?
- Is there sufficient coordination occurring at the federal level?
- Should the federal approach to juvenile justice focus on rehabilitation, accountability, or both philosophies?

The original JJDPA and its major revisions through the end of the 109th Congress will be addressed in **Appendix A** and **Appendix B**.

BACKGROUND

Juvenile justice in the United States has been predominantly the province of the states and their localities. The first juvenile court in America was founded in 1899 in Cook County, Illinois. Twenty-five years later, all but two states had enacted legislation establishing a separate juvenile court system for young offenders. The mission of these juvenile courts was to attempt to turn young delinquents into productive adults rather than merely punishing them for their crimes. This led to marked procedural and substantive differences between the adult and juvenile court systems in the states, including a focus on the offenders and not the offenses, and on rehabilitation instead of punishment.[1]

The federal government began to play a role in the states' juvenile justice systems in the 1960s and 1970s. In the Juvenile Delinquency and Youth Offenses Control Act,[2] Congress provided funds for state and local governments, through the Department of Health, Education, and Welfare, to conduct demonstration projects to research improved methods for preventing and controlling crime committed by juveniles. In 1968, Congress passed additional legislation[3] to provide direct assistance to state and local governments and to train juvenile justice personnel. To receive funding, states were required to designate a single agency to take the lead in improving delinquency prevention and control programs. Also in 1968, Congress for the first time placed juvenile justice grant authority within the purview of the Department of Justice (DOJ).

Despite these congressional efforts to provide assistance to the states as they attempted to rein in juvenile crime, juvenile arrests for violent crimes increased by 216% between 1960 and 1974.[4] This increase in juvenile violent crime outstripped the growth in the juvenile population; the under-18 population grew from 47 million in 1950 to 70 million in 1970 – an increase of only 49%.[5] It seemed apparent that the technical assistance and financial aid that Congress had provided the states was not enough to address the growing problem of juvenile crime, and many commentators maintained that there was a need for a distinct federal entity to manage the federal government's response to juvenile delinquency. In 1974, Congress addressed the issue by passing the first comprehensive piece of juvenile justice legislation, the Juvenile Justice and Delinquency Prevention Act (JJDPA).[6] The JJDPA created a number of grant programs and a new federal agency within DOJ's OJJDP, to oversee these grant programs and to coordinate the federal government-wide response to juvenile delinquency.

In the 1980s, many states responded to the public perception that juvenile crime was increasing by passing more punitive laws for juvenile offenders. Some of these laws removed certain types of juvenile crimes from the juvenile court system altogether, mandating that they be handled by the adult criminal system instead. Other laws instituted mandatory sentences for juvenile offenders convicted of certain crimes. This movement toward punishing juveniles and away from working to rehabilitate them accelerated in the 1990s, with all but three states passing laws that modified or removed traditional juvenile court confidentiality agreements, all but five states passing laws easing the transfer of juveniles into the adult criminal justice system, and a majority of states passing laws expanding sentencing options for juveniles.[7] During this period, more punitive measures were incorporated into the accepted federal funding streams for juvenile justice programs through a series of revisions to the JJDPA. These revisions are described in **Appendix A** and **Appendix B**.

JUVENILE JUSTICE HISTORY

The First Juvenile Courts

The early criminal justice system in America did not include a separate juvenile justice system. The colonists brought the British criminal justice system with them to the new world. This system included forced apprenticeship for poor and neglected children. If a juvenile committed a crime, they were first warned, shamed, or given corporeal punishment and then returned to the community. If a child committed a major criminal act, however, they were treated and tried as adults. Trials and punishment were largely based on the offender's age; anybody over the age of seven was subject to a trial in criminal court.[8] These early American laws had three fundamental features: establishing local control of the justice system, giving families the responsibility (and legal liability) for their children's actions, and distinguishing between deserving and undeserving poor people.[9]

The first Juvenile Court in the United States was established in Chicago in 1899. By 1925, all but two states had established separate juvenile justice systems.[10] The Juvenile Court of Chicago was based on the British doctrine of *parens patriae*, or the notion of the state acting in the nature of a parent. This doctrine was used to explain the state's interest in distinguishing between adults and children in its dispensation of justice. Because children are not fully imbued with developmental or legal capacity, the *parens patriae* doctrine held that the government could provide protection and treatment for children whose parents were not providing adequate care or supervision.[11] The Juvenile Court of Chicago became the model for the various state juvenile justice systems that followed it. Its key features were the definition of a juvenile as a child under the age of 16; the separation of children and adults in correctional institutions; the establishment of special, informal procedural rules, including the elimination of indictments, pleadings, and jury trials; the provision of probation officers to monitor juveniles released into the community; and the prohibition of the detention of children below the age of 12 in a jail or police station.[12]

Although delinquency among children was punished, key elements of the juvenile justice system as it was originally conceived were the welfare of the child and the concept that delinquent children could be transformed into productive citizens through treatment. This benevolent mission was clearly stated in most laws that established juvenile justice systems, and led to substantial procedural and substantive differences between juvenile and adult criminal justice systems in the states. For example, juvenile court intake considered extra-legal factors—such as the child's home situation—as well as legal factors when deciding whether to bring a case to trial, and had the discretion to handle cases informally.[13]

Additionally, these early juvenile courts did not incorporate the procedural due process protections afforded adult criminal defendants, which were deemed unnecessary as a result of the court's benevolent mission. Attorneys for the state and the youth being tried were not considered essential to the system's operation, especially in less serious cases, and judges had a broad range of dispositions at their disposal that were tailored to the best interests of the child. Judges' dispositions became part of a treatment plan for the juvenile, and this treatment continued until the juvenile was considered cured or became an adult at age 21.[14]

In 1914, the practice of *diversion*, or the official halting of formal criminal proceedings against a juvenile offender, was established with the creation of the Chicago Boy's Court. The goal of diversion was to provide treatment for juveniles outside of the formal juvenile justice system. To this end, the juvenile court in Chicago released juveniles to the supervision and authority of various community service agencies, who evaluated the youth's behavior and reported back to the Court. If the evaluation was satisfactory to the Judge, the court officially discharged the juvenile without any formal record of the proceedings.[15]

By 1930, only the federal government continued to treat children who were charged with a crime as adults.[16] This situation led the U.S. Attorney General (AG) to recommend that juveniles charged with violating federal laws be returned to their home state's juvenile justice system, a proposition that Congress agreed with.[17]

Early Federal Government Efforts

The earliest federal government involvement in juvenile delinquency occurred in 1909, when the White House held a Conference on the Care of Dependent Children. The goal of this conference was to share information about needy children across the United States and to emphasize the immediate need for action. This conference led directly to the creation of the U.S. Children's Bureau in 1912. The Children's Bureau was authorized to investigate and report on all aspects of child welfare, including the juvenile justice system.[18] In 1936, the Children's Bureau began providing the first federal subsidy program that provided child welfare grants to states. These grants were used to care for a wide array of at-risk youth, including juvenile delinquents.

The first major federal legislation addressing juvenile delinquents was enacted in 1938. The Federal Juvenile Delinquency Act of 1938 (FJDA)[19] left the state juvenile justice systems as the preferred alternative for juveniles arrested for violating federal laws, but gave the Attorney General the discretion to charge a juvenile as an adult and allowed for federal juvenile proceedings if both parties agreed to it.

In 1951, Congress amended the FJDA with the Federal Youth Corrections Act.[20] This act afforded juvenile offenders tried as adults in the federal system special rehabilitation outcomes. Apart from this revision, however, the FJDA remained essentially unchanged for 35 years until Congress passed major Juvenile Justice reform measures in the 1970s. In 1951, Congress also established the Juvenile Delinquency Bureau within the Department of Health, Education, and Welfare (HEW). The bureau's placement within HEW can be seen as a reflection of the early governmental focus on the treatment of juvenile delinquents and the prevention of delinquency, rather than on punishment.[21]

In the 1950s and 1960s, however, many observers began to question the juvenile courts' ability to successfully rehabilitate delinquents. While the system's basic goal of rehabilitating juveniles through individually tailored plans was not in question, professionals in the field grew concerned about the growing numbers of juveniles being institutionalized for treatment purposes. This concern was reflected in a series of Supreme Court rulings during the 1960s that required that juvenile court procedures become more formal in order to afford juveniles legal protections comparable to those afforded adults in criminal courts.[22]

The landmark Supreme Court ruling of this period, *In re Gault*,[23] concluded that hearings that could result in the institutionalization of children must afford the juveniles being tried the right to notice and counsel, the right to question witnesses, and the right to protection from self-incrimination. Although the Court did not include the right to appellate review in its decision, it encouraged the states to afford juveniles that protection as well.[24]

Congress responded to the increasing public awareness of juvenile crime by passing the Juvenile Delinquency and Youth Offenses Control Act of 1961.[25] This act authorized HEW to provide grants totaling $10 million annually, for three years, to states, local government entities, and private nonprofit agencies to fund demonstration projects that focused on improving the methods used to prevent and control juvenile crime. The projects funded through this initiative were focused on urban inner-cities that had the highest juvenile delinquency rates at the time.[26]

In 1968, Congress took two further actions that affected federal funding for juvenile justice. The first was the Juvenile Delinquency Prevention and Control Act,[27] which provided grant funding to the states and local government entities for the training of juvenile court personnel. These grants were to be administered by HEW. The second was the Omnibus Crime Control and Safe Streets Act,[28] which, among other things, involved DOJ in juvenile justice for the first time through the Law Enforcement Assistance Administration (LEAA), which was created in Title I of the Act. LEAA was to serve as a clearinghouse for channeling federal funding to state and local law enforcement agencies, giving states incentives to establish planning agencies, and funding a wide variety of programs ranging from education and research to local crime control initiatives.[29]

By the early 1970s, consensus began to form around the idea that the federal government's efforts to address juvenile justice were unfocused and underfunded.[30] The House Committee on Education and Labor in particular questioned the effectiveness of the Juvenile Delinquency Prevention and Control Act of 1968 and levied a number of criticisms at the way HEW implemented the act:

> The HEW administered program, during its first three years, was disappointing because of delay and inefficiency. A director of the Youth Development and Delinquency Prevention Administration was not appointed for over 18 months. Less than a third of the $150 million authorized for fiscal years 1968 through 1971 was appropriated. Furthermore, only half of the funds that were appropriated were actually expended. The funds were generally spent on underfunded, unrelated, and scattered projects. Weakness in program administration, the dominance of the Law Enforcement Assistance Administration, and inadequate funding contributed to reasons for a lack of total success.[31]

Disappointed with the way the 1968 Act was implemented, consensus began to form within Congress around the idea of creating a new federal entity to oversee the federal government's juvenile justice efforts. As the Juvenile Delinquency Prevention and Control Act's authorization was expiring in 1974, Congress moved to replace it with a more comprehensive piece of legislation.

THE JUVENILE JUSTICE AND DELINQUENCY PREVENTION ACT

The Juvenile Justice and Delinquency Prevention Act (JJDPA) was first passed by Congress in 1974[32] and was most recently reauthorized in 2002 by the 21st Century Department of Justice Appropriations Authorization Act.[33] Authorization for its main provisions expired in FY2007 and FY2008. This section analyzes the JJDPA as it stands today.

By 1974, strong momentum had developed in the public, academic, and governmental arenas toward the idea that the juvenile justice system needed to focus on preventing juvenile delinquency, deinstitutionalizing youth already in the system, and keeping juvenile offenders separate from adults offenders. Congress responded to this growing consensus by passing the Juvenile Justice and Delinquency Prevention Act of 1974. The JJDPA had three main components:

- it created a set of institutions within the federal government that were dedicated to coordinating and administering federal juvenile justice efforts;
- it established grant programs to assist the states with setting up and running their juvenile justice systems; and
- it promulgated core mandates that states had to adhere to in order to be eligible to receive grant funding.

Although the JJDPA has been amended several times over the past 30 years, it continues to feature the same three components. As it was passed in 1974, the JJDPA focused the federal government's efforts largely on preventing juvenile delinquency and on rehabilitating juvenile offenders. Subsequent revisions to the Act placed emphasis on influencing states to expand the use of sanctions and accountability measures through some existing grant programs, as well as adding new grant programs to the Act's purview. The latest reauthorization of the JJDPA, enacted by P.L. 107-273, made several changes to the Act, including consolidating various separate grant programs and modifying the language of some of the core mandates. **Appendix A** details the original JJDPA; **Appendix B** details the JJDPA's major subsequent revisions and includes a summary of the specific changes enacted by its last reauthorization.

Concentration of Federal Efforts

The original JJDPA established the Office of Juvenile Justice and Delinquency Prevention (OJJDP) within DOJ's Law Enforcement Assistance Administration[34] (LEAA) as the new clearinghouse for the federal government's efforts to influence states' juvenile justice systems. Subsequent revisions to the JJPDA designated OJJDP as a stand-alone office within DOJ and directed the Administrator to report directly to the Attorney General. Today, the JJDPA grants the Administrator of OJJDP a broad authority to coordinate the federal government's activities relating to the treatment of juvenile offenders, including programs that focus on prevention, diversion, training, treatment, rehabilitation, evaluation, research, and improvement of the states' juvenile justice systems.[35] The Administrator is charged with developing objectives, priorities, strategies, and long-term plans concerning the treatment and handling of juvenile offenders by federal agencies and by the states, and overseeing the implementation of these plans. Thus, the Administrator of OJJDP is, by statute, the lead individual in the U.S. federal government charged with developing and implementing policies that govern the treatment of juvenile offenders by federal agencies and the federal government's efforts to influence the states' juvenile justice systems.

Coordinating Council on Juvenile Justice and Delinquency Prevention

The original JJDPA established an independent organization known as the Coordinating Council on Juvenile Justice and Delinquency Prevention (Coordinating Council) to coordinate the federal government's juvenile delinquency programs. The Coordinating Council was to be composed of representatives from a broad range of federal agencies who "exercise significant decision making authority in the Federal agency involved."[36] Subsequent revisions to the JJDPA expanded the number of agencies represented on the Coordinating Council.

Today, the Coordinating Council is an independent organization within the federal government charged with coordinating all federal juvenile delinquency programs, all federal programs that deal with unaccompanied minors, and all federal programs relating to missing and exploited children.[37] The Coordinating Council is composed of the heads of all the federal agencies that touch on these broad areas, including the Attorney General, the Secretary of Health and Human Services, the Secretary of Labor, the Secretary of Education, the Secretary of Housing and Urban Development, the Administrator of OJJDP, the Director of the Office of National Drug Control

Policy, the Chief Executive Officer of the Corporation for National and Community Service, and the Commissioner of Immigration and Naturalization (now the Commissioner of Immigration and Customs Enforcement). In addition to these standing members, the Coordinating Council is composed of nine other members, of which three are appointed by the President, three are appointed by the Speaker of the House, and three are appointed by the majority leader of the Senate. These nine members are to be juvenile justice practitioners who are not officers or employees of the U.S. government, and they are to serve one- to three-year terms. The Attorney General acts as the Chairman of the Council, and the Administrator of OJJDP serves as the Vice Chairman of the Council.

In essence, the role of the Coordinating Council is to coordinate the overall federal government policy and development of objectives and priorities for federal programs dealing with juvenile delinquency and unaccompanied minors. As a function of this, the Coordinating Council is charged to examine how the various programs in the federal government are operating and to report on the degree to which federal agency funds are being used for purposes consistent with the core mandates required in the state plans.[38] The Council is also charged to review why federal agencies take juveniles into custody and to make recommendations for how to improve the federal government's practices and facilities for detaining juveniles.

Annual Report

Starting in 1988, Congress required OJJDP to produce an annual report to Congress on the agency's operations. This report, by statute, must summarize and analyze the most recent data available to the federal government concerning the detention of juveniles, describe the activities funded by OJJDP and the activities of the Coordinating Council, identify the extent to which each state complies with the core mandates and their state plan requirements, and evaluate the effectiveness of federal juvenile delinquency programs in reducing the incidences of delinquency and violent crime among juveniles.[39]

State Formula Grants

The original JJDPA authorized OJJDP to make formula grants[40] to states, which can be used to fund the planning, establishment, operation, coordination, and evaluation of projects for the development of more effective juvenile delinquency programs and improved juvenile justice systems.

Although this grant program has been modified through the intervening years, it remains in place today as one of the core components of the federal approach to influencing states' juvenile justice systems. Authorization for this program expired in FY2007, but it has continued to receive appropriations.

Funds are allocated annually among the states on the basis of relative population of people under the age of 18. However, the JJDPA sets minimum amounts that can be provided to the states depending on the total appropriation for the Formula Grant Program, which are outlined in **Table 1**. No more than 10% of the state's allocation can be used for administrative expenses, including creating the state juvenile justice plans and disbursing the grant funds. Additionally, funds used for administrative expenses must be matched by state or local funds. The JJDPA authorizes "such sums as may be necessary" through FY2007 to carry out the state formula grant program.[41]

Table 1. Minimum Formula Grant Amounts

Total Appropriation	State Minimums	Territory[a] Minimums
Less than $75,000,000	$325,000 to $400,000	$75,000 to $100,000
$75,000,000 and above	$600,000	$100,000

Source: 42 U.S.C. §5631.

Note: For any state to receive funding above the minimums, the allocation for every state or territory must exceed the appropriation they received in 2000.

a. Territory refers to the Virgin Islands of the United States, Guam, American Samoa, and the Commonwealth of the Northern Mariana Islands.

JJDPA Formula Grant Mandates[42]

To receive formula grant funding through the JJDPA, states are required to formulate plans for the administration of juvenile justice within their jurisdiction and to submit yearly reports to OJJDP concerning their progress in implementing the programs being funded. The JJDPA stipulates a list of components that must be included in state plans, funding constraints for how the state formula grants can be apportioned, and four core mandates that must be adhered to in order to receive funding.

State Plan Components

To receive state formula grant funding, states must submit a juvenile justice plan to OJJDP. Should the state fail to do so, or if the Administrator determines that the state's plan does not meet the requirements elucidated in 42 U.S.C. §5633 (a), OJJDP can make the formula grant funding available to local public and private nonprofit agencies within the state for use in activities that help the state meet the four core mandates. The following plan components are required of all states receiving funding:

- States must designate an agency to supervise the administration of the juvenile justice plan and show that this agency has the legal authority to implement the plan. States must also consult with local government entities as they formulate the plan.
- States must provide for an advisory group of 15 to 33 members that participate in the development and review of the state's juvenile justice plan.[43]
- States must provide for the analysis of juvenile delinquency issues within their jurisdiction, including a description of the services provided to address the issues and performance goals and priorities for the implementation of these services. States are also directed to formulate a plan for providing gender-specific services, a plan for providing juvenile justice services in rural areas, and a plan for providing needed mental health services to juveniles.

Formula Grant Allocation

The JJDPA places several restrictions on how the funding received through the state formula grant program can be allocated within the states and territories. At least two-thirds of the funds received through the formula grant program must be passed through to units of local government, including Indian tribes[44] and local private agencies. Private agencies must have first applied to a local unit of government for funding and been turned down before being eligible for formula grant funding, and all expenditures must be consistent with the state's plan. Funding must be distributed equitably throughout the state, including rural areas.

Additionally, at least 75% of the funds provided to the state must be used for a wide array of juvenile justice related programs, including, but not limited to:

- community based alternatives to incarceration;
- counseling, mentoring, and training programs within the juvenile justice system as well as similar community based programs and services, including aftercare and after-school programs;

- comprehensive juvenile justice and delinquency prevention programs that assist the coordination of service provision among the various players involved;
- providing services to address child abuse and neglect;
- expanding the use of probation offices;
- programs that address the relationship between juvenile delinquency and learning disabilities, and programs that help juveniles and their families overcome language barriers;
- projects designed to deter juvenile gang members from participating in illegal activities, including those that promote their involvement in lawful activities;
- substance and drug abuse prevention and treatment programs, including mental health programs;
- programs that focus on positive youth development for at-risk youth and juvenile offenders;
- programs that focus on strengthening families and providing them assistance to ensure juveniles have a nurturing home environment;
- programs that provide mental health services to juveniles at every stage of the juvenile justice process; and
- programs that encourage juvenile courts to develop a continuum of post- adjudication restraints that bridge the gap between probation and detention in a juvenile correctional facility.[45]

Core Mandates

The original JJDPA included two core requirements, or mandates, that states had to adhere to in order to receive formula grant funding. Subsequent revisions to the JJDPA expanded the list of core mandates to the four that exist today. Failure to adhere to these requirements will result in a 20% reduction of funding for each of the four mandates with which the state is not in compliance. Additionally, the state will be ineligible for future funding unless: the state agrees to spend 50% of the allocated funding to achieving compliance with whichever mandate it is noncompliant with; the Administrator of OJJDP determines that the state has achieved "substantial compliance"; or the state has demonstrated an "unequivocal commitment to achieving full compliance with such applicable requirements within a reasonable time."[46] Following are the four core mandates as they are codified today:

- Deinstitutionalization of status offences (DSO). Juveniles who are charged with or who have committed an offense that would not be a crime if committed by an adult, and juveniles who are not charged with any offenses, are not to be placed in secure detention or secure correctional facilities.[47]

- Juveniles are not to be detained or confined in any institution in which they would have contact with adult inmates. Additionally, correctional staff that work with both adult and juvenile offenders must have been trained and certified to work with juveniles.
- Juveniles are not to be detained or confined in any jail or lockup for adults, except for juveniles who are accused of nonstatus offenses. These juveniles may be detained for no longer than six hours as they are processed, waiting to be released, awaiting transfer to a juvenile facility, or awaiting their court appearance. Additionally, juveniles in rural locations may be held for up to 48 hours in jails or lockups for adults as they await their initial court appearance. Juveniles held in adult jails or lockups in both rural and urban areas are not to have contact with adult inmates, and any staff working with both adults and juveniles must have been trained and certified to work with juveniles.
- Disproportionate minority confinement. States are required to show that they are implementing juvenile delinquency prevention programs designed to reduce—without establishing or requiring numerical standards or quotas—the disproportionate number of minorities confined within their juvenile justice systems.

Juvenile Delinquency Prevention Block Grants

In addition to the formula grants, the JJDPA also authorizes OJJDP to make grants available to carry out projects designed to prevent juvenile delinquency.[48] The 21st Century Department of Justice Appropriations Authorization Act[49] folded several pre-existing grant programs into the Juvenile Delinquency Prevention Block Grant program and authorized "such sums as may be necessary" for this purpose through FY2007.[50] As a result of this consolidation, purpose areas that may be funded through the block grant program comprise a wide array of services, treatments, and interventions, including, but not limited to:[51]

- Projects that provide treatment to juvenile offenders and at risk juveniles who are victims of child abuse or neglect, or who have experienced violence at home, at school, or in their communities.

Additionally, the program can fund projects providing treatment and services to the families of these juveniles.

- Educational projects or support services for juveniles that focus on encouraging juveniles to stay in school; aiding in the transition from school to work; helping identify juveniles who have learning difficulties and disabilities both in school and in the juvenile justice system; encouraging new approaches to preventing school violence and vandalism; developing locally coordinated policies among education, juvenile justice, and social service agencies; and providing mental health services.
- Projects that expand the use of probation officers, especially for programs that permit nonviolent juvenile offenders to remain at home instead of being placed in an institution, and to ensure that juveniles complete the terms of their probation.
- Counseling, training, and mentoring programs, particularly for juveniles residing in low-income and high-crime areas.
- Community based projects and services aimed at reducing juvenile delinquency, including literacy and social service programs.
- Drug and alcohol abuse treatment programs.
- Postsecondary education and training scholarship programs for low income juveniles residing in neighborhoods with high rates of poverty, violence, and drug related crimes.
- Projects that establish an initial intake screening and evaluation of juveniles taken into custody, both to determine the likelihood that the juvenile will commit crimes in the future and to provide the appropriate interventions to prevent future crimes.
- Projects designed to prevent juveniles from participating in organized criminal gangs.

Grant funding is allocated to the eligible states based on the proportion of their population that is under the age of 18. To become eligible for these grants, states must submit an application assuring that no more than 5% of the grant will be used for administrative, evaluation, and technical assistance costs and that federal grant funding will supplement, and not supplant, state and local juvenile delinquency prevention efforts. Additionally, the state must have submitted a plan.

Part E: Developing, Testing, and Demonstrating Promising New Initiatives and Programs (Challenge Grants)

The Challenge Grants program[52] was originally added in 1992 and was modified by the 21st Century Department of Justice Appropriations Authorization Act, which authorized "such sums as may be necessary" to carry out the program through FY2007. It replaced the Demonstration Programs grant that had been created by the original JJDPA (see **Appendix A** and **Appendix B** for more information on the prior grant programs). The Challenge Grants program authorizes OJJDP to make discretionary grants to state, local, and Indian governments and private entities to carry out programs that will develop, test, or demonstrate promising new initiatives that may prevent, control, or reduce juvenile delinquency. The Administrator is charged with ensuring that these grants are apportioned in such a way as to ensure an equitable geographical distribution of these projects throughout the United States. The program is currently unauthorized, but has continued to receive appropriations.

Title V Incentive Grants for Local Delinquency Prevention Programs

The Incentive Grants for Local Delinquency Prevention program[53] authorizes OJJDP to make discretionary grants to the states that are then transmitted to units of local government in order to carry out delinquency prevention programs for juveniles who have come into contact with, or are likely to come into contact with, the juvenile justice system. Unlike the other grant programs within the JJDPA, which are authorized through FY2007, the 21st Century Department of Justice Reauthorization Act authorized "such sums as may be necessary" for the Title V grant program through FY2008. The program is currently unauthorized, but has continued to receive appropriations.

Activities that can be funded through the Title V Incentive Grants for Local Delinquency Prevention program include the following:

- alcohol and substance abuse prevention services;
- educational programs;
- child and adolescent health (as well as mental health) services;
- recreational programs;

- leadership programs;
- programs that teach juveniles that they are accountable for their actions;
- job or skills training programs; and
- other "data-driven evidence based prevention programs."

As it reviews the grant applications that it receives, OJJDP is to give priority to programs that

- include plans for service and agency coordination (including co-location of services);
- coordinate and collaborate with the Delinquency Prevention Block Grant recipients in the state;
- include innovative ways to involve the private sector in delinquency prevention activities;
- help states develop or enhance state-wide subsidy programs for early intervention and prevention of juvenile delinquency; and
- develop data-driven prevention plans and utilize evidence-based prevention strategies (including conducting program evaluations to determine the impact and effectiveness of the programs being funded).

Local government entities are eligible for funding if they are in compliance with the state plan requirements, and if they have submitted to the state's advisory group a three-year comprehensive plan outlining their plans for investing in delinquency prevention activities and for coordinating services delivered to at-risk juveniles and their families. Funding to local government entities is disbursed by the state, and these grants are conditioned on a 50% match by either the local entity or the state.

Thus, the JJDPA includes four major grant programs within its purview: the State Formula Grant program, the Delinquency Prevention Block Grant program, the Challenge Grant program, and the Title V Incentive Grants for Local Delinquency Prevention program. The first three grant programs, located within Title II of the act, were authorized through FY2007. The Title V grant program was authorized through FY2008. While these grant programs differ slightly, they each provide funding for a wide array of juvenile delinquency prevention purposes. The State Formula Grant program and the Delinquency Prevention Block Grant program feature long lists of detailed purpose areas that overlap. Conversely, the Challenge Grant and the Title V grant programs feature broadly written purpose areas that provide more discretion to OJJDP in their administration. Although this report does not include appropriations data, it is important to note that the appropriators have not funded the Delinquency Prevention Block Grant since its inception. Instead, the appropriators have continued to fund some of the grant programs repealed in 2002 either as stand-alone appropriations or as carve-outs within the Title V grant program. This issue will be discussed in greater detail in the "Issues for Congress" section of this report.

JUVENILE ACCOUNTABILITY BLOCK GRANTS

The Juvenile Accountability Block Grant (JABG) program was originally created by the FY1998 DOJ Appropriations Act (P.L. 105-119) and was appropriated each subsequent fiscal year. However, the JABG program was codified by the 21st Century Department of Justice Reauthorization Act (P.L. 107-273) in Subtitle A of Title II of the act.[54] As such it falls outside the scope of the JJDPA, but nevertheless comprises a significant component of the federal government's approach to juvenile justice. The JABG program authorizes $350 million in appropriation for each fiscal year through FY2009.

The JABG program authorizes the Attorney General to make grants to states[55] and units of local government to strengthen their juvenile justice systems and foster accountability within their juvenile populations. The program focuses resources on holding juveniles accountable for their actions and building up the juvenile justice system in the states. It also essentially signifies the high-water mark of the federal government's movement away from an emphasis on rehabilitating juveniles and toward the idea that juveniles need to be punished for their crimes; indeed, the only core mandate of the JABG program is that states must begin to implement a system of graduated sanctions[56] in order to be eligible for funding.

As originally codified, the JABG program authorized funding for 16 accountability-based purpose areas, including, but not limited to, implementing graduated sanctions; building or operating juvenile correction or detention facilities; hiring juvenile court officers, including judges, probation officers, and special advocates; and hiring additional juvenile prosecutors. The act also authorized a separate Tribal Grant program within the JABG appropriation to fund accountability-based measures aimed at strengthening the tribal juvenile justice systems. The JABG program was last authorized in

2006 by P.L. 109-162, which added a purpose area to the original 16 areas and authorized JABG at $350 million a year through FY2009.

Purpose Areas

As currently comprised, the program authorizes funding for 17 accountability based purpose areas, including, but not limited to:

- implementing graduated sanctions;
- building or operating juvenile correction or detention facilities;
- hiring and training juvenile court officers, including judges, probation officers, special advocates, juvenile prosecutors, and detention or corrections personnel;
- supporting prosecutorial initiatives aimed at curbing drug use, violence, and gangs;
- establishing juvenile drug courts and gun courts;
- establishing juvenile records and information sharing systems between the courts, schools, and social service agencies to keep better track of repeat offenders;
- using risk and needs assessments to facilitate effective early interventions for mental health and substance abuse issues;
- accountability-based school safety initiatives;
- establishing and improving pre-release and post-release programs to help juveniles reintegrate into the community; and
- restorative justice programs that emphasize the moral accountability of an offender toward their victims and the affected community.

Eligibility Requirements

The JABG program awards grants to the states; most of this funding is then sub-granted to units of local government. States and local entities must provide information about the activities that will be carried out with the grant funding and the criteria that will be used to assess whether the programs were effective (including the extent to which evidence-based practices were utilized). Additionally, states and local governments must provide assurances that the they are working toward implementing laws effecting the use of graduated sanctions for juvenile offenders.

As previously mentioned, the implementation of graduated sanctions is the only core mandate associated with the JABG program. These graduated sanctions should, at a minimum, ensure that

- sanctions are imposed on juvenile offenders for each delinquent offense they commit;
- sanctions escalate in intensity with each subsequent more serious offense;
- there is enough flexibility to tailor sanctions and services to each individual juvenile offender; and
- appropriate consideration is given when handing out sanctions to the victims of the crime and public safety in general.

States are allowed to participate in the program if their graduated sanctions are discretionary rather than mandatory, but must require each juvenile court in its jurisdiction to submit an annual report concerning the extent to which graduated sanctions were implemented and the reasons for which graduated sanctions were not applied. This information should be collected by units of local government and reported to the states, which in turn report it to the Attorney General. Eligible states and units of local government are also required to establish and convene an advisory board that is charged with recommending a coordinated enforcement plan for the use of the JABG funds awarded. The board is to include, where appropriate, members of the state or local police, the prosecutors office, the juvenile court, the probation office, the education system, the social service system, a nonprofit victim advocacy organization, and a nonprofit religious or community group.

JABG Allocation

Of the total amount appropriated for the JABG program, each state is automatically allocated 0.5%. The remaining 75% of the JABG funding is then allocated to the states in accordance to the ratio of their population of juveniles under the age of 18 to the overall population of juveniles under the age of 18 in the United States that fiscal year. The states must pass along not less than 75% of the funds they receive to units of local government, unless the state can demonstrably certify that their overall juvenile justice costs are more than

25% of the aggregate amount of juvenile justice expenditures in the state (i.e., the states expenditures plus all the units of local government expenditures) that fiscal year and that they have consulted with as many units of local government as practicable regarding their expenditures. States are required to pass along the funding to units of local government according to a formula that is based on the ratio of the local government's juvenile justice costs and the juvenile violent crimes[57] committed in their jurisdiction to the overall juvenile justice costs and juvenile violent crimes in the state.

The Attorney General is authorized to make grants directly to specially qualified units of local government if the states do not qualify or apply for JABG funding. In these cases, the AG is authorized to reserve up to 75% of that states allocation to make grants directly to units of local government that meet the funding requirements outlined above. Lastly, the AG is authorized to use the average amount allocated by the states to their units of local governments as the basis for the amounts awarded to these specially qualified units of local government.

Of the total amount awarded to a state or a unit of local government, only 5% can be used to pay for administrative costs. Funds awarded under JABG cannot be used to supplant existing funding but must instead be used to increase the amount of funding that would otherwise be available to the state juvenile justice systems. The federal share of the activities funded through a JABG grant cannot exceed 90%, except for JABG funds used to construct juvenile court or detention facilities in which case the federal share is not to exceed 50%.

ISSUES FOR CONGRESS

One of the major issues confronting the 111th Congress is the reauthorization of the JJDPA, because the Act's major provisions expired at the end of FY2007 and FY2008. Similarly, the JABG expires at the end of FY2009, and Congress may also consider its reauthorization.[58] As Congress debates reauthorizing funding for juvenile justice programs, it faces the same issues that have revolved around the juvenile justice system for more than 30 years:

- What is the appropriate federal role in an arena that has predominantly been the province of the states?

- What is the appropriate federal response to juvenile violence and juvenile crime?
- Should federal efforts to influence the states' juvenile justice systems focus on the rehabilitation of juvenile offenders, on holding juvenile offenders accountable for their actions, or some combination of both?
- Are the grant programs as currently comprised the best way to support juvenile justice efforts in the states?

The following section provides a more detailed examination of these potential issues.

Rehabilitation versus Accountability

As previously noted, the fundamental tension within the juvenile justice system over the past 30 years has been the relationship between rehabilitating juveniles and holding them accountable for their actions. To some extent, this is an arbitrary distinction in that the system as currently comprised includes both rehabilitative and accountability based programs. Nevertheless, over the years the juvenile justice system has trended away from rehabilitation. Instead, over the past few decades, the system has increasingly incorporated measures that emphasize holding juveniles accountable for their actions. For example, during the 1990s, 47 states and the District of Columbia enacted laws that made their juvenile justice systems more punitive.[59] As a result, juvenile justice can be conceptualized as a continuum that stretches philosophically *from* the rehabilitative idea that juveniles are wayward youth who can be taught to mend their ways and become contributing members of society *to* the accountability end of the spectrum which holds that juveniles must be taught to take responsibility for their actions through punishment (often in the form of graduated sanctions).

The federal juvenile justice system can thus be viewed as a pendulum that swings between these two poles; over the past 20 years, it has clearly been swinging away from rehabilitation and toward accountability through the *addition* of graduated sanctions to the JJDPA State Formula grant program's purpose areas and the *requirement* that states implement graduated sanctions in order to be eligible for JABG funding. The 111th Congress may consider whether the federal government, through its grant programs, should be focusing on rehabilitating juveniles, holding them accountable for their actions, or some combination of both of these philosophies.[60]

Expanding or Modifying the JJDPA Core Mandates

The federal government has attempted to influence the states' juvenile justice systems through the core mandates that states must comply with in order to be eligible for funding. In essence, the federal government has used grant funding as a carrot to effectuate changes in the way that states house and treat their juvenile offenders. The last modification of a core mandate occurred with the JJDPA's last reauthorization in 2002, when the disproportionate minority confinement language was modified to preclude OJJDP from using numerical benchmarks in its implementation. A possible issue for Congress to consider is whether to modify or expand the existing core mandates.[61]

Proponents of expanding the core mandates could point to the fact that the mandates have been effective in inducing states to promulgate detention standards that focus on minimizing the contact between juvenile offenders and adults and in deinstitutionalizing status offenses.[62] Opponents of expanding the mandates, however, could point to the relative ineffectiveness of the disproportionate minority confinement mandate; most states continue to detain minorities at a higher rate than their percentage of the state's juvenile population and the language has been weakened over the years to ensure that OJJDP does not require states to meet quotas in order to adhere to the mandate.[63] Should Congress choose to expand the core mandates, policy options could include

- requiring states to ensure that their delinquency prevention programs are based on solid scientific evidence such as randomized control trials,[64]
- requiring states to show that they are reducing the recidivism rates of their juvenile offenders,[65]
- expanding the number and quality of programs available for female juveniles,[66]
- requiring states to implement mental health and substance abuse screening for juveniles,[67] or
- developing and implementing gang-violence reduction initiatives.[68]

Juvenile Delinquency Prevention Block Grant

Since the JJDPA was reauthorized in 2002, there appears to have been some disparity between the authorizing legislation and the structure of the appropriations for some juvenile justice grant programs. As previously noted, this last reauthorization eliminated a number of small grant programs and consolidated most of their purpose areas into the Juvenile Delinquency Prevention Block Grant. However, the annual appropriation for OJJDP continues to follow the previous structure, and funds have been appropriated in each subsequent fiscal year for some of the grant programs that were repealed in 2002. The current disconnect between the authorization and the appropriation could present a significant challenge for OJJDP. Given this inconsistency, OJJDP employees must spend some percentage of their time reconciling the differences between the authorization and the appropriation; this may not represent the best investment of OJJDP staff time.

Additionally, because the eligibility requirements and funding mechanisms of the old grant programs and the new block grant program are different, this disparity between the authorization and the appropriation likely represents a challenge to the states and units of local government as they apply for funding. A potential issue for Congress as it reauthorizes the JJDPA includes whether the Juvenile Delinquency Prevention Block Grant should be implemented as it was authorized, whether it should be modified, or whether it should be broken up again into its component grant programs to better reflect what has been occurring with the appropriation.[69]

Overlap in Grant Programs

The current grant programs within the JJDPA overlap in a variety of ways. The State Formula Grant and the Delinquency Prevention Block Grant programs, for example, both feature a wide array of purpose areas elucidated in legislative language that are largely similar. For example, both grant programs include purpose areas for

- counseling, mentoring, and training programs;
- community based programs and services;
- after school programs;
- education programs;

- programs that expand the use of probation officers;
- substance and drug abuse prevention programs;
- mental health services;
- gang-involvement prevention programs; and
- coordinating local service delivery among the different agencies involved.

Additionally, the Delinquency Prevention Block Grant, the Challenge Grants, and the Title V Incentive Grants for Local Delinquency Prevention Programs all include language allowing OJJDP to provide funding for additional programs not included in the specific purpose areas identified. A potential issue for Congress could include whether the current overlap within the juvenile justice grant programs is appropriate. Possible policy options could include altering the current grant programs to target funding for specific activities in each grant program or consolidating the different grant programs into one large program.

The creation of new grant programs could be an alternative to modifying or consolidating the existing grant programs. Creating grant programs that are tailored to specific activities (e.g., gang-prevention, restorative justice, mentoring, mental health treatment, etc.) could provide dedicated funding streams to activities that may not otherwise receive funding if they must compete for funding in a broader grant program. However, there are limited federal resources in the juvenile justice arena, and adding grant programs without also increasing funding may take resources away from the current programs. A possible issue for the 111th Congress involves whether the existing grant programs are adequate, whether the existing grant programs should be modified, or whether new grant programs should be enacted.[70]

Coordination of Federal Efforts

The juvenile population comes into contact with a wide variety of federal programs overseen by a number different agencies. Under current law, the Administrator of OJJDP has a broad mandate to coordinate the federal government's overall response to juvenile offenders and juvenile delinquency prevention, including federal programs that focus on prevention, diversion, training, treatment, rehabilitation, evaluation, research, and improvement of the states' juvenile justice systems. Additionally, the Coordinating Council was established to help the various agencies involved in dealing with and providing treatment for juveniles better coordinate their efforts.

Some overlap exists within the federal government concerning programs that offer services for juveniles. For example, a growing body of evidence points to the relationship between child abuse or other forms of mistreatment and juvenile delinquency or other delinquent behavior such as youth violence.[71] This has led to a duplication of efforts within many federal agencies and what may sometimes be a considerable overlap in the funding opportunities available to states and local entities.[72] An example of this overlap is the body of federal funding available for youth violence prevention. Funding for youth violence programs is available within DOJ, the Department of Health and Human Services, the Department of Education, the Department of Labor, and the Department of Agriculture. Within these diverse departments, youth violence prevention funding opportunities are available for virtually every aspect of the issue: the violent youth themselves, their victims, their families, the communities they live in, the juvenile justice system that prosecutes them, and the societal factors that contribute to the violence.[73] In effect, there are a multitude of federal programs throughout the government that deal with youth violence's causes, its effects, and its ramifications. The amount of coordination that is occurring between the departments on these issues remains an open question.

Given the nexus between youth violence and juvenile justice, the coordination of these federal government programs should lie within the province of OJJDP and the Coordinating Council. The Coordinating Council, for its part, meets quarterly (for three to four hours on average) to discuss the ongoing juvenile justice related efforts within the agencies.[74] Given the extent of the overlap that exists within the federal government, some could question whether more coordination should be required across departments. A potential issue for Congress could involve how effective OJJDP and the Coordinating Council have been in coordinating the federal efforts to reduce juvenile delinquency, including efforts to address youth violence, in order to more efficiently provide treatment and services to juvenile offenders.[75]

APPENDIX A. THE JUVENILE JUSTICE AND DELINQUENCY PREVENTION ACT (JJDPA) OF 1974

The Juvenile Justice and Delinquency Prevention Act (JJDPA) was first passed by Congress in 1974[76] and was most recently reauthorized in 2002 by the 21st Century Department of Justice Appropriations Authorization Act.[77] Its provisions are currently authorized through FY2007. This appendix will analyze the original JJDPA.

The original JJDPA had three main components: it created a set of institutions within the federal government that were dedicated to coordinating and administering federal juvenile justice efforts; it established grant programs to assist the states with setting up and running their juvenile justice systems; and it promulgated core mandates that states had to adhere to in order to be eligible to receive grant funding. As it was passed in 1974, the JJDPA focused largely on preventing juvenile delinquency and on rehabilitating juvenile offenders.

Federal Government Entities Established

The JJDPA established a range of federal government entities charged with overseeing the federal government's juvenile justice efforts that continue to exist today. In addition to establishing the first federal agency dedicated to the promulgation of juvenile justice, the act established a series of institutions aimed at increasing the federal government's coordination of juvenile delinquency programs and of programs that affect juveniles generally.

The Office of Juvenile Justice and Delinquency Prevention (OJJDP)

Title II, Part A of the original JJDPA established OJJDP within DOJ's Law Enforcement Assistance Administration (LEAA) as the new clearing house for federal juvenile justice efforts. The act established the Office of the Assistant Administrator of OJJDP, who is charged with overseeing the Office and coordinating the federal government-wide juvenile justice efforts under the direction of the Administrator of the LEAA. The act endowed the Administrator with a series of powers, including the authority to require other federal entities with juvenile delinquency programs to submit information and reports to OJJDP, and charged the new entity with administering the programs that were created by the act. The act also directed the Administrator to implement the overall policy and develop the objectives and priorities for *all* federal juvenile delinquency activities as well as "all activities relating to prevention, diversion, training, treatment, rehabilitation, evaluation, research, and improvement of the juvenile justice system of the United States."[78] The LEAA Administrator, acting through the OJJDP Assistant Administrator, was thus given a broad mandate to oversee and coordinate not just the new agency's activities but all federal activities relating to the treatment of juveniles. OJJDP was required to present Congress with an annual report of its activities and of the federal government's overall juvenile delinquency programs.

Coordinating Council on Juvenile Justice and Delinquency Prevention (Coordinating Council)

The act established an independent organization known as the Coordinating Council on Juvenile Justice and Delinquency Prevention to coordinate the federal government's juvenile delinquency programs. The Coordinating Council was to be comprised of representatives from a broad range of federal agencies who "exercise significant decision making authority in the Federal agency involved,"[79] including the Attorney General, Secretary of Health, Education, and Welfare, the Secretary of Labor, Director of the Special Action Office for Drug Abuse Prevention, Secretary of Housing and Urban Development, or their respective designees. Additionally, the Coordinating Council was to include the Assistant Administrator of OJJDP and the Deputy Assistant Administrator of the National Institute for Juvenile Justice and Delinquency Prevention. The Coordinating Council was to meet a minimum of six times per year and was to report its activities as part of OJJDP's annual report.

Advisory Committee on Juvenile Justice and Delinquency Prevention (Advisory Committee)

The act established an Advisory Committee composed of 21 individuals who were to be appointed by the President to serve in an advisory capacity. These individuals were to be experts in the fields of juvenile delinquency prevention or treatment; juvenile justice administration; or community based programs and private voluntary organizations. The majority of the Advisory Committee was to be drawn from the private sector and at least one-third of the members were to be younger than 26 at the time of their appointment. The members were to serve without compensation and to meet no less than four times a year. The Advisory Committee was charged with making recommendations to the Administrator of OJJDP concerning the planning, policies, priorities, operations, and management of all juvenile delinquency programs within the federal government.

The National Institute for Juvenile Justice and Delinquency Prevention (National Institute)

The act created the National Institute to coordinate the collection, preparation, and dissemination of data regarding the treatment and control of juvenile offenders. The National Institute was charged with serving as a clearing house for all information relating to juvenile delinquency and with conducting and encouraging research on juvenile delinquency. The National Institute was also charged with training juvenile justice practitioners from every level of government and the private sector who were connected with the treatment and control of juvenile offenders. The National Institute was endowed with the power to request other federal agencies to supply the data and statistics that were necessary for its mission, and to reimburse these agencies for the expenses associated with these requests.

Federal Grant Programs for Juvenile Justice

In addition to creating entities charged with overseeing and developing the juvenile delinquency prevention programs within the federal government, the JJDPA created two main grant programs that were aimed at helping states build up and manage their juvenile justice systems and prevent juvenile delinquency. Additionally, the JJDPA created a grant program aimed at helping states handle runaway youth.

Formula Grant Program

The first federal grant program established by the JJDPA was a formula grant program for states and local governments. This formula grant program was broadly aimed at helping states improve their juvenile justice systems by providing funding that could be used to assist in the planning, establishing, operating, coordinating, and evaluating of juvenile delinquency programs. Funding under this grant program was to be allocated to states based on their relative populations of people under the age of 18, and no state was to receive less than $200,000.[80] To receive funding under this grant program, the states were required to submit plans for how they were going to disburse the funding.

The state plans were to describe a series of steps that states were to take in order to be eligible for funding, including the creation of juvenile justice entities within the state systems. States were required to pass along two-thirds of the funding to local government programs, unless granted a waiver by the Administrator, and 75% of the funds expended by the states were to be "used for advanced techniques in developing, maintaining, and expanding programs and services designed to prevent juvenile delinquency, to divert juveniles from the juvenile justice system, and to provide community based alternatives to juvenile detention and correctional facilities."[81]

In addition to these restrictions on how the money was to be spent, the JJDPA established two core mandates that states had to adhere to in order to receive funding. The first of these mandates required states to ensure that juveniles who had committed offenses that would not be crimes if they were committed by an adult (known as status offenses) not be placed in juvenile detention or correctional facilities. This has become known as the deinstitutionalization of status offenders. The second mandate required states to ensure that juveniles were not detained or confined in any institution in which they would have regular contact with adults in the criminal justice system.

Prevention and Treatment Programs Grant

The act authorized the Administrator to make grants to and enter into contracts with public and private agencies, organizations, institutions, and individuals that focused on delinquency prevention and treatment. The act authorized the Administrator to enter into these grants and contracts to, among other things, develop and implement new approaches and methods for juvenile delinquency programs; develop and maintain community based alternatives to institutionalization; develop and implement programs that diverted juveniles from the traditional correctional system; improve the delivery of services to delinquents and to at-risk youth; and implement programs aimed at keeping students in school.

Demonstration Programs Grant

The JJDPA also created a discretionary grant program aimed at supporting "innovative approaches to youth development and the prevention and treatment of delinquent behavior."[82] Grants under this program could be awarded to any state or local government agency, as well as nonprofit organizations, and were to last one year. The overarching goal of the program was to foster innovation in youth development.

Appendix B. Subsequent Revisions to the JJDPA

Between 1974 and 2001, there were a number of laws enacted that modified the JJDPA in some manner. This appendix will outline the main changes that were made to the JJDPA over the past three decades.

The Juvenile Justice Amendments of 1980 (P.L. 96-509)

In 1980, Congress made three major changes to the JJDPA and reauthorized the act through FY1984. One of the major changes enacted by P.L. 96-509 was the streamlining of the juvenile justice apparatus within DOJ; whereas the JJDPA placed OJJDP underneath the Law Enforcement Assistance Administration (LEAA) and gave the LEAA Administrator authority over the agency, under the new act's provisions the Administrator of OJJDP reported directly to the AG. In essence, this gave OJJDP a measure of independence and removed the filter between the administrator of OJJDP and the AG. Despite this, however, OJJDP remained administratively within LEAA. Another major change made to the JJPDA was the creation of a new core mandate that states were to adhere to in order to receive funding under the formula grant program: the removal of juveniles from adult jails and lockups. P.L. 96-509 also began the process of shifting the JJDPA's focus away from rehabilitation and towards sanctions, including language that called for OJJDP to focus additional attention on the problem of juveniles committing serious crimes by paying special attention to sentencing and adding resources to the juvenile court system.

The act also made a series of minor modifications to the Coordinating Council, the Advisory Committee, and the National Institute aimed at increasing the coordination of federal juvenile justice efforts and at including the perspective of juveniles into the process. Among the changes made to the JJPDA, the act allowed 7.5% of OJJDP's overall appropriation to be used for the concentration of federal juvenile delinquency efforts,[83] and it added the Director of the Bureau of Prisons, the Commissioner of the Bureau of Indian Affairs, the Commissioner for the Administration for Children, Youth, and Families, and the Director of the Youth Development Bureau to the Coordinating Council. The act directed the Advisory Committee to include at least five individuals younger than 24 years of age, at least two of whom should have been or continue to be under the jurisdiction of the juvenile justice system, and to contact and seek regular input from juveniles currently under the jurisdiction of the juvenile justice system.

The main alteration made by the act was the new requirement that states stop detaining or confining juveniles in any jail or lockup for adults in order to be eligible for the state formula grant. The act did, however, allow for the temporary detention of juveniles accused of serious crimes in such facilities where no existing acceptable alternative placement was possible, subject to the promulgation of regulations by the Administrator. Failure to achieve compliance with this mandate within five years would terminate a state's ability to receive funding unless the Administrator determined that the state was in substantial compliance with the requirements. Substantial compliance was defined as a state's achieving the removal of not less than 75% of juveniles from adult jails and lockups, and making an unequivocal commitment to achieving full compliance within two additional years.

The act also expanded the scope of the Prevention and Treatment Programs Grant to include programs that were aimed at removing juveniles from adult jails and lockups, and provided that at least 5% of the funding available under this grant program be allocated to the Virgin Islands, Guam, American Samoa, the Trust Territory of the Pacific Islands, and the Commonwealth of the Northern Mariana Islands.

The Juvenile Justice, Runaway Youth, and Missing Children's ActAmendments of 1984 Act (P.L. 98-473)

P.L. 98-473 reauthorized the JJDPA through FY1988 and formally elevated OJJDP to a stand-alone office within DOJ under the general authority of the AG. Another major change made to the JJDPA by this act was the expansion of the Prevention and Treatment Programs Grant program. The act dedicated 15% to 25% of the overall funding for state formula grants to this program, and expanded the number of purpose areas that this discretionary grant could be used for, including, but not limited to, community based alternatives to detention; diversion mechanisms including restitution and reconciliation projects; advocacy activities aimed at improving services; programs that strengthen families; prevention and treatment programs; developing a national education program aimed at reducing juvenile delinquency; developing programs aimed at fostering youth employment; and developing programs aimed at keeping youths in school. At least 30% of the funding available under this program was to be apportioned to private nonprofit agencies and institutions.

The Amendments to the Juvenile Justice and Delinquency Prevention Act of 1988 (P.L. 100-690)

In 1988, Congress reauthorized the JJDPA through FY1992. Among other things, the act required OJJDP to publish a comprehensive plan of the activities it would undertake each year in the federal register. It also required OJJDP to prepare an annual report each fiscal year providing a detailed summary and analysis of the national trends in juvenile justice, including the numbers and types of offenses with which juveniles were being charged; the rate at which juveniles were being taken into custody; the extent to which states were complying with their state plan requirements; and OJJDP and the Coordinating Council's activities. The act also required states, as part of their plans, to include information on their efforts to end the disproportionate confinement of minority youth in their detention systems, and it raised the minimum funding allocations available for states under the formula grant program. The act also directed OJJDP to include technical assistance as a purpose area for each of its grant programs and for the National Institute. The act modified the Prevention and Treatment Programs Grant program by deleting language inserted by P.L. 98-473 that required 15% to 25% of the formula grant funding be allocated to this program and by expanding the number and types of considerations required to approve applications for funding.

Gang Prevention Grant

P.L. 100-690 also established a new grant program under Part D of Title II of the JJDPA aimed at funding prevention and treatment programs for juvenile gang members. The new discretionary grant program authorized the Administrator to make grants to public and private agencies and organizations. The new grant program identified 10 broad purpose areas aimed at reducing the numbers of juveniles joining gangs and providing treatment for juveniles convicted of gang-related criminal activities.

The Juvenile Justice and Delinquency Prevention Amendments Actof 1992 (P.L. 102-586)

P.L. 102-586 reauthorized the JJDPA through FY1996. The main change enacted by this act was the elevation of disproportionate minority confinement to core mandate status. States that were not in compliance with this requirement within three years of the act's passage would no longer be eligible for formula grant funding. However, states that had shown "substantial compliance" with the requirement would be eligible for funding for two additional years. The act created a number of new grant programs within Title II of the JJDPA, including grants for community-based gang intervention, for state challenge activities, for juvenile victims of child abuse, and for mentoring. The act also added a new Title V to the JJDPA establishing a new program, the Incentive Grants for Local Delinquency Prevention Program.

The act also modified the composition of the Coordinating Council. In addition to the leaders (or their designated representatives) of the various federal agencies with a stake in the juvenile justice system, the Coordinating Council was to include nine individuals working in the field of juvenile justice who were not federal employees. They were to be appointed without regard to political affiliation. Three members were to be appointed by the President, three by the Speaker of the House, and three by the majority leader of the Senate.

Following is a description of the various grant programs that were implemented by the 1992 revision to the JJDPA.

Community Based Gang Intervention Grant

The act slightly modified the discretionary gang prevention grant authorized within Part D of Title II of the JJDPA by P.L. 100-690, renaming it the Gang-Free Schools and Communities Grant. The act also created a new grant program, the Community-Based Gang Intervention Grant. The new grant program authorized the Administrator to make grants to public and private nonprofit agencies, organizations, and institutions to reduce the participation of juveniles in gangs by engaging the community. The grant allowed funding to be provided for co-ordinating mechanisms such as regional task-forces, as well as for a variety of prevention and accountability measures. For example, on the accountability side the grant authorized funding for graduated sanctions, including the expanded use of a wide variety of interventions such as probation, mediation, restitution, community service, intensive supervision, electronic monitoring, and bootcamps, among others. On the prevention side the program authorized funding for, among other things: treatment for juvenile gang members; prevention and treatment services for substance abuse by juveniles; and services to prevent juveniles from coming into contact with the juvenile justice system again as a result of gang-related activity.

State Challenge Activities Grant

The act created another new grant program under Part E of Title II of the JJDPA, the State Challenge Activities Grant (Challenge Grant). The Challenge Grant program allowed the Administrator to designate up to 10% of a state's formula grant for this new grant program. The act defined a challenge activity as a program that is aimed at, among other things, developing policies to provide services for juveniles in the juvenile justice system; increasing community-based alternatives to detention; developing programs that replaced traditional training schools with secure settings; developing programs that prohibited gender bias within the state's juvenile justice system and ensured that female juveniles had access to a full range of services, including treatment for physical or sexual assault and education in parenting; and increasing aftercare services for juveniles coming out of placement.

Juvenile Victims of Child Abuse Grant

The act created a third new grant program under Part F of Title II of the JJDPA for Juvenile Victims of Child Abuse. This program enabled the Administrator to enter into grants with public agencies and private nonprofit organizations to provide treatment for juvenile offenders who are victims of child abuse and neglect; provide transitional services, including individual, group, and family counseling; and carry out research on juvenile child abuse issues associated with these grants.

Juvenile Mentoring Grant

The act created a fourth new grant program under Part G of Title II of the JJDPA for juvenile mentoring programs. These grants could be awarded to local educational agencies (in partnership with public or private agencies) to establish and support mentoring programs. Mentoring programs eligible for funding included programs designed to link at-risk youth with responsible adults; promote personal and social responsibility; increase educational participation; discourage the use of drugs and violence; discourage participation in gangs; and encourage participation in community service and other community activities. Grant funding could not be used to directly compensate mentors (apart from reimbursement for incidental expenses) or support litigation of any kind, among other things.

Boot Camp Grants

The act created a fifth new grant program under Part H of Title II of the JJDPA to fund the establishment of up to 10 military-style boot camps in one or more states. These boot camps were to provide highly regimented schedules involving discipline, physical training, work, and drill, and to include educational and counseling services. States receiving funding under this program would be required to provide for post-release supervision and after-care services for the juveniles participating in their boot camps.

Incentive Grants for Local Delinquency Prevention Programs (Incentive Grants)

The act created a new Title V within the JJDPA for Incentive Grants aimed at creating delinquency prevention programs at the local level. The grants would be allocated by state and passed along by each state's advisory group (as created under the state plan stipulations) to local government entities. Funding could be used to provide recreation services, tutoring and remedial education, job skills, mental health services, substance abuse services, leadership development services, and programs that teach juveniles accountability for their actions. States were required to provide a 50% match for the grants and be in compliance with the core mandates in Title II in order to receive funding under this program.

The 21st Century Department of Justice Appropriations Authorization Act of 2002 (P.0. 107-273)

P.L. 107-273 in 2002 represents the last major revision to the JJDPA. The act reauthorized OJJDP, which had remained unauthorized since FY1997 but which had been appropriated annually, through FY2007. The act also made some significant revisions to the JJDPA, most notably repealing all of the new grant programs in Title II created by P.L. 102-586 and consolidating their purpose areas within the Juvenile Justice and Delinquency Prevention Block Grant.

Among other things, the act amended the state plans section of the JJDPA and modified the disproportionate minority confinement core mandate provision. The revision to the core mandate directed the states to address the problem of disproportionate minority confinement, but stated that the states were not required to meet numerical quotas or standards in order to receive formula grant funding. The act also mandated that states enact policies requiring that individuals who work with both juveniles and adults in detention facilities be certified and trained to work with juveniles. In addition, the act added a number of additional stipulations to the state plans, including, among other things:

- that states notify appropriate public agencies within 24 hours of a child's apprehension for a status offense;
- that states specify up to 5% of their formula grant funding for incentive grants to reduce probation officer case loads; and
- that states establish systems and policies to incorporate child protective services records into juvenile case files and to ensure that child welfare records are available to the court.

If states failed to comply with any of the four core mandates they would have their formula grant funding reduced by not less than 20% for each mandate with which they were not in compliance. Additionally, states would be ineligible to receive any formula funding unless they agreed to spend 50% of the funding they received on achieving compliance with whichever core mandate they were non-compliant with, unless the Administrator determined that the state had achieved substantial compliance with the mandate.

Juvenile Delinquency Prevention Block Grant

Perhaps the major structural change enacted by P.L. 107-273 was the elimination of the series of grant programs that had been created within Title II of the JJDPA: the Gang-Free Schools and Communities Grant; the Community Based Gang Intervention Grant; the States Challenge Activities Grant; the Juvenile Victims of Child Abuse Grant; the Juvenile Mentoring Grant; and the Boot Camps Grant. In their stead, the act created a Juvenile Delinquency Prevention Block Grant aimed at funding programs that reduced juvenile delinquency that incorporated most of the general purpose areas that had been eligible for funding under the previous grant programs. Included under this broad umbrella were 25 purpose areas that run the gamut of juvenile delinquency prevention, including, but not limited to, treatment programs; counseling programs; educational programs; programs that expanded the use of probation officers; community-based programs; drug-prevention programs; and gang-prevention programs.

ACKNOWLEDGMENTS

A previous version of this report was authored by Blas Nuñez-Neto.

Author Contact Information

Kristin M. Finklea
Analyst in Domestic Security
kfinklea@crs.loc.gov, 7-6259

End Notes

[1] U.S. Department of Justice, Office of Juvenile Justice and Delinquency Prevention, *Juvenile Justice: A Century of Change*, National Report Series, December 1999, p. 2. Hereafter referred to as OJJDP, *A Century of Change*.

[2] P.L.87-274.

[3] P.L. 90-445.

[4] U.S. Department of Justice, Office of Juvenile Justice and Delinquency Prevention, "The JJDP Act: A Second Look," *Juvenile Justice*, vol. II, no. 2, Fall/Winter 1995.

[5] Federal Interagency Forum on Child and Family Statistics 1998, *America's Children: Key National Indicators of Well-Being*, at http://www.childstats.gov/pdf/ac1998/ac_98.pdf.

[6] P.L. 93-415.

[7] OJJDP, *A Century of Change*, p. 5.

[8] Karen Hess and Robert Drowns, *Juvenile Justice*, 4th Ed., Thomas Wadsworth, Belmont, CA, 2004, p. 7. Hereafter referred to as Hess and Drowns, *Juvenile Justice*.

[9] Grossberg, Michael, "Changing Conceptions of Child Welfare in the United States, 1020-1935," Chapter 1 in Margaret K. Rosenheim, Franklin E. Zimring, David S. Tanenhaus, and Bernardine Dorhn, eds., *A Century of Juvenile Justice*, University of Chicago Press, Chicago, IL, 2002, p. 6. Hereafter referred to as *A Century of Juvenile Justice*, Ch. 1.

[10] U.S. Department of Justice, Office of Juvenile Justice and Delinquency Prevention, *Juvenile Offenders and Victims: 1999 National Report*, 1999, p. 86, available at http://www.ncjrs.org/html/ojjdp/nationalreport99/toc.html. Hereafter referred to as OJJDP, *1999 National Report*.

[11] OJJDP, *1999 National Report*, p. 86.

[12] Hess and Drowns, *Juvenile Justice*, pp. 15-16.

[13] OJJDP, *1999 National Report*, p. 86.

[14] OJJDP, *1999 National Report*, p. 87.

[15] Hess and Drowns, *Juvenile Justice*, p. 18.

[16] National Commission on Law Observance and Enforcement, *Report on the Child Offender in the Federal System of Justice*, 1931, p. 2.
[17] H.Rept. 958, 72nd Cong., 1st. Sess. 2, accompanying the bill enacted as 47 Stat. 301 (1932).
[18] *A Century of Juvenile Justice*, Ch. 1, pp. 27-29.
[19] 52 Stat. 764 (1938), 18 U.S.C. 921 to 927 (1940 ed.).
[20] 64 Stat. 1086 (1950), 18 U.S.C. 5005 to 5026 (1952 ed.).
[21] Hess and Drowns, *Juvenile Justice*, p. 21.
[22] OJJDP, *A Century of Change*, p. 3.
[23] 387 U.S. 1, 87 S. Ct. 1428 (1967).
[24] Other Supreme Court rulings that have directly impacted juvenile justice include *Kent v. United States* (383 U.S. 541, 1966), *In re Winship* (397 U.S. 358, 1970), *McKeiver v. Pennsylvania* (403 U.S. 528, 1971), *Breed v. Jones* (421 U.S. 519, 1975), *Oklahoma Publishing Company v. District Court in and for Oklahoma City* (430 U.S. 308, 1977), *Smith v. Daily Mail Publishing Company* (443 U.S. 97, 1979), and *Schall v. Martin* (467 U.S. 253, 1984).
[25] P.L. 87-274.
[26] U.S. Department of Justice, Office of Juvenile Justice and Delinquency Prevention, "The JJDP Act: A Second Look," *Juvenile Justice*, Vol. II, No.2, Fall/Winter 1995, p.12.
[27] P.L. 90-445.
[28] P.L. 90-351.
[29] LEAA has since been succeeded by the Office of Justice Programs (OJP).
[30] U.S. Department of Justice, Office of Juvenile Justice and Delinquency Prevention, "The JJDP Act: A Second Look," *Juvenile Justice*, Vol. II, No.2, Fall/Winter 1995, p.13.
[31] U.S. Congress, House Committee on Education and Labor, *Juvenile Justice and Delinquency Prevention Amendments of 1977*, H.Rept. 95-313, pp. 35-36.
[32] P.L. 90-415.
[33] P.L. 107-273.
[34] LEAA was established to serve as a clearinghouse for channeling federal funding to state and local law enforcement agencies. LEAA gave states incentives to establish planning agencies and funded a wide variety of programs spanning from education and research to local crime control initiatives.
[35] 42 U.S.C. §5614.
[36] P.L. 93-415, §206(a-b).
[37] 42 U.S.C. §5616.
[38] The JJDPA required states to formulate juvenile justice plans and adhere to certain mandates in order to receive formula grant funding; see discussion below.
[39] 42 U.S.C. §5617.
[40] See 42 U.S.C. §5631.
[41] 42 U.S.C. §5671(a)(1).
[42] This entire section references 42 U.S.C. §5633.
[43] The make up of this group should include at least one local elected official, representatives from the various state agencies involved in preventing, responding to, and treating juvenile delinquency, and other individuals working or volunteering in the field. A majority of the advisory group cannot be employed by the federal, state, or local government, one fifth of the members must be younger than 24, and at least 3 of the members must be within the jurisdiction of the juvenile justice system. 42 U.S.C. §5633 (a)(3).
[44] Indian tribes must comply with the four core mandates in order to be eligible for funding.
[45] 42 U.S.C. §5633(a)(9).
[46] 42 U.S.C. §5633 (c).
[47] The most common status offence is truancy.
[48] 42 U.S.C. §5651-5656.
[49] P.L. 107-273.

[50] See **Appendix B** for more information on the changes enacted by the 21st Century Department of Justice Appropriations Authorization Act, P.L. 107-273.

[51] The purpose areas noted here show the breadth of activities that can be funded through this grant program. There are 25 purpose areas in all, and the last purpose area authorizes funding for "other activities that are likely to prevent juvenile delinquency." 42 U.S.C. §5652. Although it was authorized through FY2007, this program has not received appropriations to date.

[52] 42 U.S.C. §5661-5662.

[53] 42 U.S.C. §5781-5784.

[54] JABG was codified within the Omnibus Crime Control and Safe Streets Act of 1968 (42 U.S.C. 3796ee); as such it resides outside the immediate purview of the JJDPA despite the fact that it is administered by OJJDP.

[55] Under this subheading, the word state refers to the 50 states as well as the District of Columbia and the Commonwealth of Puerto Rico. Additionally, the Virgin Islands, American Samoa, Guam, and the Northern Mariana Islands are collective considered to be 1 state for the purposes of JABG allocations.

[56] Graduated sanctions should be designed so that sanctions are imposed on a juvenile for each delinquent offense and escalate in intensity with each subsequent, more serious, offense. There should be "sufficient flexibility" to allow for individualized sanctions and services for juvenile offenders. Additionally, "appropriate consideration" should be given to public safety and the victims of the crime. 42 U.S.C. §3796ee-2(d).

[57] Violent crimes under this section include murder, non-negligent manslaughter, forcible rape, robbery, and aggravated assault.

[58] Legislation has been introduced in the 111th Congress that would reauthorize the JJDPA (S. 678, the Juvenile Justice And Delinquency Prevention Reauthorization Act of 2009) as well as the JABG (H.R. 1514, the Juvenile Accountability Block Grants Program Reauthorization Act of 2009).

[59] *A Century of Change*, p. 5.

[60] Legislation has been introduced in the 111th Congress that would increase the ability to use juvenile justice grant money for rehabilitative purposes (S. 678, the Juvenile Justice And Delinquency Prevention Reauthorization Act of 2009), while other legislation would maintain the current trend toward a focus on accountability (H.R. 1514, the Juvenile Accountability Block Grants Program Reauthorization Act of 2009).

[61] Legislation introduced in the 111th Congress to reauthorize the JJDPA (S. 678) has not yet included additions to the four core mandates. Proposed legislation would—among other things—modify State reporting requirements, which could in turn aid in clarifying and meeting core requirements on reducing disproportionate minority contact with the juvenile justice system and preventing youth awaiting trial from being held in adult facilities.

[62] See Office of Juvenile Justice and Delinquency Prevention, *The Mandates*, Fact Sheet, March 1994, at http://www.ncjrs.gov/txtfiles/fs-9407.txt.

[63] See Eileen Poe-Yamagata and Michael A. Jones, *And Justice for Some*, Building Blocks for Youth, at http://www.buildingblocksforyouth.org/justiceforsome/jfs.pdf.

[64] For more information on the uses of randomized control trials evaluate government programs, see CRS Report RL33301, *Congress and Program Evaluation: An Overview of Randomized Controlled Trials (RCTs) and Related Issues*, by Clinton T. Brass, Blas Nuñez-Neto, and Erin D. Williams.

[65] See Federal Advisory Committee on Juvenile Justice, *2006 Annual Request for Information Final Report*, Appendix 2, available at http://www.facjj.org/docs/APPENDIX_2-4_FACJJ_2006_Annual_Request_for_Information_10-16- 06.doc. Hereafter referred to as FACJJ Report.

[66] FACJJ Report.

[67] FACJJ Report.

[68] FACJJ Report.

[69] Legislation introduced in the 111th Congress to reauthorize the JJDPA (S. 678) has not yet included modifications to the general structure of the Juvenile Delinquency Prevention Block Grant. Rather, proposed legislation would increase the scope of the projects that grant money-receiving entities may conduct.

[70] Legislation introduced in the 111th Congress to reauthorize the JJDPA (S. 678) would create a new incentive grant program for states to receive federal funding. The proposed legislation would provide funding for activities such as increasing the use of evidence based or promising prevention programs, improving the involvement of professional personnel in reducing juvenile delinquency, and establishing a partnership between juvenile justice agencies and mental health authorities.

[71] While some studies show smaller effect sizes for the link between child abuse and youth violence than others, there is nevertheless a significant correlation between the maltreatment of juveniles and subsequent delinquent or violent behavior. U.S. Public Health Service, Office of the Surgeon General, *Youth Violence: A Report of the Surgeon General's Office*, 2001, pp. 65-72.

[72] See, for example, Janet Wiig with John A. Tuell, *Guidebook for Juvenile Justice and Child Welfare System Coordination and Integration*, Child Welfare League of America, 2004.

[73] From a CRS Congressional Distribution Memo, *Federal Youth Violence Programs*, Blas Nuñez-Neto, Coordinator. Available upon request.

[74] See Coordinating Council on Juvenile Justice and Delinquency Prevention, *Meetings*, available at http://www.juvenilecouncil.gov/meetings.html.

[75] Several pieces of legislation introduced in the 111th Congress directly address juvenile justice policy coordination. For example, the Juvenile Justice and Delinquency Prevention Act (S. 678) would provide for the addition of several members (the Administrator of the Substance Abuse and Mental Health Services Administration, the Secretary of Defense, the Secretary of Agriculture, and representatives from the mental health fields) to OJJDP's Coordinating Council on Juvenile Justice and Delinquency Prevention. The additional members could assist in coordinating issues identified as tangential to juvenile delinquency, such as mental health. Also, the Youth PROMISE Act (H.R. 1064, S. 435) would replace the current Coordinating Council as currently outlined under JJDPA; in its place, the act would establish an Advisory Panel to assist the Administrator of OJJDP in assessing evidence-based and promising practices as well as existing and needed resources for preventing and reducing juvenile delinquency and criminal street gang activity.

[76] P.L. 90-415.

[77] P.L. 107-273.

[78] P.L. 93-415, §204(a).

[79] P.L. 93-415, §206(a-b).

[80] The Virgin Islands, Guam, American Samoa, and the Trust Territory of the Pacific Islands were to receive no less than $50,000.

[81] P.L. 93-415, §223(a)(10).

[82] P.L. 93-415, §401.

[83] This meant, in essence, that OJJDP could use 7.5% of the overall appropriation for its own administrative costs in ensuring that the grants that were awarded were effectively concentrating federal funding on the issues that were considered to be most important.

In: Perspectives on Juvenile Offenders
Editors: Owen B. Hahn
ISBN: 978-1-60876-819-6

Chapter 6

JUVENILE TRANSFER LAWS: AN EFFECTIVE DETERRENT TO DELINQUENCY?

Richard E. Redding
Office of Juvenile Justice and Delinquency Prevention,
U.S. Dept. of Justice

Beginning in the 1980s, many States passed legal reforms designed to get tough on juvenile crime. One important reform was the revision of transfer (also called waiver or certification) laws (Griffin, 2003) to expand the types of offenses and offenders eligible for transfer from the juvenile court for trial and sentencing in the adult criminal court.[1] These reforms lowered the minimum age for transfer, increased the number of transfer-eligible offenses, or expanded prosecutorial discretion and reduced judicial discretion in transfer decisionmaking (Fagan and Zimring, 2000; Redding, 2003, 2005). In 1979, for example, 14 States had automatic transfer statutes requiring that certain juvenile offenders be tried as adults; by 1995, 21 States had such laws, and by 2003, 31 States (Steiner and Hemmens, 2003). In addition, the age at which juvenile court jurisdiction ends was lowered to 15 or 16 years in 13 States (see Snyder and Sickmund, 2006), although very recently, some States have reduced the scope of transfer laws (Bishop, 2004), and one State has raised the age at which juvenile court jurisdiction ends from 16 to 18.

In the wake of these legislative changes, the number of youth convicted of felonies in criminal courts and incarcerated in adult correctional facilities has increased (Redding, 2003), reaching a peak in the mid-1990s and then declining somewhat (Snyder and Sickmund, 2006) due, in part, to the decrease in juvenile crime. An estimated 4,100 youth were committed to State adult prisons in 1999, representing 1 percent of new prison commitments (Snyder and Sickmund, 2006). Sixty-one percent of these youth were incarcerated for person offenses, 23 percent for property offenses, 9 percent for drug offenses, and 5 percent for public order offenses (e.g., weapons possession) (Snyder and Sickmund, 2006). Transferred juveniles, particularly those convicted of violent offenses, typically receive longer sentences than those sentenced in the juvenile court for similar crimes (Bishop, 2000; Kupchik, Fagan, and Liberman, 2003; Myers, 2005; Virginia Department of Criminal Justice Services, 1996). But, they may be released on bail for a considerable period of time while they await trial in the criminal court (Myers, 2005), and many youth incarcerated in adult facilities serve no longer than the maximum time they would have served in a juvenile facility (Bishop, 2000; Fritsch, Caeti, and Hemmens, 1996; Myers, 2001). Seventy-eight percent were released from prison before their 21st birthday, and 95 percent were released before their 25th birthday, with an average of 2 years, 8 months of time served on their sentences (Snyder and Sickmund, 2006).

A Message from OJJDP

In an effort to strengthen the sanctions for serious juvenile crimes, a number of States have enacted laws increasing the types of offenders and offenses eligible for transfer from the juvenile court to the adult criminal court for trial and potential sentencing.

These laws have lowered the minimum transfer age, increased the number of offenses eligible for transfer, and limited judicial discretion, while expanding prosecutorial discretion for transfers.

Among the principal goals of such transfer laws are the deterrence of juvenile crime and a reduction in the rate of recidivism, but what does the research indicate about their effectiveness in addressing these ends?

Several studies have found higher recidivism rates for juveniles convicted in criminal court than for similar offenders adjudicated in juvenile courts. The research is less clear, however, in regard to whether transfer laws deter potential juvenile offenders.

This Bulletin provides an overview of research on the deterrent effects of transferring youth from juvenile to criminal courts, focusing on large-scale comprehensive OJJDP-funded studies on the effect of transfer laws on recidivism.

It is our hope that the information provided in this Bulletin will help inform public discussion and policy decisions on the transfer of juvenile offenders to adult criminal courts.

TYPES OF TRANSFER LAWS

While the age at which juveniles can be transferred to the adult system varies across States, most States will transfer youth ages 14 and older who have committed a serious violent offense. Typically, there are four categories of offenses for which juveniles of a certain age may be transferred: (a) any crime, (b) capital crimes and murder, (c) certain violent felonies, and (d) certain crimes committed by juveniles with prior records (Snyder and Sickmund, 2006). (See Griffin, 2003, and Snyder and Sickmund, 2006, for recent comprehensive lists of States, recent transfer statutes, and statutory requirements.)

There are three types of transfer laws, all of which are referred to in this Bulletin: legislative (automatic transfer), judicial-discretionary (judicial transfer), and prosecutorial-discretionary (prosecutorial direct-file). Each type defines the kind of juvenile offender eligible for transfer under the statute, typically specifying certain offenses and minimum age criteria. Most States have two or three coexisting types of transfer laws (Redding and Mrozoski, 2005). For example, 40 States and the District of Columbia have judicial and prosecutorial transfer statutes, with the prosecutorial statutes often applicable only to older and more serious offenders (Sanborn, 2003).

Automatic transfer laws, currently in effect in 29 States (Snyder and Sickmund, 2006), require transfer of a juvenile if statutory criteria are met (for example, alleged commission of a violent felony by juveniles 14 years of age and older). Under these laws, the case either originates in criminal court, or originates in juvenile court and is then transferred to criminal court. Judicial transfer laws, currently in 45 States and the District of Columbia (Snyder and Sickmund, 2006), vest discretion with the juvenile court judge to decide whether a juvenile should be transferred after the prosecution files a transfer motion. Prosecutorial direct-file laws, currently in 14 States and the District of Columbia (Snyder and Sickmund, 2006), vest the discretion with prosecutors, allowing them to decide whether to file charges in the juvenile or criminal court. Twenty-five States also have reverse waiver laws (Snyder and Sickmund, 2006). In a reverse waiver jurisdiction, the criminal court judge has the discretion to transfer the defendant back to the juvenile court (or to treat the defendant as a juvenile for sentencing purposes).

General and Specific Deterrence

The nationwide policy shift toward transferring juvenile offenders to the criminal court is based largely on the assumption that more punitive, adult criminal sanctions will act as a deterrent to juvenile crime. In terms of specific deterrence—in other words, whether trying and sentencing juvenile offenders as adults decreases the likelihood that they will reoffend—six large-scale studies have found higher recidivism rates among juveniles convicted for violent offenses in criminal court when compared with similar offenders tried in juvenile court. With respect to general deterrence—whether transfer laws deter any would-be juvenile offenders—the picture is less clear. The studies on this issue have produced somewhat conflicting findings; however, the bulk of the empirical evidence suggests that transfer laws have little or no general deterrent effect.

This Bulletin reviews all of the extant research on the general and specific deterrent effects of transferring juveniles to adult criminal court (Redding, 2005), focusing in particular on recent large-scale studies on specific deterrence funded by the Office of Juvenile Justice and Delinquency Prevention (Fagan, Kupchik, and Liberman, 2003; Lane et al., 2002; Lanza-Kaduce et al., 2005). It also identifies gaps in the field's knowledge base, notes challenges for further research, and discusses whether effective deterrence may be achieved through transfer.

General Deterrence: Do Transfer Laws Prevent Juvenile Crime?

Two studies conducted in the 1980s found that transfer laws did not lower juvenile crime rates. Jensen and Metsger's (1994) time-series analysis for the years 1976 to 1986 found a 13-percent increase in arrest rates for violent crime committed by 14- to 18-year-olds in Idaho after the State implemented its transfer law in 1981. In comparison, between 1982 and 1986, the arrest rates for similarly aged juveniles decreased in the neighboring States of Montana and Wyoming (which retained transfer procedures similar to those Idaho had before 1981). In a similar time-series analysis comparing juvenile arrest rates between 1974 and 1984 in New York and Philadelphia, Singer and McDowall (1988) found that a 1978 New York State law that automatically sent violent juvenile offenders to criminal court (by lowering the ages for criminal court jurisdiction to 13 for murder and 14 for assault, arson, burglary, kidnapping, and rape) had no deterrent effect on violent juvenile crime. The law was applied widely and publicized extensively in the media.[2] Although limited, evidence available at the time suggested that juvenile offenders in New York were aware of the law (Singer and McDowall, 1988).

On the other hand, the results of a multistate analysis for the years 1978 to 1993 suggest that adult sanctions, under certain conditions, may have moderate deterrent effects on juvenile crime (Levitt, 1998). Controlling for demographic and economic variables, the researchers compared the juvenile arrest rates for violent crime across States as a function of each State's minimum age for criminal court jurisdiction to the relative punitiveness of its juvenile and criminal justice systems. Punitiveness is defined as the ratio of the number of incarcerated offenders to the number of total offenders in each State system for different age groups. Researchers found relative decreases in youth crime as youth reached the age of criminal responsibility, but only in those States in which juvenile and criminal justice systems differed significantly in severity of punishment. This suggests that significantly more punitive punishments meted out by criminal courts may deter youth from offending once they reach the age of criminal responsibility.

Two multistate studies reached a different conclusion. Examining data on all felony arrests in the State of Florida between 1989 and 2002, including each offender's age and arrest history, Lee and McCrary (2005) evaluated the effect of turning age 18 on criminal offending. This study found that young people did not lower their offending rates upon turning age 18, suggesting that the prospect of adult sanctions was not a deterrent.

Steiner and Wright (2006) examined the effects of prosecutorial transfer laws in the 14 States that had such laws as of 2003.[3] These States enacted their laws at different times (between 1975 and 2000), thereby providing data over different historical time periods. Using time-series analyses, researchers compared monthly juvenile arrest rates for violent index crime (homicide, rape, robbery, and aggravated assault) for each month in the 5 years before and the 5 years after each State enacted its prosecutorial transfer law. In addition, 2 States were selected as controls for each of the 14 target States. The control States resembled the target States in size, location, and juvenile arrest rates, but implemented no transfer law during or near the relevant time period. The study found that transfer laws had no general deterrent effect. Only in Michigan did juvenile crime decrease after the State enacted its prosecutorial transfer law; in the other 13 States, juvenile crime either remained constant or increased after the enactment of the law (see also Risler, Sweatman, and Nackerud, 1998).

A few researchers have interviewed juvenile offenders about the effects of transfer. Before the widespread expansion of transfer laws, Glassner and colleagues (1983) reported the results of interviews with a small number of juvenile offenders in New York, who said they had decided to stop offending once they reached the age at which they knew they could be tried as adults.

Researchers in another small-scale study (Redding and Fuller, 2004) interviewed 37 juvenile offenders who had been charged with murder or armed robbery and automatically tried as adults in Georgia. The study examined their knowledge and perceptions of transfer laws and criminal sanctions. Georgia had undertaken a public awareness campaign to inform juveniles about the State's new automatic transfer law. Nevertheless, juvenile offenders reported being unaware of the law; only 8 of the 37 youth knew that juveniles who committed serious crimes could be tried as adults. Even among those who knew about the law, none expected that it would be enforced against them for the serious crime they had committed. Many thought they would only get light sentences (e.g., a sanction of probation, boot camp, or a several-month stay in a juvenile detention facility) from the juvenile court. These results are consistent with those from a Canadian study (Peterson-Badali, Ruck, and Koegl, 2001) finding that only 22 of the 53 juvenile offenders interviewed thought that they would receive a serious punishment if caught.

Seventy-five percent of the transferred juveniles interviewed by Redding and Fuller (2004) felt that their experiences in the adult criminal justice system had taught them the serious consequences of committing crimes. As one juvenile explained, "[Being tried as an adult] showed me it's not a game anymore. Before, I thought that since I'm a juvenile I could do just about anything and just get 6 months if I got caught" (Redding and Fuller, 2004:39). Seventy-five percent of the juvenile offenders said that if they had known they could be tried and sentenced as adults, they may not have committed the crime (Redding and Fuller, 2004).

In sum, the limited empirical research on the general deterrent effect of juvenile transfer is somewhat inconsistent and does not permit strong conclusions. The bulk of the evidence suggests that transfer laws, at least as currently implemented and publicized, have little or no general deterrent effect in preventing serious juvenile crime. Substantial further research is needed to examine whether transfer laws have—or, under the appropriate conditions, could have—a general deterrent effect. In particular, it is important to examine the following questions:

- Are juveniles aware of transfer laws?
- Do they believe the laws will be enforced against them?
- Does this awareness and belief deter criminal behavior?

In conjunction with such research, there is a need to implement and evaluate well-targeted public awareness campaigns on the State and local levels designed to apprise juveniles of the legal consequences of committing serious crimes (Redding and Fuller, 2004). Public awareness campaigns have proved effective in reducing adult crime in some contexts (e.g., Elder et al., 2004; Johnson and Bowers, 2003).

Potential Deterrence

It is possible that transfer laws resulting in significant adult sentences might have general deterrent effects if would-be juvenile offenders were made aware of such laws and if the laws were widely implemented. With respect to adult offenders, studies "plainly suggest that when potential offenders are made aware of substantial risks of being punished, many of them are induced to desist" (Von Hirsch et al., 1999:47). However, research with adults suggests that the severity of punishment appears to have little or no effect on crime rates (Pratt and Cullen, 2005; Robinson and Darley, 2004), perhaps because potential offenders typically have much more information about the likelihood of being arrested than they do about likely sentences (Von Hirsch et al., 1999). Studies show that the general public knows little about potential sentences and tends to underestimate their severity (Robinson and Darley, 2004; Von Hirsch et al., 1999). In addition, offenders tend to discount punishment as an uncertain future event, whereas the short-term rewards of crime are more powerful pull factors (Wilson and Herrnstein, 1985). "[F]uture contingent costs may be discounted less, if their magnitude is sufficiently great *and* their likelihood of being incurred increases. Severe sentencing policies thus might possibly have an impact if coupled with much higher probabilities of conviction" (Von Hirsch et al., 1999:48).

Although studies of juvenile offenders are few in number, they suggest that arrests and sanctions have deterrent effects. For example, Mocan and Rees (2005) examined self-reported delinquency data (for drug selling, assault, robbery, burglary, and theft) for 14,942 adolescents from the 1995 National Longitudinal Study of Adolescent Health. They compared county-level arrests (of adults and juveniles) for violent crime reported in 1993 with county-level juvenile crime rates in 1995, thus providing a measure of the deterrent effects of arrest rates on subsequent juvenile crime rates. They found that the arrest rate had a general deterrent effect on the crimes of drug dealing and assault; for each additional arrest, there was a 3.6-percent decrease in the likelihood that juveniles would sell drugs and a 6.6-percent decrease in the likelihood that they would commit an assault. According to Mocan and Rees (2005:344), "this pattern of results runs counter to claims that at-risk young Americans are so present-oriented that they do not respond to incentives and sanctions."

Similarly, Smith and Gartin (1989) found that being arrested reduced recidivism among youthful male offenders, particularly first-time offenders. A 2003 study of serious juvenile offenders incarcerated in a maximum security facility found a negative relationship between their sentence severity and self-reported intent to reoffend and a positive correlation between their self-reported intent and the number of offenses they actually committed after their release. Researchers found evidence that these offenders made "some explicit calculations about the advantages and disadvantages of committing future crimes" (Corrado et al., 2003:197).

Criminal sanctions will only have deterrent effects if potential offenders: (1) believe there is a significant likelihood of getting caught, (2) believe there is a significant likelihood of receiving a substantial sentence, and (3) consider the risk of the penalty when deciding whether to offend (see Von Hirsch et al., 1999). It is useful to consider, however, each of the necessary preconditions for successful deterrence in the context of juvenile offending. A law can act as a deterrent only if the targeted population is aware that the law exists and believes that it will be enforced.

Redding and Fuller (2004) found that few violent juvenile offenders knew that they could be tried as adults, none thought it would happen to them, and few thought they would face serious punishment. Moreover, few reported thinking about the possibility of getting caught when they committed the offense. Indeed, it seems that offenders generally underestimate the risk of arrest (Robinson and Darley, 2004). Juveniles' psychosocial immaturity, including their tendency to focus on the short-term benefits of their choices (Beckman, 2004; Scott, Reppucci, and Woolard, 1995; Steinberg and

Cauffman, 1996), may reduce the likelihood that they will perceive the substantial risk of being arrested or punished as an adult (Schneider and Ervin, 1990).

Specific Deterrence

To date, six published studies have been conducted to examine the specific deterrence effects of transfer. These large-scale studies indicate that youth tried in adult criminal court generally have greater recidivism rates after release than those tried in juvenile court. It is unclear, however, whether transfer affects recidivism for nonviolent property or drug offenders.

Fagan (1996) examined the recidivism rates of 800 randomly selected 15- and 16-year-old juvenile offenders charged with robbery or burglary during 1981–82. Controlling for eight variables (race, gender, age at first offense, prior offenses, offense severity, case length, sentence length, and court), as well as for time residing in the community, researchers compared offenders charged in New Jersey's juvenile courts with offenders charged in New York's criminal courts under that State's automatic transfer law (under which 16 is the age of full criminal responsibility). Both areas shared similar demographic, socioeconomic, and crime- indicator characteristics. Thus, the study provides a comparison of recidivism rates as a function of whether cases were processed in the juvenile or criminal court, without the sample selection problems inherent in studies comparing cases within a single jurisdiction where prosecutors or judges decide which cases to transfer.

A higher percentage of youth who were tried for robbery in criminal court were rearrested (91 percent) than those tried for robbery in juvenile court (73 percent). Of youth who were rearrested, those tried in the criminal court also were rearrested sooner and more often. However, there were no differences in recidivism rates (in terms of the percent rearrested, rearrest rate, and time to rearrest) for burglary offenders tried in the criminal court versus those tried in juvenile court. The findings on robbery offenders suggest that criminal court processing alone, irrespective of whether youth are incarcerated in juvenile or adult facilities, produces a higher recidivism rate. This finding is emphasized by the parallel finding that even those youth sentenced to probation in criminal court had a substantially higher recidivism rate than those incarcerated in the juvenile justice system (see also Mason and Chang, 2001).

Juveniles with the highest recidivism rates were those who were incarcerated after being tried in the criminal court. The study indicated that, overall, youth adjudicated in juvenile court had a 29-percent lower risk of rearrest than those tried in criminal court. Drug offenses were the one exception. Criminal court adjudication substantially reduced the risk of rearrest in those cases.

Bishop and colleagues (1996) compared the 1-year recidivism rate of 2,738 juvenile offenders transferred to criminal court in Florida in 1987 with a matched sample of 2,738 juvenile offenders who had not been transferred. Florida relies almost exclusively on prosecutorial transfer. These transfer decisions are largely offense-driven and made soon after arrest, before the prosecutor has much information about the youth's background. Therefore, it is less likely that the youth retained in the juvenile justice system had lower recidivism rates due to variables other than those controlled for in the analysis, such as the youth's mental health status or amenability to treatment (Bishop and Frazier, 2000). The study controlled for seven variables (race, gender, age, number of referrals to juvenile court, most serious prior offense, number of charges, and most serious charge). Researchers found that the rearrest rates were higher (0.54 versus 0.32 offenses per person, per year of time living in the community) among transferred youth. Also, the average time to reoffending was shorter (135 versus 227 days) for the transferred youth across seven offense types (including violent felonies, property offenses, and minor misdemeanors).

Following the same Florida offenders 7 years after the initial study by Bishop et al. (1996), Winner et al. (1997) compared transferred versus nontransferred offenders matched for gender, age, race, and offending history. They found that the rearrest rates were higher and the time to reoffending shorter (adjusting for time residing in the community following release from incarceration) among those who had been transferred to criminal court. The exception was transferred property felons who had lower recidivism rates than similar offenders who remained under juvenile court jurisdiction.

Myers (2001, 2003) examined the 18-month recidivism rates of 494 juvenile offenders charged with robbery or aggravated assault in Pennsylvania in 1994, using a statistical model to control for the possibility that the transferred juveniles were the more serious offenders in the first place (and therefore more likely to recidivate) or those less amenable to treatment in the juvenile system. The study controlled for age at referral, race, geographical location, school and family status, various indices of prior offending history, use of a weapon, and various case-processing variables. Youth who were judicially transferred to criminal court were twice as likely to be rearrested, and were rearrested more quickly (and often for more serious offenses) upon their return to the community, than youth who were retained in the juvenile justice system during the same period.

Finally, two recent large-scale studies funded by OJJDP are particularly informative:

RECENT OJJDP-FUNDED STUDIES

Lanza-Kaduce and colleagues (2005) conducted a second Florida study that included 950 young adult offenders.[4] Half of the offenders had been prosecutorially transferred to the criminal court in 1995 or 1996 for offenses they had committed as juveniles; the other half had remained in the juvenile system. This resulted in a sample of 475 matched pairs of transferred and retained cases.

The cases were drawn from six urban and rural judicial circuits in Florida that differed considerably in their rates of transfer. The cases were matched within each judicial circuit (thus controlling for geographical effects in case processing and decisionmaking) along seven relevant demographic, criminal history, and offense variables: age, gender, race, number of previous juvenile referrals, most serious prior offense, offense, and number of charges. In addition, a subset of this group, consisting of 315 best matched pairs, were further matched according to an offense seriousness index created by examining local records to obtain data about 12 other case characteristics: prior juvenile referrals, multiple charges at arrest, multiple incidents involved in the case, charge consolidation, legal problems during case processing, gang involvement, codefendants or accomplices, property loss or damage, victim injury, use of weapons, felony charges, and the presence of mitigating and aggravating factors. The measure of recidivism was the number of offenses committed after youth turned age 18, and data analyses were conducted on the 475 matched pairs, as well as on the subset of 315 best matched pairs.

Transferred Juveniles More Likely to Offend

The Lanza-Kaduce study expands on the earlier Florida studies (i.e., Bishop et al., 1996; Winner et al., 1997). It includes reoffense types and a detailed matching on relevant case and offense characteristics (see Frazier et al., 1999). Its recidivism data draws on information from two different State databases. To reduce a potential lack of comparability in recidivism measures between transfers and juvenile court retainees due to differences in decision-making and recordkeeping between the two systems, it examines offending after age 18. "The focus on adult recidivism . . . captures the persistence of a criminal career into adulthood—a pivotal policy concern" (Lanza-Kaduce et al., 2005:64). Moreover, the data "include cases transferred in 1995 and 1996, after the 'get tough' idea was fully entrenched in the American culture and after prosecutorial transfer had been used in Florida for a long time" (Lanza-Kaduce et al., 2005:65).

Like the earlier Florida studies, this study found that transferred offenders, particularly violent offenders, were significantly more likely to reoffend.

- Overall, 49 percent of the transferred offenders reoffended, compared with 35 percent of the retained offenders.
- For violent offenses, 24 percent of the transferred offenders reoffended, compared with 16 percent of the retained offenders.
- For drug offenses, 11 percent of the transferred offenders reoffended, compared with 9 percent of the retained offenders.
- For property offenses, 14 percent of the transferred offenders reoffended, compared with 10 percent of the retained offenders.

The results were virtually identical for the subset of 315 best matched pairs. In addition, researchers conducted paired-comparison analyses in which each matched pair was the unit of analysis. This analysis classified each pair according to whether both offenders reoffended (21 percent of cases), only the transferred offender reoffended (29 percent of cases), only the retained offender reoffended (15 percent of cases), or neither reoffended (36 percent of cases).[5] Again, the results were virtually identical for the subgroup of best-matched pairs. However, the study failed to replicate the 1997 Florida study finding of lower recidivism rates among transferred property offenders (Winner et al., 1997).

In addition to the recidivism study, the Florida research group conducted detailed interviews with 144 serious male offenders between the ages of 17 and 20, half of whom had been transferred and the other half of whom were retained in the juvenile system (Bishop and Frazier, 2000; Lane et al., 2002). Eighty-three percent had more than one prior arrest, 60 percent began offending before the age of 14, and 47 percent had committed a violent offense as their most serious current offense. Interviews were conducted in four "deep-end" juvenile correctional institutions (i.e., 9–36 month placements in highly secure juvenile correctional facilities designed for high- and medium-risk offenders) and eight adult prisons in Florida (mostly youthful offender facilities designed to house young adults up to age 24), with youth at different stages in serving their sentence. Of the 71 youth who had been transferred to the adult system, 63 also had prior experience in the juvenile system. Fifty-eight percent of the youth rated the deep-end juvenile placements as beneficial, 33 percent rated the adult prison as beneficial, 20 percent rated the less restrictive juvenile dispositions (for example, probation, placement in low-restrictive residential programs) as beneficial, and 12 percent rated adult probation as beneficial.

The youth rated the deep-end juvenile programs the most beneficial largely because these programs provided intensive, long-term job skills training and treatment. In addition, the lengthier period of incarceration gave them more time to consider their futures and the consequences of reoffending, suggesting that the longer sanctions had an impact (Lane et al., 2002). But "[o]ften when adult sanctions were perceived as being beneficial, the benefit was not attributed to anything gained from the disposition. Rather, many youth indicated that they expected to remain crime-free because their experiences in the adult system had been so horrible. Youth who believed the adult sanctions would keep them from committing crimes primarily pointed to three reasons: pain and denigration, time spent in prison, and fear of future consequences, especially tougher sentences. Paradoxically, most of those who said the adult experience was negative also mentioned pain, denigration, and/or anger, but they gave these as reasons why the adult dispositions had made matters worse. Others attributed a negative impact to adult sanctions because they 'learned more crime while there'" (Lane et al., 2002:444). While a substantial minority of the youth said that prison had taught them a lesson—declaring that they would not reoffend because they did not want to endure the pain of imprisonment again— 61 percent said that prison had either no impact or a negative impact on their behaviors (Lane et al., 2002:448). Overall, the "findings call into question the practice of [incarcerating juveniles in adult prison and] 'skipping' the deep-end juvenile programs when sentencing youth for serious crimes" (p. 452).

In another OJJDP-sponsored study, Fagan and colleagues (2003) extended and largely replicated previous research (Fagan, 1996). This time, they examined the timeat-risk (i.e., residing in the community) recidivism rates for 2,382 15- and 16-yearold juveniles charged in 1992 or 1993 with robbery, burglary, or assault. The 2003 study used a larger sample drawn from more counties in each State as well as more detailed measures of important variables, such as offenders' prior juvenile record. The study compared those charged in selected counties in northern New Jersey, where such cases originate in the juvenile court, with those charged in matched counties in New York, where such cases originate in the criminal court. The New York and New Jersey counties are contiguous, and part of a large metropolitan area that shares common demographic, economic, and social characteristics as well as similar criminogenic influences and crime rate characteristics. Thus, the study design allows for comparison of recidivism rates as a function of whether cases are processed in juvenile court or criminal court, without the sample selection problems inherent in designs that compare cases retained in the juvenile court with those transferred in a single jurisdiction wherein decisionmakers decide which cases to transfer. All cases were followed for a 7-year period until 2000, by which time almost all of the offenders had served their sentences and had spent at least 2 years living in the community. The study statistically controlled for a variety of relevant demographics (age, gender, ethnicity), case and offense characteristics (for example, most serious charge, weapon use, whether detained, case length), criminal history variables (age at first arrest, number of prior arrests, previous incarcerations), and sentence length. It used statistical techniques that analyzed recidivism in different ways (first rearrest, severity of rearrest charges, time until rearrest, likelihood of subsequent incarceration).

Greater Likelihood of Rearrest

The study found a 100-percent greater likelihood of rearrest for a violent offense and a 47-percent greater likelihood of rearrest for a property offense, among the New York juveniles whose cases were processed in the criminal court than for the New Jersey juveniles. They also had a greater number of rearrests for such offenses and a 26-percent greater chance of being reincarcerated. The pattern of findings was even stronger for first-time offenders. For drug offense rearrests, however, the results were reversed, with the juveniles tried in juvenile court having a 31-percent greater likelihood of rearrest for drug offenses. Finally, the study found that the differences in recidivism were unrelated to periods of incarceration in adult versus juvenile facilities. Thus, incarceration in adult prisons "does not seem to be responsible for the criminogenic effect of adult court processing" (Fagan et al., 2003:66).

These findings fully replicate those of the earlier Fagan (1996) study, except with respect to property offenses. The 1996 study found no difference in recidivism rates for burglary, whereas the 2003 study found that criminal court processing increased the recidivism rates for property offenses.

Transfer Found to Increase Recidivism

In sum, to date, six large-scale studies have been conducted on the specific deterrent effects of transfer. These studies used large sample sizes (between 494 and 5,476 participants), different methodologies (natural experiment across two jurisdictions, matched groups within the same jurisdictions, or statistical controls), multiple measures of recidivism, and were conducted in five jurisdictions (Florida, New Jersey, New York, Minnesota, Pennsylvania) having different types of transfer laws (automatic, prosecutorial, or judicial). The strong consistency in results across the studies is all the more compelling given that they used different samples and methodologies, thereby providing a degree of convergent validity for the findings. All of the studies found higher recidivism rates among offenders who had been transferred to criminal court, compared with those who were retained in the juvenile system. This held true even for offenders who only received a sentence of probation from the criminal court. Thus, the extant research provides sound evidence that transferring juvenile offenders to the criminal court does not engender community protection by reducing recidivism. On the contrary, transfer substantially increases recidivism. A recent review of the extant research on transfer conducted by the Centers for Disease Central arrived at the same conclusion (McGowan et al., 2007). Only two apparent exceptions challenge this pattern of findings. For nonviolent property offenders, the effects of transfer remain unclear, with one study finding that transfer had no effect on recidivism (Fagan, 1996) and another finding that transfer decreased recidivism (Winner et al., 1997), but with two studies (conducted in the same jurisdiction as the first two studies) finding that it increased recidivism (Fagan et al., 2003; Lanza-Kaduce et al., 2005). In addition, with respect to drug offenders, two studies (Fagan, 1996; Fagan et al., 2003) found decreased recidivism rates among those tried in the criminal court.

Challenges for Future Research

Important challenges for future research are to determine: (1) whether transfer differentially impacts recidivism as a function of offense type (violent offenses, property offenses, drug offenses), and (2) what features of the criminal justice system increase recidivism, an important question for policymaking. These challenges raise such questions as the following:

- Can changes be made in the criminal court processing and adult system sanctions of juveniles to make them less detrimental? What are they?
- In what ways should the juvenile justice system guard against those features of the criminal justice system that serve to increase recidivism?
- How can States' blended sentencing systems, which allow the juvenile courts to impose adult sentences in certain cases (see Redding and Howell, 2000), incorporate the best features of the juvenile and criminal justice systems, while avoiding the negative effects of criminal justice system processing?

Why Do Juveniles Tried as Adults Have Higher Recidivism Rates?

Experts (see Bazemore and Umbreit, 1995; Myers, 2003; Thomas and Bishop, 1984; Winner et al., 1997) have identified several possible explanations for the higher recidivism rates of violent juvenile offenders tried in criminal court as compared to those adjudicated in juvenile court:

- The stigmatization and other negative effects of labeling juveniles as convicted felons.
- The sense of resentment and injustice juveniles feel about being tried and punished as adults.
- The learning of criminal mores and behavior while incarcerated with adult offenders.
- The decreased focus on rehabilitation and family support in the adult system.

A felony conviction also results in the loss of a number of civil rights and privileges (see Redding, 2003), further reducing the opportunities for employment and community reintegration.

Findings from several studies (Fagan, 1996; Fagan, Kupchik and Liberman, 2003) show that criminal court processing alone, even without the imposition of any criminal sentence, increases recidivism. Juveniles' sense of injustice at criminal court processing may cause them to react defiantly by reoffending, and it may further harden an emergent criminal self-concept (see Sherman, 1993; Thomas and Bishop, 1984; Winner et al., 1997). "The concept of fairness appears to be an important variable in an individual's perception of sentence severity and its subsequent relationship to future recidivism" (Corrado et al., 2003:183). Furthermore, it appears that many adolescents with conduct disorders already have a sense of having been dealt an unfair hand by authority figures (Chamberlain, 1998). Bishop and Frazier (2000) interviewed 95 serious and chronic juvenile offenders in Florida, roughly half of whom were transferred to the criminal court and were incarcerated in adult correctional facilities, and half of whom had been adjudicated in the juvenile court and were incarcerated in maximum-security juvenile facilities. According to the authors, many of the juveniles felt a strong sense of injustice about being tried as adults:

> *Many experience the court process not so much as a condemnation of their behavior as a condemnation of them. Unlike the juvenile court, the criminal court failed to communicate that young offenders retain some fundamental worth. What the youths generally heard was that they were being punished not only because their behavior was bad but also because they were personifications of their behavior. Far from viewing the criminal court and its officers as legitimate, the juvenile offenders we interviewed saw them more often as duplicitous and manipulative, malevolent in intent, and indifferent to their needs. It was common for them to experience a sense of injustice and, then, to condemn the condemners (Bishop and Frazier, 2000:263).*

These findings are consistent with those of Redding and Fuller (2004), who found that juveniles tried as adults clearly felt that transfer laws were unfair. Many felt that their juvenile status and immaturity dictated that they should be tried as juveniles, despite the serious crimes they had committed. They also did not understand why the legal system was trying them as adults, and they saw themselves as being treated differently from other similarly situated juveniles. Both perceptions contributed to their sense of unfairness, perhaps leading to greater cynicism about the legal system as a result of being incarcerated (see Piquero et al., 2005).

Some studies indicate that prison incarceration "does not seem to be responsible for the criminogenic effect of adult court processing" (Fagan, Kupchik, and Liberman, 2003:66). One reason for the increased recidivism of these offenders, however, might be the reduced opportunities for meaningful rehabilitation in adult prison. Forst, Fagan, and Vivona's 1989 study, for example, found that youth in juvenile facilities gave higher marks than youth in adult facilities to the available treatment and case management services. Youth in juvenile detention described these services as helpful in providing counseling, enabling them to obtain needed services, encouraging participation in programs, teaching the consequences of rule breaking, and deepening their understanding of their problems. Similarly, in a recent study comparing the experiences of youths in adult versus juvenile correctional facilities in a large Northeastern State, all of whom had been tried in adult criminal court, Kupchik (2007) found that youths in juvenile facilities reported far more positive, mentoring-style staff-inmate interactions than did the youths in adult facilities. However, youths in adult facilities reported having greater access to counseling and educational services, perhaps because of the larger size of the adult facilities.

Bishop and Frazier's recent Florida study (2000) vividly portrays the differences between juvenile and adult correctional facilities. They found that the juvenile correctional institutions were treatment- oriented and adhered to therapeutic models of rehabilitation (Bishop and Frazier, 2000:255). "Compared to the criminal justice system, the juvenile system seems to be more reintegrative in practice and effect" (Bishop and Frazier, 2000:265). Youths in juvenile facilities had positive feelings about the staff, who they felt cared about them and taught them appropriate behaviors. Most of the juveniles incarcerated in juvenile facilities felt conf ident that they would not reoffend, often crediting the staff with helping them make this positive change. Conversely, only a third of the juveniles in adult prisons said that they would not reoffend.

Juveniles in adult prison reported that much of their time was spent learning criminal behavior from the inmates and proving how tough they were. They also were much more fearful of being victimized than they had been when incarcerated in juvenile facilities, and more than 30 percent had been assaulted or had witnessed assaults by prison staff. Indeed, Beyer (1997) paints a bleak picture of life in adult prison for juveniles, who are at greater risk for suicide, as well as for physical and sexual abuse from older inmates.

As compared with those in juvenile facilities, juveniles incarcerated in adult prison are eight times more likely to commit suicide, five times more likely to be sexually assaulted, and almost twice as likely to be attacked with a weapon by inmates or beaten by staff (Beyer, 1997). Because juveniles in adult prisons are exposed to a criminal culture in which inmates commit crimes against each other, these institutions may socialize delinquent juveniles into true career criminals. In an older study about life in prison (Eisikovits and Baizerman, 1983), violent juvenile offenders reported that their daily survival required finding ways to fit into the inmate culture, dealing with difficult and authoritarian relationships with adult inmates, and adjusting to the institution by accepting violence as a part of daily life and, thus, becoming even more violent.

Finally, Redding and Fuller (2004) found that juveniles whose jail or prison experiences were worse than they had expected, and those who reported witnessing or experiencing violence while incarcerated, were less likely to say that their incarceration would deter them from committing crimes in the future. This finding raises the possibility that incarceration in adult facilities may have brutalizing effects on juveniles, which may partly account for their increased recidivism. (The term "brutalization effect" describes the finding that homicide rates in a State often increase after an execution (Bowers, 1998), perhaps because executions model and communicate that violence is an acceptable and psychologically cathartic alternative.) Likewise, juveniles' brutal experiences in adult prison may teach the wrong lessons about the acceptability and psychological benefits of criminal conduct, particularly violent crime, while also contributing to their sense of being treated unfairly, both of which may increase recidivism. Further research is needed on this issue.

Implications for Policymakers and Practitioners

The research findings on juvenile transfer have the potential to impact both policy and practice. In a recent study, Hensl and Redding (2005) found that juvenile court judges who were knowledgeable about the ineffectiveness of transfer in reducing recidivism were somewhat less likely to transfer juvenile offenders to the criminal court. This finding suggests that educating judges, prosecutors, court personnel, and legislators about the research on transfer may reduce the number of cases transferred to criminal court or the number of transferred cases that result in criminal sanctions. The Miami-Dade

County Public Defender's Office developed the Juvenile Sentencing Advocacy Project, which produced a 350-percent increase in the number of transferred cases receiving a juvenile rather than an adult sanction from criminal court judges (Mason, 2000). In Florida, which has had some of the most aggressive transfer policies in the Nation, the number of juveniles prosecuted in the criminal court decreased by two-thirds between 1996 and 2003 (whereas the total number of juvenile court cases decreased by only 9 percent), apparently due, in part, to research disseminated showing the counter-deterrent effects of transfer (Bishop, 2004). Moreover, in the last several years, some States have reduced the scope of transfer laws to make fewer juvenile offenders eligible for prosecutorial or judicial transfer (Bishop, 2004; Griffin, 2003).

Yet in Florida, for example, the data show that the transferred cases were generally no more serious, and sometimes were less serious, than the cases retained in the juvenile justice system (Lanza-Kaduce, Frazier, and Bishop, 1999). Forty-three percent of the 1,100 juveniles incarcerated in adult prisons for offenses committed when they were 15 years old or younger had not previously been committed to a juvenile justice program (Annino, 2000). Thus, the juvenile justice system never had an opportunity to rehabilitate these youth before they were transferred to the adult system, despite the fact that serious juvenile offenders in Florida report that intensive juvenile placements are relatively more beneficial than either adult prison or mild juvenile sanctions (Lane et al., 2002).

But Florida is not unique in transferring first-time offenders to the criminal court. Transfer laws, particularly automatic transfer laws, often target first-time offenders, even though they do not pose the greatest recidivism risk or threat to community safety. The frequency of offending, instead of the seriousness of the first offense, best predicts overall recidivism and the risk for committing a subsequent violent offense (see Bishop, 2004; Piquero, 2000; Redding, 1997). To best achieve reductions in recidivism, the overall number of juvenile offenders transferred to the criminal justice system should be minimized. Moreover, those who are transferred should be the chronic repeat offenders—rather than first-time offenders—particularly in cases where the first-time offense is a violent offense.

CONCLUSION

Most practitioners would agree, consistent with the extant research, that it is important that the juvenile courts' response to juvenile offenders be calibrated to have sufficient effectiveness as a deterrent while not being overly punitive. The practice of transferring juveniles for trial and sentencing in adult criminal court has, however, produced the unintended effect of increasing recidivism, particularly in violent offenders, and thereby of promoting life-course criminality (Scott, 2000). But, if it was indeed true that transfer laws had a deterrent effect on juvenile crime, then some of these offenders would not have offended in the first place. Although the limited extant research falls far short of providing definitive conclusions, the bulk of the empirical evidence suggests that transfer laws, as currently implemented, probably have little general deterrent effect on would-be juvenile offenders.

REFERENCES

Annino, P. G. (2000). Children in adult prisons: A call for a moratorium. *Florida State University Law Review, 28*, 471–90.

Bazemore, G. & Umbriet, M. (1995). Rethinking the sanctioning function in juvenile court: Retributive or restorative responses to youth crime. *Crime and Delinquency, 41*, 296-316.

Beckman, M. (2004). Crime, culpability, and the adolescent brain. *Science, 305*, 596-99.

Beyer, M. (1997). Experts for juveniles at risk of adult sentences. In *More than meets the eye: Rethinking assessment, competency and sentencing for a harsher era of juvenile justice,* edited by P. Puritz, A. Capozello, and W. Shang, 1–22. Washington, DC: American Bar Association, Juvenile Justice Center.

Bishop, D. M. (2000). Juvenile offenders in the adult criminal justice system. In *Crime and justice: A review of research, vol. 27*, edited by M. Tonry, 81–165. Chicago, IL: University of Chicago Press.

Bishop, D. M. (2004). Injustice and irrationality in contemporary youth policy. *Criminology and Public Policy, 3*, 633-44.

Bishop, D. M. & Frazier, C. E. (2000). Consequences of transfer. In *The changing borders of juvenile justice: Transfer of adolescents to the criminal court,* edited by J. Fagan and F.E. Zimring, 227–76. Chicago, IL: University of Chicago Press.

Bishop, D. M., Frazier, C. E., Lanza-Kaduce, L. & Winner, L. (1996). The transfer of juveniles to criminal court: Does it make a difference? *Crime and Delinquency, 42*, 171-91.

Bowers, W. C. (1998). Deterrence, brutalization, and the death penalty: Another examination of Oklahoma's return to capital punishment. *Criminology, 36*, 711-33.

Chamberlain, P. (1998). *Family connections: A treatment foster care model for adolescents with delinquency.* Eugene, OR: Northwest Media.

Corrado, R. R., Cohen, I. M., Glackman, W. & Odgers, C. (2003). Serious and violent young offenders' decisions to recidivate: An assessment of five sentencing models. *Crime and Delinquency, 49*, 179-200.

Eisikovits, Z. & Baizerman, M. (1983). "Doin' time": Violent youth in a juvenile facility and in an adult prison. *Journal of Offender Counseling, Services, and Rehabilitation, 6(3)*, 5-20.

Elder, R. W., Shults, R. A., Sleet, D. A., Nicholas, J. L., Thompson, R. S. & Rajab, W. 2004. Effectiveness of mass media campaigns for reducing drinking and driving and alcohol-involved crashes: A systemic review. *American Journal of Preventive Medicine, 27(1)*, 57-65.

Fagan, J. A. (1996). The comparative advantage of juvenile versus criminal court sanctions on recidivism among adolescent felony offenders. *Law and Policy, 18*, 77-113.

Fagan, J., Kupchik, A. & Liberman, A. (2003). *Be careful what you wish for: The comparative impacts of juvenile versus criminal court sanctions on recidivism among adolescent felony offenders.* Public Law Research Paper No. 03–61. New York: Columbia University Law School.

Fagan, J. & Zimring, F. E., eds. (2000). *The changing borders of juvenile justice: Transfer of adolescents to the criminal court.* Chicago, IL: University of Chicago Press.

Forst, M., Fagan, J. & Vivona, S. T. (1989). Youth in prisons and training schools: Perceptions and consequences of the treatment-custody dichotomy. *Juvenile and Family Court Journal, 40*, 1-14.

Frazier, C. E., Bishop, D. M., Lanza-Kaduce, L. & Marvasti, A. (1999). Juveniles in criminal court: Past and current research from Florida. *Quinnipiac Law Review, 18*, 573-96.

Fritsch, E. J., Caeti, T. J. & Hemmens, C. (1996). Spare the needle but not the punishment: The incarceration of waived youth in adult prisons. *Crime and Delinquency, 42*, 593-609.

Glassner, B., Ksander, M., Berg, B. & Johnson, B. D. (1983). A note on the deterrent effect of juvenile versus adult jurisdiction. *Social Problems., 31*, 219-21.

Griffin, P. (2003). *Trying and sentencing juveniles as adults: An analysis of state transfer and blended sentencing laws.* Pittsburgh, PA: National Center for Juvenile Justice.

Hensl, K. B. & Redding, R. E. (2005). (March). *The relationship among juvenile court judges' personal characteristics and attitudes, juvenile offender characteristics, and judicial transfer decisions.* Paper presented at the American Psychology-Law Society annual conference. La Jolla, CA.

Jensen, E. L. & Metsger, L. K. (1994). A test of the deterrent effect of legislative waiver on violent juvenile crime. *Crime and Delinquency, 40*, 96-104.

Johnson, S. D. & Bowers, K. J. (2003). Opportunity is in the eye of the beholder: The role of publicity in crime prevention. *Criminology and Public Policy, 2*, 497-524.

Kupchik, A. (2007). The correctional experiences of youth in adult and juvenile prisons. *Justice Quarterly, 24*, 247-70.

Kupchik, A., Fagan, J. & Liberman, A. (2003). Punishment, proportionality, and jurisdictional transfer of adolescent offenders: A test of the leniency gap hypothesis. *Stanford Law and Policy Review, 14*, 57-83.

Lane, J., Lanza-Kaduce, L., Frazier, C. E. & Bishop, D. M. (2002.)Adult versus juvenile sanctions: Voices of incarcerated youths. *Crime and Delinquency, 48*, 43 1-55.

Lanza-Kaduce, L., Frazier, C. E. & Bishop, D. M. (1999). Juvenile transfers in Florida: The worst of the worst? *University of Florida Journal of Law and Public Policy, 10*, 277–312.

Lanza-Kaduce, L., Lane, J., Bishop, D. M. & Frazier, C. E. (2005). Juvenile offenders and adult felony recidivism: The impact of transfer. *Journal of Crime and Justice, 28*, 59-77.

Lee, D. S. & McCrary, J. (2005). *Crime, punishment, and myopia.* Working Paper 11491. Cambridge, MA: National Bureau of Economic Research.

Levitt, S. D. (1998). Juvenile crime and punishment. *Journal of Political Economy, 106*, 1156-85.

Mason, C. A. (2000). *Juvenile sentencing advocacy project: Evaluation report.* Miami, FL: Miami-Dade County Public Defender's Office.

Mason, C. A. & Chang, S. (2001). *Rearrest rates among youth incarcerated in adult court.* Miami, FL: Miami-Dade County Public Defender's Office.

McGowan, A., Hahn, R., Liberman, A., Crosby, A., Fullilove, M., Johnson, R., Moscicki, E., Price, L., Snyder, S., Tuma, F., Lowry, J., Briss, P., Cory, S. & Stone, G. (2007). Effects on violence of laws and policies facilitating the transfer of juveniles from the juvenile justice system to the Adult System. *American Journal of Preventive Medicine, 32*, S7-S28.

Mocan, H. N. & Rees, D. I. (2005). Economic conditions, deterrence, and juvenile crime: Evidence from micro data. *American Law and Economics Review, 7*, 319-49.

Myers, D. L. (2001). *Excluding violent youths from juvenile court: The effectiveness of legislative waiver.* New York: LFB Scholarly.

Myers, D. L. (2003). The recidivism of violent youths in juvenile and adult court: A consideration of selection bias. *Youth Violence and Juvenile Justice, 1*, 79-101.

Myers, D. L. (2005). *Boys among men: Trying and sentencing juveniles as adults.* Westport, CT: Praeger.

Peterson-Badali, M., Ruck, M. D. & Koegl, C. J. (2001). Youth court dispositions: Perceptions of Canadian juvenile offenders. *International Journal of Offender Therapy and Comparative Criminology, 45*, 593-605.

Piquero, A. R. (2000). Assessing the relationships between gender, chronicity, seriousness, and offense skewness in criminal offending. *Journal of Criminal Justice, 28*, 103-16.

Piquero, A. R., Fagan, J., Mulvey, E. P., Steinberg, L. & Odgers, C. (2005). Developmental trajectories of legal socialization among serious adolescent offenders. *Journal of Criminal Law and Criminology, 96*, 267-98.

Pratt, T. C. & Cullen, F. T. (2002). Assessing macro-level predictors and theories of crime: A meta-analysis. In *crime and justice: A review of research, vol. 32,* edited by M. Tonry, 373–450. Chicago, IL: University of Chicago Press.

Redding, R. E. (1997). Juveniles transferred to criminal court: Legal reform proposals based on social science research. *Utah Law Review, 3*, 709-97.

Redding, R. E. (2003). The effects of adjudicating and sentencing juveniles as adults: research and policy implications. *Youth Violence and Juvenile Justice, 1*, 128-55.

Redding, R. E. (2005). Adult punishment for juvenile offenders: Does it reduce crime? In *Handbook on Children, Culture and Violence,* edited by Nancy Dowd, Dorothy Singer, and Robin Fretwell Wilson, 375-95. Thousand Oaks, CA: Sage Publications, Inc.

Redding, R. E. & Fuller, E. J. (2004). (summer). What do juvenile offenders know about being tried as adults?: Implications for deterrence. *Juvenile and Family Court Journal,* 35-45.

Redding, R. E. & Howell, J. C. (2000). Blended sentencing in American juvenile courts. In *The changing borders of juvenile justice: Transfer of adolescents to the criminal court,* edited by J. Fagan and F.E. Zimring, 145–80. Chicago, IL: University of Chicago Press.

Redding, R. E. & Mrozoski, B. S. (2005). Adjudicatory and dispositional decision-making in juvenile justice. In *Juvenile delinquency: Prevention, assessment, and intervention,* edited by K. Heilbrun, N. Goldstein, and R. Redding, 232-56. New York: Oxford University Press.

Risler, E. A., Sweatman, T. & Nackerud, L. (1998). Evaluating the Georgia legislative waiver's effectiveness in deterring juvenile crime. *Research on Social Work Practice, 8*, 657-67.

Robinson, P. H. & Darley, J. M. (2004). Does criminal law deter? A behavioral science investigation. *Oxford Journal of Legal Studies, 24(2)*, 173-205.

Sanborn, J. B. (2003). Hard choices or obvious ones: Developing policy for excluding youth from juvenile court. *Youth Violence and Juvenile Justice, 1*, 198-214.

Schneider, A. L. & Ervin, L. (1990). Specific deterrence, rational choice, and decision heuristics: Applications in juvenile justice. *Social Science Quarterly, 71*, 585-601.

Scott, E. S. (2000). The legal construction of adolescence. *Hofstra Law Review, 29*, 547-98.

Scott, E. S., Reppucci, N. D. & Woolard, J. L. (1995). Evaluating adolescent decision making in legal contexts. *Law and Human Behavior, 19*, 221-44.

Sherman, L. W. (1993). Defiance, deterrence, and irrelevance: A theory of the criminal sanction. *Journal of Research in Crime and Delinquency, 30*, 445-73.

Singer, S. I. & McDowall, D. (1988). Criminalizing delinquency: The deterrent effects of the New York juvenile offender law. *Law and Society Review, 22*, 521-35.

Smith, D. A. & Gartin, P. R. (1989). Specifying specific deterrence: The influence of arrest on future criminal activity. *American Sociological Review, 54*, 94-105.

Snyder, H. N. & Sickmund, M. (2006). *Juvenile offenders and victims: 2006 national report.* Washington, DC: U.S. Department of Justice, Office of Justice Programs, Office of Juvenile Justice and Delinquency Prevention.

Steinberg, L. & Cauffman, E. (1996). Maturity of judgment in adolescence: Psychosocial factors in adolescent decisionmaking. *Law and Human Behavior, 20*, 249-72.

Steiner, B. & Hemmens, C. (2003). (spring). Juvenile waiver 2003: Where are we now? *Juvenile and Family Court Journal, 54(2)*, 1-24.

Steiner, B. & Wright, E. (2006). Assessing the relative effects of state direct file waiver laws on violent juvenile crime: Deterrence on irrelevance? *Journal of Criminal Law and Criminology, 96*, 1451-77.

Thomas, C. W. & Bishop, D. M. (1984). The impact of legal sanctions on delinquency: A longitudinal comparison of labeling and deterrence theories. *Journal of Criminal Law and Criminology, 75*, 1222-45.

Virginia Department of Criminal Justice Services. (1996). *Juvenile murder in Virginia: A study of arrests and convictions.* Richmond, VA: Virginia Department of Criminal Justice Services.

Von Hirsch, A., Bottoms, A. E., Burney, E. & Wikstrom, P. O. (1999). *Criminal deterrence and sentence severity: An analysis of recent research.* Oxford, England: Hart.

Wilson, J. Q. & Herrnstein, R.J . (1985). *Crime and human nature.* New York: Simon and Schuster.

Winner, L., Lanza-Kaduce, L., Bishop, D. M. & Frazier, C. E. (1997). The transfer of juveniles to criminal court: Reexamining recidivism over the long term. *Crime and Delinquency, 43*, 548-63.

ACKNOWLEDGMENTS

Richard, E. Redding, J. D., Ph.D., is professor of law at Chapman University School of Law. Portions of this bulletin were adapted with the permission of the publisher from Redding (2005:375–94). The author would like to thank Charles Frazier and Aaron Kupchik for their helpful comments and editorial suggestions.

SHARE WITH YOUR COLLEAGUES

you reprint, please cite OJJDP and the authors of this Bulletin. We are also interested in your feedback, such as how you received a copy, how you intend to use the information, and how OJJDP materials meet your individual or agency needs. Please direct your comments and questions to:

Juvenile Justice Clearinghouse
Publication Reprint/Feedback
P.O. Box 6000
Rockville, MD 20849–6000
800–851–3420
301–519–5600 (fax)
Web: tellncjrs.ncjrs.gov

This Bulletin was prepared under contract number 2005F–065 from the Office of Juvenile Justice and Delinquency Prevention (OJJDP), U.S. Department of Justice.

The Office of Juvenile Justice and Delinquency Prevention is a component of the Office of Justice Programs, which also includes the Bureau of Justice Assistance; the Bureau of Justice Statistics; the Community Capacity Development Office; the National Institute of Justice; the Office for Victims of Crime; and the Office of Sex Offender Sentencing, Monitoring, Apprehending, Registering, and Tracking (SMART).

End Notes

[1] Seventeen States currently have "blended sentencing" laws (see Redding and Howell, 2000) that permit the criminal court, after its adjudication of the youthful offender, to impose juvenile sentences in certain cases. Fifteen States permit the juvenile court to impose limited criminal sanctions (Snyder and Sickmund, 2006).

[2] In addition, brochures were sent to public schools announcing the law and the legal risks juvenile offenders faced, and juvenile court judges warned youth about the risks of committing violent offenses (S. Singer, 2004, personal communication).

[3] These States included Arizona, Arkansas, California, Colorado, Florida, Georgia, Louisiana, Michigan, Montana, Nebraska, Oklahoma, Vermont, Virginia, and Wyoming.

[4] This is the most recent in a series of studies conducted by the Florida research group. These studies, which have been funded by the Florida Department of Justice and OJJDP, are part

of an ongoing research program, beginning in the mid-1980s, studying the effects of transfer in Florida. For an overview of the Florida research program, see Frazier et al., 1999.

[5] The total does not equal 100 because of rounding.

In: Perspectives on Juvenile Offenders
Editors: Owen B. Hahn
ISBN: 978-1-60876-819-6

Chapter 7

PSYCHIATRIC DISORDERS OF YOUTH IN DETENTION

Linda A. Teplin, Karen M. Abram, Gary M. McClelland, Amy A. Mericle, Mina K. Dulcan and Jason J. Washburn

Office of Juvenile Justics and Delinquency Prevention
U.S. Dept. of Justice

The juvenile justice system faces a significant challenge in identifying and responding to the psychiatric disorders of detained youth. In 2001, more than 104,000 juvenile offenders were in custody in juvenile residential placement facilities (Sickmund, Sladky, and Kang, 2004). Understanding the psychiatric disorders of juvenile detainees is an important step toward meeting their needs. Providing such youth with psychiatric services may be critical to breaking the cycle of recidivism. Without sound data on the prevalence of psychiatric disorders, however, defining the best strategies to use and allocating the juvenile justice system's scarce mental health resources are difficult.

EARLIER RESEARCH

Although epidemiological data are key to understanding the psychiatric disorders of juvenile detainees, few empirical studies exist. Table 1 (page 3) lists studies published in the United States since 1990 that have examined the diagnostic characteristics of incarcerated and detained juveniles. These studies do not provide data that are sufficiently comprehensive to guide juvenile justice policy in this area. Six studies in table 1 present rates of multiple disorders, and four of those examine patterns of psychiatric comorbidity among juvenile detainees (Domalanta et al., 2003; Duclos et al., 1998; Pliszka et al., 2000; Shelton, 2001). However, the studies' findings are inconsistent. The prevalence of major affective disorder in the studies varies from 5 percent to 88 percent; substance use disorders from 20 percent to 88 percent; and psychosis from 12 percent to 45 percent. Such inconsistencies may arise from discrepancies in methodology:

Sampling strategies. Samples varied substantially among the studies. Some studies used random samples. Others relied on nonrandom samples, for example, consecutive admissions over a specified time period. Only a few studies reported racial and ethnic differences; some studies did not report the racial or ethnic composition of the sample. Females were excluded entirely from some investigations.

Small samples. Some severe disorders have low base rates, between 1 and 4 percent. Low base rates require large sample sizes to generate reliable estimates (Cohen, 1988). Sample sizes among the studies varied substantially. Many of the studies sampled too few subjects to generate reliable rates, even for the more common disorders. Most studies did not have enough participants in key demographic subgroups to compare participants by gender, race and ethnicity, or age.

A Message from OJJDP

A significant number of youth in detention suffer from psychiatric disorders. To address the needs of such offenders, justice officials need to know the kinds of disorders that are most common and their prevalence among juvenile detainees.

Research indicates that providing detained youth with mental health services may reduce recidivism, but identifying and responding to such mental health needs are challenging.

This Bulletin draws on research conducted by the Northwestern Juvenile Project, which measured the prevalence of alcohol, drug, and mental disorders among youth detained at the Cook County Juvenile

Temporary Detention Center in Illinois. The study examined the prevalence of psychiatric disorders among youth by gender, race and ethnicity, and age.

According to the study, nearly two-thirds of males and three-quarters of females met diagnostic criteria for one or more psychiatric disorders. Many of these youth had two or more disorders.

Youth with serious mental disorders should receive appropriate treatment while they are detained. This Bulletin presents information that can help the juvenile justice system detect youth with psychiatric disorders and respond with an integrated system of services.

Measurement. Some studies in table 1 used nonstandard or untested instruments, did not assess if the disorder impaired the ability of juveniles to function, or reported data on only one category of diagnoses (e.g., substance use disorders, anxiety disorders, personality disorders).

The Northwestern Juvenile Project

The Northwestern Juvenile Project was designed to overcome these methodological limitations. It includes a random sample of juvenile detainees ages 10–18 and a widely accepted and reliable measurement tool, the Diagnostic Interview Schedule for Children (DISC) Version 2.3 (Shaffer et al., 1996), to measure diagnoses of alcohol, drug, and mental disorders. It also uses accepted criteria for identifying functional impairment (Friedman et al., 1996).

Estimates are presented for demographic subgroups (gender, race and ethnicity, and age) for six categories of disorders: affective (major depressive episode, dysthymia, manic episode); psychosis; anxiety (panic, separation anxiety, overanxious, generalized anxiety, obsessive-compulsive disorders); attention-deficit/hyperactivity disorder (ADHD); disruptive behavior (oppositional-defiant and conduct disorders); and substance use (alcohol and drug disorders).

Methods

Subjects were a randomly selected sample of male and female youth who were arrested and subsequently detained at the Cook County Juvenile Temporary Detention Center (Cook County Detention Center) in Illinois between November 20, 1995, and June 14, 1998. The sample was stratified by gender, race and ethnicity (African American, non-Hispanic white, Hispanic), age (10–13 or 14–18 years old), and legal status (processed as a juvenile or an adult). The final sample (N =1,829) comprised 1,172 males (64.1 percent) and 657 females (35.9 percent), 1,005 African Americans (54.9 percent), 524 Hispanics (28.7 percent), 296 non-Hispanic whites (16.2 percent), and 4 detainees of other racial and ethnic groups (0.2 percent). The mean age of participants was 14.9 years old.

Similar to national trends for juvenile detainees, approximately 90 percent of the Cook County Detention Center detainees were male and most were racial or ethnic minorities: African American (77.9 percent), Hispanic (16.0 percent), non-Hispanic white (5.6 percent), and other racial or ethnic groups (0.5 percent). Their age and offense distributions were also similar to other U.S. juvenile detainees (Sickmund, Sladky, and Kang, 2004).

Although no single site can represent the nation, Illinois' criteria for detaining juveniles are similar to other states'. Pretrial detention is allowed if a juvenile needs protection, is likely to flee, or is considered a danger to the community (Grisso, Tomkins, and Casey, 1988; Illinois Criminal Justice Information Authority, 1997). Details of the data collection and sampling procedures can be found in Teplin et al., 2002, and Abram et al., 2003.

Statistical Analysis

Because the sample was stratified by gender, race and ethnicity, age, and legal status, prevalence estimates were weighted to reflect the detention center's population. A simplified version of the results are presented in this Bulletin. Details of the statistical analyses and the results can be found in Teplin et al., 2002, and Abram et al., 2003.

Psychiatric Diagnoses

The DISC Version 2.3 assesses affective disorders, anxiety disorders, disruptive behavior disorders, substance use disorders, and psychosis within the past 6 months (Bravo et al., 1993; Shaffer et al., 1996).

Diagnoses of psychosis and ADHD required special management. The psychosis module of the DISC is a broad symptom screen and does not generate a specific diagnosis. Instead, it flags subjects if they indicate any essential symptoms of psychosis or at least three associated symptoms. More than one-quarter of the subjects scored positive on the screen. To minimize false positive diagnoses, these subjects were counted as psychotic only if their symptoms persisted for at least 1 week; they had not used alcohol, drugs, or medication during this time; and the psychiatrist or clinical psychologist who reviewed the case judged that the symptoms were probably indicative of psychosis. Twelve subjects met these criteria. The study counted as psychotic another eight subjects who, although they denied symptoms, appeared to have auditory hallucinations, thought disorders, or delusions during their interviews.

ADHD among youth is difficult to assess via self-report and is particularly challenging to diagnose among delinquent youth (Schwab-Stone et al., 1996; Thompson et al., 1996). The *Diagnostic and Statistical Manual of Mental Disorders*, third edition, revised *(DSM–III–R)* (American Psychiatric Association, 1987), requires that ADHD symptoms be present before age 7. Most subjects who reported symptoms of ADHD could not remember when their symptoms began. To reduce the risk of underreporting ADHD, rates were calculated in the conventional manner (requiring that the subject report that symptoms were present before age 7) and by counting the disorder as present regardless of the reported age of onset, as long as the duration criterion was met. (This Bulletin presents only the latter rates; the former are available from the authors.) Details on the DISC can be found in Teplin et al., 2002, and Abram et al., 2003.

Rates of disorder using *DSM–III–R* criteria with and without diagnostic-specific or global functional impairment were examined. The rates were substantially similar. (Tables are available from the authors.) Rates of *DSM–III–R* diagnoses without impairment are presented in the following tables.

FINDINGS

Table 2 (page 7) shows that nearly two-thirds of males and nearly three-quarters of females met the diagnostic criteria for one or more of the disorders listed. Overall rates excluding conduct disorder were also calculated because many of its symptoms are related to delinquent behaviors. Excluding conduct disorder, overall rates decreased only slightly.

Prevalence by Gender

The most common disorders among males and females were substance use and disruptive behavior. One-half of males and almost one-half of females met criteria for a substance use disorder; more than 40 percent of males and females met the criteria for disruptive behavior disorders. More than one-fourth of females and almost one-fifth of males met the criteria for one or more affective disorders.

Table 2 reports the female-to-male odds ratios. Females had significantly higher odds than males of having any disorder, any disorder except conduct disorder, any affective disorder, major depressive episode, any anxiety disorder, panic disorder, separation anxiety disorder, overanxious disorder, and substance use disorder other than alcohol or marijuana.

Significantly more females (56.5 percent) than males (45.9 percent) met criteria for two or more of the following disorders: major depressive, dysthymic, manic, psychotic, panic, separation anxiety, overanxious, generalized anxiety, obsessive-compulsive, ADHD, conduct, oppositional defiant, alcohol, marijuana, and other substance use. Approximately one-fifth of females (17.3 percent) and males (20.4 percent) had only one disorder (Abram et al., 2003).

Figures 1 and 2 (page 8) indicate substantial comorbidity for females and males. (Psychoses were omitted from this analysis because there were so few cases.) Patterns of overlap differ somewhat by gender. Nearly one-third of females (29.5 percent) and males (30.8 percent) had substance use disorders and ADHD or disruptive behavior disorders; approximately half of these also had anxiety disorders, affective disorders, or both. Significantly more females (47.8 percent) than males (41.6 percent) had two or more of the following types of disorders: affective, anxiety, substance use, and ADHD or disruptive behavior. Significantly more females (22.5 percent) than males (17.2 percent) had three or more types of disorders. Additional information is available in Abram et al., 2003.

Table 1. Published Studies of Psychiatric Disorders in Incarcerated, Detained, and Secured Juvenile Populations in the United States, From 1990 to 2003

Author(s)/Year	Sample*	Diagnostic Measures*	Major Findings*
Davis et al., 1991	**Participants:** Youth in a state residential facility ***N*:** 173 **Age:** N/R **Gender:** N/R **Race/ethnicity:** Equally divided between white and nonwhite	Clinical interview (*DSM–III–R* criteria)	**Affective:** Dysthymia: 17%; MDD: 15% **SUD/AUD:** Alcohol abuse disorder: 34%; alcohol dependence disorder: 12%; drug abuse disorder: 45%; drug dependence disorder: 19% **CD:** 81% **Other:** ADD: 19%; adjustment disorder: 18%; any developmental disorder: 17%; any PD: 17%; ODD: 5%
Forehand et al., 1991	**Participants:** Youth in a juvenile prison ***N*:** 52 **Age:** 16 **Gender:** Male **Race/ethnicity:** African American: 63%; white: 37%	DISC–2	**Affective:** MDD: 33% **CD:** Group delinquency: 58%; solitary aggression: 23% **Anxiety:** Overanxious: 40% **Other:** ADD: 27%
Eppright et al., 1993	**Participants:** Youth in a juvenile detention center ***N*:** 100 **Age:** 14.6 **Gender:** 21 females; 79 males **Race/ethnicity:** African American: 32%; white: 68%	DICA–R; SCID–II	**CD:** 87% **Other:** Antisocial PD: 75%; avoidant PD: 4%; borderline PD: 27%; dependent PD: 7%; histrionic PD: 3%; narcissistic PD: 8%; obsessive-compulsive PD: 2%; paranoid PD: 17%; passive aggressive PD: 14%; schizoid PD: 1%; schizotypal PD: 0%; self-defeating PD: 2%
Rohde, Mace, and Seeley, 1997	**Participants:** Youth in a secure detention facility ***N*:** 60 **Age:** 14.9 **Gender:** 16 females; 44 males **Race/ethnicity:** African American: 2%; Asian/Pacific Islander: 2%; Hispanic: 7%; American Indian: 5%; white: 83%; other: 2%	K–SADS–PL (additional items added for *DSM–III–R* criteria)	Lifetime (%) / Current (%) **Affective** Dysthymia 8 / 8 MDD 40 / 23 **SUD/AUD** Alcohol abuse 7 / 2 Alcohol dependence 42 / 18 Hard drug abuse 7 / 2 Hard drug dependence 33 / 17 Marijuana abuse 5 / 3 Marijuana dependence 43 / 23 **CD** 73 / 73 **Anxiety** 18 / 10 **Other** ADHD 17 / 13 ODD 17 / 2
Steiner, Garcia, and Mathews, 1997	**Participants:** Violent incarcerated youth ***N*:** 85 **Age:** 16.6 **Gender:** Male **Race/ethnicity:** African American: 38%; Hispanic: 27%; white: 30%; other: 5%	Psychiatric Diagnostic Interview–Revised	**Anxiety:** 20% met "partial criteria" for PTSD; 32% met full criteria.
Timmons-Mitchell et al., 1997	**Participants:** Institutionalized delinquents ***N*:** 50 **Age:** 15.7 for females; 15.9 for males **Gender:** 25 females; 25 males **Race/ethnicity:** N/R **Other:** Of the total sample of 173 subjects, 50 were interviewed using DISC.	DISC (modified)	Male (%) / Female (%) **Psychosis** 16 / 12 **Affective** 72 / 88 **SUD** 88 / 56 **CD** 100 / 96 **Anxiety** 52 / 72 **Other** ADHD 76 / 68 Eating disorder 0 / 16 Sleep disorder 68 / 72

(continued)

Table 1. (Continued)

Author(s)/Year	Sample*	Diagnostic Measures*	Major Findings*
Cauffman et al., 1998	**Participants:** Incarcerated wards ***N*:** 189 **Age:** 17.2 for females; 16.6 for males **Gender:** 96 females; 93 males **Race/ethnicity:** Male (%) Female (%) African American 38 21 Hispanic 27 29 White 30 23 Other 5 27	Psychiatric Diagnostic Interview—Revised (PTSD module only)	**Anxiety:** PTSD: 32% (male); 49% (female)
Duclos et al., 1998	**Participants:** Youth in a detention facility ***N*:** 150 **Age:** 15 (median) **Gender:** 65 females; 85 males **Race/ethnicity:** 100% American Indian, specific group(s) N/R **Other:** 77% status offenders	DISC 2.3; CIDI	Male (%) Female (%) Total (%) **Affective** Dysthymia 0 0 0 MDD 6 16 10 **SUD/AUD** 37 39 38 **CD** 21 11 17 **Anxiety (any)** 2 13 7 Generalized 0 8 3 Overanxious 0 13 5 PTSD 2 0 1 **Other** ODD 1 3 2 ADHD 6 11 8 **Comorbidity**† 17 27 21
Atkins et al., 1999	**Participants:** Youth in a detention facility ***N*:** 75 **Age:** 15.5 **Gender:** 4 females; 71 males **Race/ethnicity:** African American: 77%; non-Hispanic white: 23%	DISC 2.3	**Psychosis:** 45% **Affective:** 24% **SUD:** 20% **CD:** 40% **Anxiety:** 33% **Other:** ODD: 15%; ADHD: 1% **Comorbidity:** Mean of 2.4 diagnoses per youth
Erwin et al., 2000	**Participants:** Youth in a secure juvenile treatment facility ***N*:** 51 **Age:** 17.5 **Gender:** Male **Race/ethnicity:** African American: 28%; Hispanic: 12%; white: 57%	Clinician-Administered PTSD Scale for Children and Adolescents	**Anxiety:** Lifetime PTSD: 45%; current PTSD: 18%
Pliszka et al., 2000	**Participants:** Youth in a detention center ***N*:** 50 **Age:** 15.4 **Gender:** 5 females; 45 males **Race/ethnicity:** N/R	DISC 2.3	**Affective (any):** 42%; MDD: 20%; mania: 20% **SUD:** Alcohol dependence: 28%; marijuana dependence: 46%; other: 14% **CD:** 60% **Other:** ADHD: 18%; ODD: 24% **Comorbidity**‡
Aarons et al., 2001	**Participants:** Adjudicated youth ***N*:** 419 **Age:** 16.9 **Gender:** 34% female; 66% male **Race/ethnicity:** African American: 21%; Asian/Pacific Islander: 9%; Hispanic: 29%; non-Hispanic white: 34%; biracial: 4%; other: 3% **Other:** Participants from a subsample (*n*=1,036) of a larger study titled "Patterns of Care"; age and race based on the total subsample	CIDI (SUD module only)	Lifetime (%) Past Year (%) **SUD/AUD (any)** 62 37 AUD 49 28 Amphetamine 23 10 Cannabis 46 15 Cocaine 2 0.5 Hallucinogen 9 3 Opiate 0.5 0

Table 1. (Continued)

Author(s)/Year	Sample*	Diagnostic Measures*	Major Findings*
Garland et al., 2001	**Participants:** Adjudicated youth *N*: 478 **Age:** 16.9 **Gender:** 74 females; 404 males **Race/ethnicity:** African American: 21%; Asian/Pacific Islander: 6%; Hispanic: 26%; white: 39%; mixed: 5%; other: 3% **Other:** Participants from a subsample (*n*=1,618) of a larger study titled "Patterns of Care"; age and race based on total subsample	Computer-assisted DISC–IV	**Affective (any):** 7%; dysthymia: 0%; hypomania: 1%; MDD: 5%; mania: 2% **CD:** 30% **Anxiety (any):** 9%; generalized anxiety: 1%; obsessive-compulsive: 2%; panic: 0%; PTSD: 3%; separation anxiety: 4%; social phobia: 2% **Other:** Any DBD: 48%; ADHD: 13%; ODD: 15%
Shelton, 2001	**Participants:** Youth in commitment and detention facilities *N*: 312 **Age:** 12–20 (mean or median N/R) **Gender:** 60 females; 252 males **Race/ethnicity:** African American: 57%; Hispanic and other: 17%; white: 26%	DISC; C–GAS	**Psychosis:** 32% **Affective:** 17% **SUD:** 37% **Anxiety:** 58% **Other:** Any DBD: 40%; miscellaneous disorders: 18% **Comorbidity:**[§]
McCabe et al., 2002	**Participants:** Adjudicated youth *N*: 625 **Age:** 16.2 **Gender:** 112 females; 513 males **Race/ethnicity:** African American: 19%; Asian/Pacific Islander: 12%; Hispanic: 30%; white: 29%; biracial/other: 9% **Other:** Participants from a larger study titled "Patterns of Care" (*n*=1,715)	Computer-assisted DISC–IV (selected modules); CIDI Substance Abuse Module	Male (%) / Female (%) **Affective (any)** 5 / 16 MDD 3 / 14 Mania 1 / 3 **SUD** 37 / 28 **CD** 33 / 38 **Anxiety (any)** 8 / 15 PTSD 2 / 7 Separation 4 / 10 **Other** Any DBD 49 / 64 ADHD 15 / 21 ODD 30 / 42 **Comorbidity** 38 / 28
Wasserman et al., 2002	**Participants:** Youth in secure facilities *N*: 292 **Age:** 17 **Gender:** Male **Race/ethnicity:** African American: 54%; Hispanic: 16%; white: 28%; other: 2%	Voice DISC–IV	**Affective (any):** 10%; dysthymic: 1%; hypomanic: 1%; MDD: 8%; manic: 2% **SUD (any):** 50%; alcohol abuse: 17%; alcohol dependence: 13%; marijuana abuse: 15%; marijuana dependence: 26%; other substance abuse: 4%; other substance dependence: 13% **CD:** 32% **Anxiety (any):** 20%; agoraphobia: 5%; generalized anxiety: 2%; obsessive-compulsive: 5%; panic: 5%; PTSD: 5%; specific phobia: 9%; social phobia: 2% **Other:** Any DBD: 33%; ADHD: 2%
Domalanta et al., 2003	**Participants:** Youth in a detention center *N*: 1,024 **Age:** 14.9 for females; 15.3 for males **Gender:** 274 females; 750 males **Race/Ethnicity:** Male (%) / Female (%) African American 42 / 33 Hispanic 35 / 37 White 19 / 23 Other 4 / 7	Patient health questionnaire	Male (%) / Female (%) / Total (%) **Affective (any)** 26 / 31 / MDD 10 / 10 / Mood NOS 12 / 13 / Other mood 4 / 8 / **SUD** 43 / 36 / **AUD** 27 / 27 / **Anxiety** Other 8 / 12 / Panic 5 / 8 / Somatoform 12 / 22 / **Comorbidity**** / / 38

Notes: Treatment studies are not included; only diagnoses reported by each study are displayed. Percentages are rounded to the nearest whole number. Mean age in years is reported unless unavailable or otherwise indicated.

*ADD = attention-deficit disorder; ADHD = attention-deficit/hyperactivity disorder; AUD = alcohol use disorder; CD = conduct disorder; C–GAS = Children's Global Assessment Scale; CIDI = Composite International Diagnostic Interview; DBD = disruptive behavior disorder; DICA–R = Diagnostic Interview for Children and Adolescents–Revised; DISC = Diagnostic Interview Schedule for Children; *DSM = Diagnostic and Statistical Manual of Mental Disorders;* K–SADS–PL= Kiddie-Schedule for Affective Disorders, Present and Lifetime Version; MDD = major depressive disorder; NOS = not otherwise specified; N/R = not reported; ODD = oppositional-defiant disorder; PD = personality disorder; PTSD = posttraumatic stress disorder; SCID = Structured Clinical Interview for *DSM;* SUD = substance use disorder

† Of the 21% with two or more disorders, 83% had SUD and DBD.

‡ Among those with mania, 82% had CD, 36% had alcohol dependence, 64% had marijuana dependence, and 45% had other substance dependence. Among those with MDD, 80% had CD, 20% had alcohol dependence, and 60% had marijuana dependence.

§ Anxiety and DBD: 28%; anxiety and psychotic: 21%; anxiety and affective: 14%; anxiety and SUD: 25%; DBD and psychotic: 14%; DBD and affective: 9%; DBD and SUD: 19%; psychotic and affective: 1%; psychotic and SUD: 15%; affective and SUD: 7%.

** Among those with MDD, 49% had substance abuse and 39% had alcohol abuse. Among those with alcohol abuse, 14% had MDD and 83% had substance abuse. Among those with substance abuse, 12% had MDD and 55% had alcohol abuse.

Prevalence by Race and Ethnicity

Tables 3 and 4 (pages 9 and 10) show the prevalence rates of disorders for males and females by race and ethnicity. Table 3 indicates that among males, non-Hispanic whites had the highest rates for many disorders and African Americans had the lowest. Compared with African Americans, non-Hispanic whites had significantly higher rates of any disorder, any disorder except conduct disorder, any disruptive behavior disorder, conduct disorder, any substance use disorder, and substance use disorder other than alcohol or marijuana. The only disorder for which African Americans had significantly higher rates than non-Hispanic whites was separation anxiety disorder. Hispanics had significantly higher rates than non-Hispanic whites of any anxiety disorder and separation anxiety disorder. Compared with African Americans, Hispanics had higher rates of panic disorder, obsessive-compulsive disorder, and substance use disorder other than alcohol or marijuana. Non-Hispanic whites had higher rates than Hispanics of any disorder, any disruptive behavior disorder, conduct disorder, and substance use disorder other than alcohol or marijuana.

Table 4 compares prevalence rates among females by race and ethnicity. Compared with African American females, non-Hispanic white females had significantly higher rates of any disorder, any disorder except conduct disorder, any disruptive behavior disorder, conduct disorder, and all substance use disorders. Compared with Hispanic females, non-Hispanic white females had higher rates of any disorder except conduct disorder. Hispanic females had higher rates of generalized anxiety disorder than either African American or non-Hispanic white females. Compared with African American females, Hispanic females had higher rates of all disruptive behavior disorders, alcohol use disorder, substance use disorder other than alcohol or marijuana, and alcohol and drug use disorders.

Among females, significantly more non-Hispanic whites (63.1 percent) had two or more types of disorders than African Americans (42.6 percent). Among males also, significantly more non-Hispanic whites (53.1 percent) had two or more types of disorders than African Americans (40.7 percent). The odds of having comorbid disorders were higher than expected for most racial and ethnic subgroups, except when base rates of disorders were already high or when there were few participants in a category (Abram et al., 2003).

Prevalence by Age

Tables 5 and 6 (pages 11 and 12) show the prevalence of disorders for males and females by age. Table 5 indicates that among males, the youngest age group had the lowest rates of many disorders, including any disorder, any disorder except conduct disorder, generalized anxiety disorder, and all the substance use disorders. The 14–15 age group had higher rates of psychotic disorders than the 16-and-older age group. Significantly more males age 16 and older (41.2 percent) had two or more types of disorders than males age 13 and younger (27.0 percent). Similarly, more males age 14 and 15 (45.3 percent) had two or more types of disorders than males age 13 and younger (Abram et al., 2003).

Table 6 indicates that patterns of disorders are different for females than for males. The oldest female age group had significantly lower rates of oppositional-defiant disorder than the younger age groups. Compared with the older age groups, the youngest age group had significantly lower rates of any substance use disorder and marijuana use disorder. Among females, there were no significant age differences in the prevalence of comorbid disorder types.

Table 2. Six-Month Prevalence and Odds Ratios of *DSM–III–R* Diagnoses, by Gender

Disorder	Male (%) (*n*=1,170)	Female (%) (*n*=656)	Female-to-Male Odds Ratios
Any of the listed disorders	66.3	73.8	1 .43†
Any except conduct disorder	60.9	70.0	1.49†
Any affective disorder	18.7	27.6	1.66†
Major depressive episode	13.0	21.6	1.85†
Dysthymia	12.2	15.8	1.34
Manic episode	2.2	1.8	0.81
Psychotic disorders	1.0	1.0	0.98
Any anxiety disorder	21.3	30.8	1.64†
Panic disorder	0.3	1.5	5.65†
Separation anxiety disorder	12.9	18.6	1.55†
Overanxious disorder	6.7	12.3	1.95†
Generalized anxiety disorder	7.1	7.3	1.03
Obsessive-compulsive disorder	8.3	10.6	1.31
Attention-deficit/ hyperactivity disorder*	16.6	21.4	1.37
Any disruptive behavior disorder	41.4	45.6	1.19
Oppositional-defiant disorder	14.5	17.5	1.25
Conduct disorder	37.8	40.6	1.12
Any substance use disorder	50.7	46.8	0.86
Alcohol use disorder	25.9	26.5	1.03
Marijuana use disorder	44.8	40.5	0.84
Other substance use disorder	2.4	6.9	3.00†
Alcohol and other drug use disorders	20.7	20.9	1.01

Notes: The odds ratios show the relative likelihood of one group having a disorder compared with another group. For the female-to-male odds ratios, odds ratios greater than 1.0 indicate that females had higher odds of having a specific disorder than males; ratios less than 1.0 show that females had lower odds of having the disorder.

*Attention-deficit/hyperactivity disorder is reported without the criterion of onset before age 7 because caretaker information is not available and self-reporting of symptoms before age 7 is unreliable.

† Odds ratios are significant at $p < .05$.

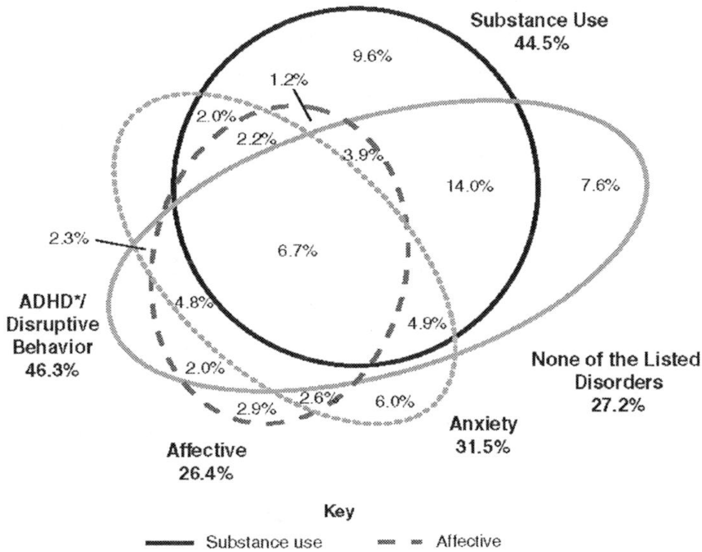

Note: Detail may not total 100% due to rounding.
*Attention-deficit/hyperactivity disorder.

Figure 1. Comorbidity Among Females, by Disorder.

Comorbidity of Substance Use Disorders and Major Mental Disorders

More than one-tenth of males (10.8 percent) and 13.7 percent of females had a major mental disorder (psychosis, manic episode, or major depressive episode) and a substance use disorder (Abram et al., 2003). These disorders were examined in depth because detention centers are mandated to treat major mental disorders and because comorbidity complicates treatment.

Prevalence of Substance Use Disorders among Youth with Major Mental Disorders

Compared with participants with no major mental disorder,[1] females and males with any major mental disorder had significantly greater odds of having substance use disorders. Two subcategories of major mental disorder were examined: psychosis or manic episode (combined because there were too few cases to analyze separately and because these disorders have similar symptoms) and major depressive episode. Most odds ratios for these subcategories were statistically significant, except when cell sizes were small.

Gender differences. Among youth with major mental disorders (n=305), more than half of females and nearly three-quarters of males had any substance use disorder. Differences between females and males (and the corresponding odds ratios) were not statistically significant.

Racial and ethnic differences. Among females with major mental disorders, significantly more non-Hispanic whites and Hispanics had drug and alcohol use disorders than did African Americans (50.0 percent and 43.4 percent, respectively, versus 21.3 percent). Significantly more Hispanic females had alcohol use disorders than did African Americans (52.5 percent versus 26.6 percent). Among males with major mental disorders, no significant differences existed relative to race and ethnicity.

Age differences. Among females with major mental disorders, no significant differences existed by age. Among males, nearly 90 percent of those age 16 and older with a major mental disorder also had a substance use disorder, significantly more than males ages 10–13 and 14–15 (55.2 percent and 60.6 percent, respectively).

Prevalence of Major Mental Disorders among Youth with Substance Use Disorders

Nearly 30 percent of females and more than 20 percent of males with any substance use disorder also had a major mental disorder. Among youth with drug and alcohol use disorders, more than one-third of females and more than one-quarter of males had a major mental disorder. There were no significant differences by gender, race and ethnicity, or age.

Compared with participants with no substance use disorder (the residual category), females and males with any substance use disorder had significantly greater odds of having any major mental disorder and its subcategory, major depressive episode. Among males, odds ratios for psychosis or a manic episode were significant for alcohol use disorder and comorbid drug and alcohol use disorders.

Relative Onset of Major Mental Disorders and Substance Use Disorders

One-quarter of females (27.2 percent) and males (25.0 percent) reported that their major mental disorder preceded their substance use disorder by more than 1 year. One-tenth of females (9.8 percent) and 20.7 percent of males reported that their substance use disorder preceded their major mental disorder by more than 1 year. Nearly two-thirds of females (63.0 percent) and 54.3 percent of males developed their disorders within the same year. Findings were similar for subcategories of disorders.

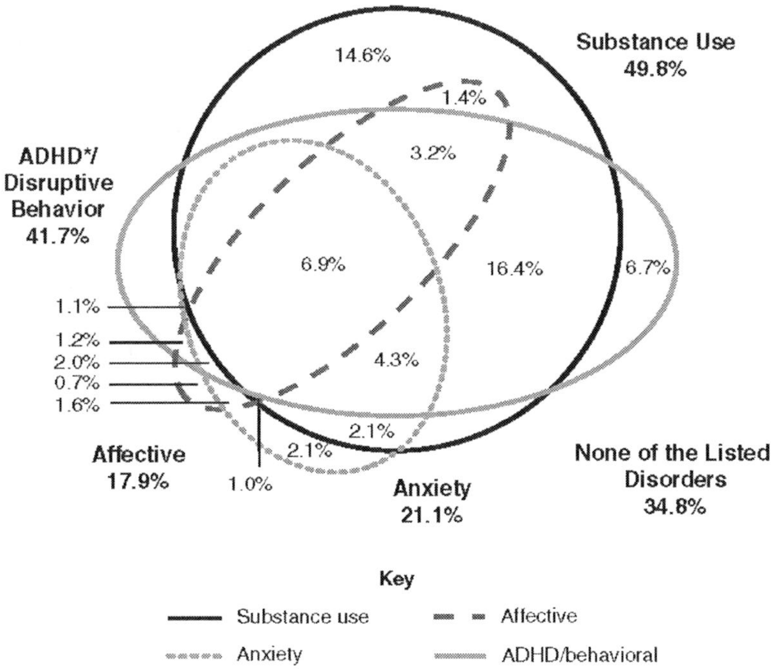

Note: Detail may not total 100% due to rounding.
*Attention-deficit/hyperactivity disorder.

Figure 2. Comorbidity Among Males, by Disorder.

Table 3. Six-Month Prevalence of *DSM–III–R* Diagnoses for Males, by Race and Ethnicity

Disorder	African American (%) (*n*=574)	Non-Hispanic White (%) (*n*=207)	Hispanic (%) (*n*=386)	Overall Significance	Specific Tests*
Any of the listed disorders	64.6	82.0	70.4	< .001	White > African American; white > Hispanic
Any except conduct disorder	59.4	72.9	65.3	.009	White > African American
Any affective disorder	18.6	13.8	21.5	.19	
Major depressive episode	12.5	9.5	16.6	.20	
Dysthymia	12.2	9.5	13.3	.53	
Manic episode	2.5	0.5	1.4	.27	
Psychotic disorders	1.0	2.6	0.7	.19	
Any anxiety disorder	20.9	14.4	25.5	.05	Hispanic > white
Panic disorder	0.1	0.5	1.0	.04	Hispanic > African American
Separation anxiety disorder	12.7	5.9	15.5	.02	African American > white; Hispanic > white
Overanxious disorder	6.9	2.9	7.0	.16	
Generalized anxiety disorder	7.5	2.5	7.2	.08	
Obsessive-compulsive disorder	6.5	9.3	17.0	.01	Hispanic > African American
Attention-deficit/ hyperactivity disorder†	17.0	20.9	13.7	.18	

Table 3. (Continued)

Disorder	African American (%) (*n*=574)	Non-Hispanic White (%) (*n*=207)	Hispanic (%) (*n*=386)	Overall Significance	Specific Tests*
Any disruptive behavior disorder	39.8	60.3	43.3	< .001	White > African American; white > Hispanic
Oppositional-defiant disorder	14.4	19.4	13.6	.23	
Conduct disorder	35.6	59.9	41.7	< .001	White > African American; white > Hispanic
Any substance use disorder	49.1	62.6	55.4	.01	White > African American
Alcohol use disorder	24.6	30.1	30.8	.28	
Marijuana use disorder	44.4	53.8	45.4	.11	
Other substance use disorder	0.5	21.1	6.0	< .001	White > African American; white > Hispanic; Hispanic > African American
Alcohol and other drug use disorders	20.4	24.0	21.7	.65	

* Specific tests are performed only if the alpha for the overall test is less than .05.

† Attention-deficit/hyperactivity disorder is reported without the criterion of onset before age 7 because caretaker information is not available and self-reporting of symptoms before age 7 is unreliable.

ANALYSIS

Data gathered by the Northwestern Juvenile Project indicate that youth with psychiatric and substance use disorders pose a challenge for the juvenile justice system. Even when conduct disorder was excluded, 60 percent of male and 70 percent of female juvenile detainees met diagnostic criteria for one or more psychiatric disorders. Comorbidity was common. To the extent that

Cook County is typical, the findings suggest that on an average day, as many as 72,000 detained youth have at least one psychiatric disorder; 47,000 detained youth have two or more types of psychiatric disorders; and more than 12,000 detained youth have both a major mental disorder and a substance use disorder.

Table 4. Six-Month Prevalence of *DSM–III–R* Diagnoses for Females, by Race and Ethnicity

Disorder	African American (%) (*n*=430)	Non-Hispanic White (%) (*n*=89)	Hispanic (%) (*n*=136)	Overall Significance	Specific Tests*
Any of the listed disorders	70.9	86.1	75.9	.01	White > African American
Any except conduct disorder	67.4	83.9	69.5	.01	White > African American; white > Hispanic
Any affective disorder	26.2	23.4	28.7	.68	
Major depressive episode	19.7	19.0	22.8	.70	
Dysthymia	15.5	17.9	17.2	.80	
Manic episode	1.9	1.1	2.1	.85	
Psychotic disorders	0.9	0.0	2.1	.29†	
Any anxiety disorder	31.2	30.0	32.6	.92	
Panic disorder	0.9	3.4	2.8	.17	
Separation anxiety disorder	18.9	14.5	21.7	.41	
Overanxious disorder	12.5	11.1	13.2	.90	
Generalized anxiety disorder	6.6	4.4	13.1	.03	Hispanic > African American; Hispanic > White
Obsessive-compulsive disorder	10.3	12.4	10.6	.84	

Table 4. (Continued)

Disorder	African American (%) (n=430)	Non-Hispanic White (%) (n=89)	Hispanic (%) (n=136)	Overall Significance	Specific Tests*
Attention-deficit/ hyperactivity disorder‡	20.0	22.2	29.3	.08	
Any disruptive behavior disorder	39.4	61.6	56.5	<.001	White > African American; Hispanic > African American
Oppositional-defiant disorder	15.8	17.8	26.2	.03	Hispanic > African American
Conduct disorder	34.3	58.9	50.2	<.001	White > African American; Hispanic > African American
Any substance use disorder	42.3	61.9	51.7	.002	White > African American
Alcohol use disorder	21.2	39.2	34.0	<.001	White > African American; Hispanic > African American
Marijuana use disorder	37.8	53.4	44.7	.02	White > African American
Other substance use disorder	0.9	20.0	14.7	<.001	White > African American; Hispanic > African American
Alcohol and other drug use disorders	17.2	35.1	28.3	<.001	White > African American; Hispanic > African American

* Specific tests are performed only if the alpha for the overall test is less than .05.

† Test computed with one degree of freedom because of empty cells.

‡ Attention-deficit/hyperactivity disorder is reported without the criterion of onset before age 7 because caretaker information is not available and self-reporting of symptoms before age 7 is unreliable.

The prevalence of psychiatric disorders among youth entering the juvenile justice system may be greater than that of detainees, as reflected in this study. The sample included only detainees; it excluded youth who were not detained because their charges were less serious, because they were immediately released, or because they were referred directly to the mental health system.

Moreover, under reporting of symptoms and impairments by youth is common, especially for disruptive behavior disorders (Schwab-Stone et al., 1996).

Comparing these findings with studies of youth in the general population is difficult because published estimates for the latter vary widely depending on the sample, the method, the source of data, and whether functional impairment was required for diagnosis (Roberts, Attkisson, and Rosenblatt, 1998). Despite these differences, the overall rates presented here are substantially higher than the median rate (15 percent) reported by Roberts, Attkisson, and Rosenblatt (1998) and the rates of other recent investigations (Costello et al., 1996b; Simonoff et al., 1997; Shaffer et al., 1996; and Turner and Gil, 2002). The rates of comorbidity reported here are also substantially higher than those reported in community samples (Angold, Costello, and Erkanli, 1999; Costello et al., 1996a; Costello et al., 1999; Kessler and Walters, 1998; Lewinsohn, Gotlib, and Seeley, 1995).

Of particular concern are the high rates of depression and dysthymia among detained youth,[2] which are also higher than rates in the general population (Costello et al., 1996a; Costello et al., 1996b; Garrison et al., 1997; Kessler and Walters, 1998; McGee et al., 1992; Simonoff et al., 1997; Turner and Gil, 2002). Depressive disorders, which are a risk factor for suicide and attempted suicide, are difficult to detect and treat in the corrections milieu. Overall, the prevalence rates presented here are comparable to rates in other high-risk populations, such as maltreated or runaway youth (Famularo, Kinscherff, and Fenton, 1992; Feitel et al., 1992).

The comorbidity of substance use disorders is also of particular concern. Among the disorders assessed, detainees are more likely to have substance use plus ADHD or disruptive behavior disorders than any other combination. Half of these detainees also have an affective or anxiety disorder. Among adolescent substance users, these internalizing disorders are associated with more severe substance use (Riggs et al., 1999; Whitmore et al., 1997) but better treatment outcomes (Randall et al., 1999).

Table 5. Six-Month Prevalence of *DSM–III–R* Diagnoses for Males, by Age

Disorder	13 and Younger (%) (*n*=315)	14–15 Years Old (%) (*n*=361)	16 and Older (%) (*n*=494)	Overall Significance	Specific Tests*
Any of the listed disorders	52.7	68.0	67.3	.001	14 and 15 years > 13 and younger; 16 and older > 13 and younger
Any except conduct disorder	44.9	63.4	61.8	< .001	14 and 15 years > 13 and younger; 16 and older > 13 and younger
Any affective disorder	13.0	21.2	17.7	.09	
Major depressive episode	7.5	14.8	12.4	.06	
Dysthymia	7.3	14.5	11.2	.08	
Manic episode	1.6	2.6	2.0	.80	
Psychotic disorders	0.0	2.1	0.3	.01[†]	14 and 15 years > 16 and older
Any anxiety disorder	17.7	23.0	20.6	.42	
Panic disorder	0.8	0.1	0.3	.25	
Separation anxiety disorder	10.0	14.5	12.0	.40	
Overanxious disorder	4.8	5.1	8.4	.25	
Generalized anxiety disorder	1.3	5.9	9.2	.001	14 and 15 years > 13 and younger; 16 and older > 13 and younger
Obsessive-compulsive disorder	6.0	9.4	7.8	.43	
Attention-deficit/ hyperactivity disorder[‡]	12.5	20.9	13.8	.06	

Table 5. (Continued)

Disorder	13 and Younger (%) (*n*=315)	14–15 Years Old (%) (*n*=361)	16 and Older (%) (*n*=494)	Overall Significance	Specific Tests*
Any disruptive behavior disorder	32.9	43.5	41.2	.06	
Oppositional-defiant disorder	10.7	18.2	12.1	.08	
Conduct disorder	30.8	41.1	36.4	.10	
Any substance use disorder	28.3	51.3	54.4	< .001	14 and 15 years > 13 and younger; 16 and older > 13 and younger
Alcohol use disorder	12.9	25.6	28.7	< .001	14 and 15 years > 13 and younger; 16 and older > 13 and younger
Marijuana use disorder	25.1	46.9	46.8	< .001	14 and 15 years > 13 and younger; 16 and older > 13 and younger
Other substance use disorder	0.8	2.5	2.6	.01	14 and 15 years > 13 and younger; 16 and older > 13 and younger
Alcohol and other drug use disorders	10.2	21.5	22.0	< .001	14 and 15 years > 13 and younger; 16 and older > 13 and younger

* Specific tests are performed only if the alpha for the overall test is less than .05.

† Test computed with one degree of freedom because of empty cells.

‡ Attention-deficit/hyperactivity disorder is reported without the criterion of onset before age 7 because caretaker information is not available and self-reporting of symptoms before age 7 is unreliable.

The data highlight an important paradox regarding race and ethnicity. More than one-half of the youth in the juvenile justice system are African American or Hispanic. Therefore, most delinquent youth with psychiatric disorders are minorities. The prevalence of many single and comorbid disorders, however, is highest among non-Hispanic whites. Thus, non-Hispanic white youth in the juvenile justice system may, on average, be more dysfunctional (have greater psychiatric morbidity) than minorities.

Table 6. Six-Month Prevalence of *DSM–III–R* Diagnoses for Females, by Age

Disorder	13 and Younger (%) (*n*=56)	14–15 Years Old (%) *n*=353)	16 and Older (%) (*n*=247)	Overall Significance	Specific Tests*
Any of the listed disorders	66.7	72.2	77.6	.18	
Any except conduct disorder	64.7	67.4	74.8	.13	
Any affective disorder	20.7	27.9	28.8	.50	
Major depressive episode	13.0	21.6	23.4	.27	
Dysthymia	10.4	15.6	17.2	.46	
Manic episode	3.9	1.4	1.9	.45	
Psychotic disorders	0.0	0.6	1.8	.21†	
Any anxiety disorder	26.6	32.6	29.2	.55	
Panic disorder	1.9	1.7	1.0	.75	
Separation anxiety disorder	18.1	19.7	17.2	.77	
Overanxious disorder	7.1	13.8	11.4	.34	
Generalized anxiety disorder	3.8	7.1	8.4	.51	
Obsessive-compulsive disorder	10.4	11.8	8.8	.51	
Attention-deficit/ hyperactivity disorder‡	26.6	22.7	18.5	.30	
Any disruptive behavior disorder	44.7	50.0	39.6	.11	

Table 6. (Contiuned)

Disorder	**13 and Younger (%) (*n*=56)**	**14–15 Years Old (%) *n*=353)**	**16 and Older (%) *n*=247)**	**Overall Significance**	**Specific Tests***
Oppositional-defiant disorder	30.5	20.2	10.7	<.001	13 years and younger > 16 and older; 14 and 15 > 16 and older
Conduct disorder	33.0	45.3	35.7	.06	
Any substance use disorder	30.5	45.8	52.0	.02	14 and 15 years > 13 and younger; 16 and older > 13 and younger
Alcohol use disorder	16.7	25.4	30.3	.16	
Marijuana use disorder	24.8	41.3	43.3	.04	14 and 15 years > 13 and younger; 16 and older > 13 and younger
Other substance use disorder	5.9	5.3	9.5	.52	
Alcohol and other drug use disorders	11.5	21.8	22.0	.20	

* Specific tests are performed only if the alpha for the overall test is less than .05.

† Test computed with one degree of freedom because of empty cells.

‡ Attention-deficit/hyperactivity disorder is reported without the criterion of onset before age 7 because caretaker information is not available and self-reporting of symptoms before age 7 is unreliable.

Females had higher rates than males of many single and comorbid psychiatric disorders, including major depressive episodes, some anxiety disorders, and substance use disorders other than alcohol and marijuana (e.g., cocaine and hallucinogens). These findings confirm those of earlier studies of adult female detainees and females with conduct disorder (Lewis et al., 1991; Teplin, Abram, and McClelland, 1996; Wasserman et al., 2005).

In contrast to the general population, males did not have significantly higher odds of ADHD than females. This may reflect a greater prevalence of attentional problems among females in detention compared with those in the general population, or a possible unreliability of the ADHD diagnosis.

The youngest age group (13 and younger) had the lowest prevalence rates of most disorders, consistent with studies of youth in the general population (Cohen, Cohen, and Brook, 1993; Kandel et al., 1997; Newman et al., 1996; Simonoff et al., 1997). Many youth in the juvenile justice system may develop new or additional disorders as they grow older. Although comorbidity of major mental and substance use disorders is more prevalent among older detainees, this study found no dominant sequence of onset, suggesting that multiple pathways to disorders exist.

Limitations

This study provides a snapshot of the subjects' psychopathology immediately after arrest and detention. It cannot show whether mental disorder causes delinquency, increases the likelihood of arrest and detention, or is merely a frequent trait among delinquent youth. Some symptoms may be a reaction to detention. Moreover, the rates might differ somewhat using *DSM–IV* rather than *DSM–III–R* criteria. The findings are drawn from one site only and may pertain only to youth in urban detention centers with a similar demographic composition. Finally, because interviewing caretakers was not feasible, the data are subject to the limitations of self-reporting. Despite these constraints, the study has implications for future research on delinquent youth and for the juvenile justice system.

Future Research

Further research is needed to determine the most common pathways to comorbidity, critical periods of vulnerability, and how these factors differ by gender, race and ethnicity, and age. Longitudinal studies that identify the most common developmental sequences would demonstrate when primary and secondary preventive interventions might prove most beneficial (Nottlemann and Jensen, 1995).

Females are increasingly arrested for violent crimes, and they make up a growing proportion of delinquent youth (Office of Juvenile Justice and Delinquency Prevention, 2001; Snyder and Sickmund, 1999). Understanding psychiatric morbidity and associated risk factors among delinquent females could help improve treatment and reduce the cycle of disorder and dysfunction. Earlier studies of conduct-disordered youth (many of whom become delinquent) suggest that females have a greater persistence of emotional disorder and worse outcomes than males (Loeber and Stouthamer-Loeber, 1998; Zoccolillo, 1992). Moreover, problem behaviors among females often persist beyond adolescence. As they grow older, delinquent females may become suicidal, addicted to alcohol or drugs, enmeshed in violent relationships, and unable to care for their children (Lewis et al., 1991; Zoccolillo, 1992). Delinquent females also engage in sexual activity at an earlier age than nonoffenders, placing them at greater risk for unintended pregnancy and the human immunodeficiency virus (Gender-Specific Programming for Girls Advisory Committee, 1998).

Longitudinal studies are needed to examine why some delinquent youth develop new psychopathology and others do not, to investigate protective factors, and to determine how vulnerability and risk differ by key variables such as gender and race and ethnicity. Many youth in the juvenile justice population will develop new disorders as they grow older. Risk factors for the development of disorders are common among delinquent youth (Werner, 1989). These factors include physical and sexual abuse, a troubled family environment, parental substance abuse, poverty, poor education, neighborhood disintegration, and neglect.

Delinquent youth have few protective factors to offset these risks (Cocozza, 1992). Thus, most youth in the juvenile justice system are at great risk for psychopathology, problem behaviors, and even early death (Lattimore, Linster, and MacDonald, 1997; Loeber et al., 1999; Teplin et al., 2005). Longitudinal data on the subjects described in this Bulletin are being collected. Future papers will address persistence and change in psychiatric disorders (including onset, remission, and recurrence), comorbidity, associated functional impairments, and how these disorders affect risk behaviors that may lead to rearrest.

Implications for Juvenile Justice

Research findings indicate that a substantial number of youth in detention need mental health services. Youth with serious mental disorders have a constitutional right to receive treatment while detained. Providing mental health services to youth in detention and redirecting them to the mental health system after release may help prevent their return to the correctional system (Dembo et al., 1997; National Research Council and Institute of Medicine, 2001). However, providing services within the juvenile justice system poses a number of challenges.

Mental health screening

Identifying youth who need mental health services is a significant first step. Experts recommend that youth be screened for psychiatric problems within 24 hours of admission to a juvenile facility. At a minimum, screening should address acute mental health problems (including psychosis), the risk for suicide or harm to self, the use of psychiatric medications, substance abuse, and the risk for assaultive behavior. Youth who disclose such information should have appropriate legal protections (Wasserman et al., 2003).

Many detention centers do not routinely screen for psychiatric problems (Goldstrom et al., 2001). Only recently have specialized screening tools been developed to assess the mental health needs of youth entering the juvenile justice system (Dembo et al., 1996; Grisso, 1999; Grisso et al., 2001); these instruments need further testing and evaluation.

Mental health services

Youth in need of mental health services require access to them while in detention (Costello and Jameson, 1987; Wasserman et al., 2003). Detention centers should train personnel to detect mental disorders that are overlooked at intake or that arise during incarceration (Dembo et al., 1997; Hayes, 2000; Ulzen and Hamilton, 1998). Furthermore, personnel need to know how to make appropriate referrals once they suspect a disorder may be present.

Although fewer in number, females in detention have greater service needs than males. Earlier studies indicate that females with problem behaviors may have worse outcomes than males (Lewis et al., 1991; Loeber and Stouthamer-Loeber, 1998; Zoccolillo, 1992). Services should be developed to address the unique needs of this growing population.

Community services

Youth typically do not remain in detention for long. Most detainees return to their communities within 2 weeks (Snyder and Sickmund, 1999). Ideally, those with mental disorders should be linked to community mental health services prior to their release (Cocozza and Skowyra, 2000; Faenza, Siegfried, and Wood, 2000). However, youth in the juvenile justice system are disproportionately minority, impoverished, and poorly educated, and many lack social networks—characteristics known to limit the type and scope of mental health services provided to youth (Kataoka, Zhang, and Wells, 2002; McKay, McCadam, and Gonzales, 1996). Juvenile justice administrators need to form collaborative relationships with education, child welfare, mental health, and substance abuse service systems to ensure that youth have adequate access to care after their release.

Because many youth in detention suffer from psychiatric disorders and pose a challenge to the juvenile justice system, research is needed to better understand the comorbidity of psychiatric disorders, psychiatric disorders among females involved in the juvenile justice system, and the long-term outcomes of detained youth with mental disorders. These youth will continue to overburden the juvenile justice system, and eventually the adult justice system, until it is better able to detect them and respond with an integrated system of appropriate services during detention and after release.

References

Aarons, G. A., Brown, S. A., Hough, R. L., Garland, A. F. & Wood, P. A. (2001). Prevalence of adolescent substance use disorders across five sectors of care. *Journal of the American Academy of Child and Adolescent Psychiatry, 40*, 419–426.

Abram, K. M., Teplin, L. A., McClelland, G. M. & Dulcan, M. K. (2003). Comorbid psychiatric disorders in youth in juvenile detention. *Archives of General Psychiatry, 60*, 1097–1108.

American Psychiatric Association. (1987). *Diagnostic and Statistical Manual of Mental Disorders: DSM–III–R.* Washington, DC: American Psychiatric Association.

Angold, A., Costello, E. J. & Erkanli, A. (1999). Comorbidity. *Journal of Child Psychology and Psychiatry, 40*, 57-87.

Atkins, D. L., Pumariega, A. J., Rogers, K., Montgomery, L., Nybro, C., Jeffers, G. & Sease, F. (1999). Mental health and incarcerated youth. I: Prevalence and nature of psychopathology. *Journal of Child and Family Studies, 8*, 193-204.

Bravo, M., Woodbury-Farina, M., Canino, G. J. & Rubio-Stipec, M. (1993). The Spanish translation and cultural adaptation of the Diagnostic Interview Schedule for Children (DISC) in Puerto Rico. *Culture, Medicine and Psychiatry, 17*, 329-344.

Cauffman, E., Feldman, S., Waterman, J. & Steiner, H. (1998). Posttraumatic stress disorder among female juvenile offenders. *Journal of the American Academy of Child and Adolescent Psychiatry, 37*, 1209-1216.

Cocozza, J. J. (1992). *Responding to the Mental Health Needs of Youth in the Juvenile Justice System.* Seattle, WA: National Coalition for the Mentally Ill in the Criminal Justice System.

Cocozza, J. J. & Skowyra, K. R. (2000). Youth with mental health disorders: Issues and emerging responses. *Juvenile Justice, 7*, 3-13.

Cohen, J. (1988). *Statistical Power Analysis for the Behavioral Sciences,* 2d ed. Hillsdale, NJ: Lawrence Earlbaum Associates.

Cohen, P., Cohen, J. & Brook, J. (1993). An epidemiological study of disorders in late childhood and adolescence—II. Persistence of disorders. *Journal of Child Psychology and Psychiatry, 34*, 869-877.

Costello, E. J., Angold, A., Burns, B. J., Erkanli, A., Stangle, D. K. & Tweed, D. L. (1996a). The Great Smoky Mountains Study of Youth: Functional impairment and serious emotional disturbance. *Archives of General Psychiatry, 53*, 1137-1143.

Costello, E. J., Angold, A., Burns, B. J., Stangle, D. K., Tweed, D. L., Erkanli, A. & Worthman, C. M. (1996b). The Great Smoky Mountains Study of Youth: Goals, design, methods and the prevalence of DSM–III–R disorders. *Archives of General Psychiatry, 53*, 1129-1136.

Costello, E. J., Erkanli, A., Federman, E. & Angold, A. (1999). Development of psychiatric comorbidity with substance abuse in adolescents: Effects of timing and sex. *Journal of Clinical Child Psychology, 28*, 298–311.

Costello, J. C. & Jameson, E. J. (1987). Legal and ethical duties of health care professionals to incarcerated children. *The Journal of Legal Medicine, 8*, 191–263.

Davis, D. L., Bean, G. J., Schumacher, J. E. & Stringer, T. L. (1991). Prevalence of emotional disorders in a juvenile justice institutional population. *American Journal of Forensic Psychology, 9*, 5-17.

Dembo, R., Schmeidler, J., Borden, P., Turner, G., Sue, C. C. & Manning, D. (1996). Examination of the reliability of the Problem Oriented Screening Instrument for Teenagers (POSIT) among arrested youths entering a juvenile assessment center. *Substance Use and Misuse, 31*, 785-824.

Dembo, R., Schmeidler, J., Pacheco, K., Cooper, S. & Williams, L. W. (1997). The relationships between youth's identified substance use, mental health or other problems at a juvenile assessment center and their referrals to needed services. *Journal of Child and Adolescent Substance Abuse, 6*, 23-54.

Domalanta, D. D., Risser, W. L., Roberts, R. E. & Risser, J. M. H. (2003). Prevalence of depression and other psychiatric disorders among incarcerated youths. *Journal of the American Academy of Child and Adolescent Psychiatry, 42*, 477-484.

Duclos, C. W., Beals, J., Novins, D. K., Martin, C., Jewett, C. S. & Manson, S. M. (1998). Prevalence of common psychiatric disorders among American Indian adolescent detainees. *Journal of the American Academy of Child and Adolescent Psychiatry, 37*, 866-873.

Eppright, T. D., Kashani, J. H., Robison, B. D. & Reid, J. C. (1993). Comorbidity of conduct disorder and personality disorders in an incarcerated juvenile population. *American Journal of Psychiatry, 150*, 1233-1236.

Erwin, B. A., Newman, E., McMackin, R. A., Morrissey, C. & Kaloupek, D. G. (2000). PTSD, malevolent environment, and criminality among criminally involved male adolescents. *Criminal Justice and Behavior, 27*, 196–215.

Faenza, M., Siegfried, C. & Wood, J. (2000.) *Community Perspectives on the Mental Health and Substance Abuse Treatment Needs of Youth Involved in the Juvenile Justice System.* Alexandria, VA: National Mental Health Association and the U.S. Department of Justice, Office of Justice Programs, Office of Juvenile Justice and Delinquency Prevention.

Famularo, R., Kinscherff, R. & Fenton, T. (1992). Psychiatric diagnoses of maltreated children: Preliminary findings. *Journal of the American Academy of Child and Adolescent Psychiatry, 31*, 863-867.

Feitel, B., Margetson, N., Chamas, J. & Lipman, C. (1992). Psychosocial background and behavioral and emotional disorders of homeless and runaway youth. *Hospital and Community Psychiatry, 43*, 155-159.

Forehand, R., Frame, C. L., Wierson, M., Armistead, L. & Kempton, T. (1991). Assessment of incarcerated juvenile delinquents: Agreement across raters and approaches to psychopathology. *Journal of Psychopathology and Behavioral Assessment, 13*, 17-25.

Friedman, R. M., Katz-Leavy, J. W., Manderscheid, R. W. & Sondheimer, D. L. (1996). Prevalence of serious emotional disturbance in children and adolescents. In *Mental Health, United States, 1996,* edited by R.W. Manderscheid and M. A. Sonnenschein. Rockville, MD: U.S. Department of Health and Human Services.

Garland, A. F., Hough, R. L., McCabe, K. M., Yeh, M., Wood, P. A. & Aarons, G. A. (2001). Prevalence of psychiatric disorders in youths across five sectors of care. *Journal of the American Academy of Child and Adolescent Psychiatry, 40*, 409-418.

Garrison, C. Z., Waller, J. L., Cuffe, S. P., McKeown, R. E., Addy, C. L. & Jackson, K. L. (1997). Incidence of major depressive disorder and dysthymia in young adolescents. *Journal of the American Academy of Child and Adolescent Psychiatry, 36*, 458-465.

Gender-Specific Programming for Girls Advisory Committee. (1998). *Guiding Principles for Promising Female Programming: An Inventory of Best Practices.* Washington, DC: U.S. Department of Justice, Office of Justice Programs, Office of Juvenile Justice and Delinquency Prevention.

Goldstrom, I., Jaiquan, F., Henderson, M., Male, A. & Manderscheid, R. W. (2001). The availability of mental health services to young people in juvenile justice facilities: A national study. In *Mental Health, United States, 2000,* edited by R.W. Manderscheid and M.J. Henderson. Rockville, MD: U.S. Department of Health and Human Services.

Grisso, T. (1999). Juvenile offenders and mental illness. *Psychiatry, Psychology and Law, 6*, 143-151.

Grisso, T., Barnum, R., Fletcher, K. E., Cauffman, E. & Peuschold, D. (2001). Massachusetts Youth Screening Instrument for mental health needs of juvenile justice youths. *Journal of the American Academy of Child and Adolescent Psychiatry, 40*, 541-548.

Grisso, T., Tomkins, A. & Casey, P. (1988). Psychosocial concepts in juvenile law. *Law and Human Behavior, 12*, 403-437.

Hayes, L. M. (2000). Suicide prevention in juvenile facilities. *Juvenile Justice, 7*, 24-32.

Illinois Criminal Justice Information Authority. (1997). *Trends and Issues 1997.* Chicago, IL: Illinois Criminal Justice Information Authority.

Kandel, D. B., Johnson, J. G., Bird, H. R., Canino, G., Goodman, S. H., Lahey, B. B., Regier, D. A. & Schwab-Stone, M. (1997). Psychiatric disorders associated with substance use among children and adolescents: Findings from the Methods for the Epidemiology of Child and Adolescent Mental Disorders (MECA) Study. *Journal of Abnormal Child Psychology* 25:12 1–132.

Kataoka, S. H., Zhang, L. & Wells, K. B. (2002). Unmet need for mental health care among U.S. children: Variation by ethnicity and insurance status. *American Journal of Psychiatry, 159*, 1548-1555.

Kessler, R. C. & Walters, E. E. (1998). Epidemiology of DSM–III–R major depression and minor depression among adolescents and young adults in the National Comorbidity Survey. *Depression and Anxiety, 7*, 3-14.

Lattimore, P. K., Linster, R. L. & MacDonald, J. M. (1997). Risk of death among serious young offenders. *Journal of Research in Crime and Delinquency, 34*, 187-209.

Lewinsohn, P. M., Gotlib, I. H. & Seeley, J. R. (1995). Adolescent psychopathology, IV: Specificity of psychosocial risk factors for depression and substance abuse in older adolescents. *Journal of the American Academy of Child and Adolescent Psychiatry, 34*, 1221-1229.

Lewis, D. O., Yeager, C. A., Cobham-Portorreal, C. S., Klein, N., Showalter, C. & Anthony, A. (1991). A follow-up of female delinquents: Maternal contributions to the perpetuation of deviance. *Journal of the American Academy of Child and Adolescent Psychiatry, 30*, 197-201.

Loeber, R., DeLamatre, M., Tita, G., Cohen, J., Stouthamer-Loeber, M. & Farrington, D. P. (1999). Gun injury and mortality: The delinquent backgrounds of juvenile victims. *Violence and Victims, 14*, 339-352.

Loeber, R. & Stouthamer-Loeber, M. (1998). Development of juvenile aggression and violence. *American Psychologist, 53*, 242–259.

McCabe, K. M., Lansing, A. E., Garland, A. & Hough, R. (2002). Gender differences in psychopathology, functional impairment, and familial risk factors among adjudicated delinquents. *Journal of the American Academy of Child and Adolescent Psychiatry, 41*, 860-867.

McGee, R., Feehan, M., Williams, S. & Anderson, J. (1992). DSM–III disorders from age 11 to age 15 years. *Journal of the American Academy of Child and Adolescent Psychiatry, 31*, 50-59.

McKay, M. M., McCadam, K. & Gonzales, J. J. (1996). Addressing the barriers to mental health services for inner city children and their caretakers. *Community Mental Health Journal, 32*, 353-361.

National Research Council and Institute of Medicine. (2001). *Juvenile Crime, Juvenile Justice*. Washington, DC: National Academy Press.

Newman, D. L., Moffitt, T. E., Caspi, A., Magdol, L., Silva, P. A. & Stanton, W. R. (1996). Psychiatric disorder in a birth cohort of young adults:

Prevalence, comorbidity, clinical significance, and new case incidence from ages 11 to 21. *Journal of Consulting and Clinical Psychology, 64*, 552–562.

Nottlemann, E. D. & Jensen, P. S. (1995). Comorbidity of disorders in children and adolescents. *Advances in Clinical Child Psychology, 17*, 109-155.

Office of Juvenile Justice and Delinquency Prevention. 2001. Census of Juveniles in Residential Placement Databook. Retrieved March 26, 2002, from the Web: www.ojjdp.ncjrs.org/ojstatbb/cjrp.

Pliszka, S. R., Sherman, J. O., Barrow, M. V. & Irick, S. (2000). Affective disorder in juvenile offenders: A preliminary study. *American Journal of Psychiatry, 157*, 130-132.

Randall, J., Henggeler, S. W., Pickrel, S. G. & Brondino, M. J. (1999). Psychiatric comorbidity and the 16-month trajectory of substance-abusing and substance-dependent juvenile offenders. *Journal of the American Academy of Child and Adolescent Psychiatry, 38*, 1118–1124.

Riggs, P. D., Mikulich, S. K., Whitmore, E. A. & Crowley, T. J. (1999). Relationship of ADHD, depression, and non-tobacco substance use disorders to nicotine dependence in substance-dependent delinquents. *Drug and Alcohol Dependence, 54*, 195-205.

Roberts, R. E., Attkisson, C. & Rosenblatt, A. (1998). Prevalence of psychopathology among children and adolescents. *American Journal of Psychiatry, 155*, 715-725.

Rohde, P., Mace, D. E. & Seeley, J. R. (1997). The association of psychiatric disorders with suicide attempts in a juvenile delinquent sample. *Criminal Behavior and Mental Health, 7*, 187-200.

Schwab-Stone, M. E., Shaffer, D., Dulcan, M., Jensen, P. S., Fisher, P., Bird, H. R., Goodman, S. H., Lahey, B. B., Lichtman, J. H., Canino, G., Rubio-Stipec, M. & Rae, D. S. (1996). Criterion validity of the NIMH Diagnostic Interview Schedule for Children Version 2.3 (DISC–2.3). *Journal of the American Academy of Child and Adolescent Psychiatry, 35*, 878-888.

Shaffer, D., Fisher, P., Dulcan, M., Davies, M., Piacentini, J., Schwab-Stone, M. E., Lahey, B. B., Bourdon, K., Jensen, P. S., Bird, H. R., Canino, G. & Regier, D. A. (1996). The NIMH Diagnostic Interview Schedule for Children Version 2.3 (DISC–2.3): Description, acceptability, prevalence rates, and performance in the MECA Study. *Journal of the American Academy of Child and Adolescent Psychiatry, 35*, 865-877.

Shelton, D. (2001). Emotional disorders in young offenders. *Journal of Nursing Scholarship, 33*, 259-263.

Sickmund, M., Sladky, T. J. & Kang, W. (2004). Census of juveniles in residential placement databook. Retrieved August 10, 2004, from the Web: www.ojjdp.ncjrs.org/ojstatbb/cjrp.

Simonoff, E., Pickles, A., Meyer, J. M., Silberg, J. L., Maes, H. H., Loeber, R., Rutter, M., Hewitt, J. K. & Eaves, L. J. (1997). The Virginia Twin Study of Adolescent Behavioral Development: Influences of age, sex, and impairment on rates of disorder. *Archives of General Psychiatry, 54*, 801-808.

Snyder, H. N. & Sickmund, M. (1999). *Juvenile Offenders and Victims: 1999 National Report.* Report. Washington, DC: U.S. Department of Justice, Office of Justice Programs, Office of Juvenile Justice and Delinquency Prevention.

Steiner, H., Garcia, I. G. & Mathews, Z. (1997). Post-traumatic stress disorder in incarcerated juvenile delinquents. *Journal of the American Academy of Child and Adolescent Psychiatry, 36*, 357-365.

Teplin, L. A., Abram, K. M. & McClelland, G. M. (1996). Prevalence of psychiatric disorders among incarcerated women: I. Pretrial jail detainees. *Archives of General Psychiatry, 53*, 505–5 12.

Teplin, L. A., Abram, K. M., McClelland, G. M., Dulcan, M. K. & Mericle, A. A. (2002.)Psychiatric disorders in youth in juvenile detention. *Archives of General Psychiatry, 59*, 1133-1143.

Teplin, L. A., McClelland, G. M., Abram, K. A. & Mileusnic, D. (2005). Early violent death among delinquent youth: A prospective longitudinal study. *Pediatrics, 115*, 1586-1593.

Thompson, L. L., Riggs, P. D., Mikulich, S. K. & Crowley, T. J. (1996). Contribution of ADHD symptoms to substance problems and delinquency in conduct-disordered adolescents. *Journal of Abnormal Child Psychology, 24*, 325-347.

Timmons-Mitchell, J., Brown, C., Schulz, S. C., Webster, S. E., Underwood, L. A. & Semple, W. E. (1997). Comparing the mental health needs of female and male incarcerated juvenile delinquents. *Behavioral Sciences and the Law, 15*, 195–202.

Turner, R. J. & Gil, A. G. (2002). Psychiatric and substance use disorders in South Florida: Racial/ ethnic and gender contrasts in a young adult cohort. *Archives of General Psychiatry, 59*, 43–50.

Ulzen, T. P. M. & Hamilton, H. (1998). The nature and characteristics of psychiatric comorbidity in incarcerated adolescents. *Canadian Journal of Psychiatry, 43*, 57-63.

Wasserman, G. A., Jensen, P., Ko, S. J., Cocozza, J., Trupin, E., Angold, A., Cauffman, E. & Grisso, T. (2003). Mental health assessments in juvenile justice: Report on the Consensus Conference. *Journal of the American Academy of Child and Adolescent Psychiatry, 42*, 751-761.

Wasserman, G. A., McReynolds, L. S., Ko, S. J., Katz, L. M. & Carpenter, J. R. (2005). Gender differences in psychiatric disorders at juvenile probation intake. *American Journal of Public Health, 95*, 131–137.

Wasserman, G. A., McReynolds, L. S., Lucas, C. P., Fisher, P. & Santos, L. (2002). The voice DISC–IV with incarcerated male youths: Prevalence of disorder. *Journal of the American Academy of Child and Adolescent Psychiatry, 41*, 314-321.

Werner, E. E. (1989). High-risk children in young adulthood: A longitudinal study from birth to 32 years. *American Journal of Orthopsychiatry 59*, 72–81.

Whitmore, E. A., Mikulich, S. K., Thompson, L. L., Riggs, P. D., Aarons, G. A. & Crowley, T. J. (1997). Influences on adolescent substance dependence. *Drug and Alcohol Dependence 47*, 87–97.

Zoccolillo, M. (1992). Co-occurrence of conduct disorder and its adult outcomes with depressive and anxiety disorders: A review. *Journal of the American Academy of Child and Adolescent Psychiatry 31*, 547–556.

ACKNOWLEDGMENTS

Linda A. Teplin, Ph.D., is the Owen L. Coon Professor of Psychiatry and Behavioral Sciences and Director, Psycho-Legal Studies Program, Feinberg School of Medicine, Northwestern University, Chicago. Karen M. Abram, Ph.D., is Assistant Professor, Feinberg School of Medicine, Northwestern University. Gary M. McClelland is Research Assistant Professor, Feinberg School of Medicine, Northwestern University. Amy A. Mericle, Ph.D., is Postdoctoral Fellow, School of Medicine, Department of Psychiatry, University of California, San Francisco. Mina K. Dulcan, Ph.D., is Professor of Psychiatry and Behavioral Sciences and Pediatrics, Fein-berg School of Medicine, Northwestern University, and Head of Child and Adolescent Psychiatry, Children's Memorial Hospital. Jason J. Washburn, Ph.D., is Assistant Professor, Feinberg School of Medicine, Northwestern University.

This Bulletin was prepared under grant number 1999.JE.FX.1001 from the Office of Juvenile Justice and Delinquency Prevention, U.S. Department of Justice.

Points of view or opinions expressed in this document are those of the authors and do not necessarily represent the official position or policies of OJJDP or the U.S. Department of Justice.

The Office of Juvenile Justice and Delinquency Prevention is a component of the Office of Justice Programs, which also includes the Bureau of Justice Assistance, the Bureau of Justice Statistics, the National Institute of Justice, and the Office for Victims of Crime.

End Notes

[1] Relevant analyses regarding major mental disorders are available from authors.

[2] Although not included in table 2, combined prevalence rates of major depressive episode and dysthymia were 17 percent for males and 24 percent for females.

CHAPTER SOURCES

The following chapters have been previously published:

Chapter 1 – This is an edited, excerpted and augmented edition of a United States Department of Justice, Office of Justice Programs, Office of Juvenile Justice and Delinquency Prevention, Juvenile Justice Bulletin, dated February 2009.

Chapter 2 – This is an edited, excerpted and augmented edition of a United States Department of Justice, Office of Justice Programs, Office of Juvenile Justice and Delinquency Prevention Bulletin, dated November 2008.

Chapter 3 – This is an edited, excerpted and augmented edition of a United States Department of Justice, Office of Justice Programs, Office of Juvenile Justice and Delinquency Prevention, Juvenile Justice Bulletin, dated February 2008.

Chapter 4 - This is an edited, excerpted and augmented edition of a United States Department of Justice, Office of Justice Programs, Office of Juvenile Justice and Delinquency Prevention, Juvenile Justice Bulletin, dated April 2009.

Chapter 5 – This is an edited, excerpted and augmented edition of a United States Congressional Research Service publication, Report Order Code RL33947, dated April 14, 2009.

Chapter 6 - This is an edited, excerpted and augmented edition of a United States Department of Justice, Office of Justice Programs, Office of Juvenile Justice and Delinquency Prevention, Juvenile Justice Bulletin, dated August 2008.

Chapter 7 - This is an edited, excerpted and augmented edition of a United States Department of Justice, Office of Justice Programs, Office of Juvenile

Justice and Delinquency Prevention, Juvenile Justice Bulletin, dated April 2006.

INDEX

A

accomplices, 139
accountability, x, 88, 89, 95, 105, 106, 109, 121, 123, 127
accounting, 7, 53
acute, 183
adaptation, 185
ADHD, 159, 161, 162, 165, 176, 181, 189, 190
adjudication, 6, 34, 53, 100, 138, 155
administration, 94, 98, 99, 105, 115
administrative, 98, 102, 108, 128
administrators, 3, 26, 184
adolescence, 153, 154, 182, 185
adolescents, 15, 30, 39, 136, 145, 149, 150, 153, 185, 186, 187, 188, 189, 190
adulthood, 140, 191
adults, xi, 59, 60, 61, 64, 65, 75, 81, 88, 89, 91, 92, 93, 95, 101, 110, 117, 119, 122, 124, 129, 132, 134, 135, 136, 141, 144, 145, 151, 152, 153, 188
advocacy, 5, 26, 107, 119, 151
affective disorder, 15, 158, 161, 162, 168, 172, 174, 177, 179
African American, ix, 6, 15, 38, 40, 43, 44, 45, 46, 47, 48, 49, 160, 166, 167, 170, 172, 173, 174, 175, 178
after-school, 99
aggression, 188
aid, 23, 90, 127, 134, 146
aiding, 102
air, 13
alcohol, viii, ix, 4, 10, 14, 34, 37, 38, 39, 40, 41, 42, 43, 44, 45, 46, 47, 48, 49, 102, 103, 150, 158, 159, 161, 162, 165, 166, 167, 170, 180, 182
alcohol abuse, 102, 166
alcohol dependence, 166
alcohol use, viii, ix, 37, 38, 43, 165, 167, 170
alpha, 173, 175, 178, 180
alternative, 93, 112, 119, 147
alternatives, 99, 117, 119, 122
American Psychiatric Association, 29, 34, 161, 184
anger, 16, 141
anxiety, 16, 159, 161, 162, 166, 168, 172, 174, 176, 177, 179, 180, 191
anxiety disorder, 159, 161, 162, 166, 168, 172, 174, 176, 177, 179, 180, 191
apathy, 32
appellate review, 93
appendix, 114, 118
application, 102
applied research, 30
appropriations, xi, 88, 98, 103, 105, 111, 127
armed robbery, 34, 134
arrest, ix, x, 34, 57, 58, 59, 60, 61, 64, 67, 68, 69, 70, 71, 72, 73, 74, 75, 76, 77, 78, 79, 80, 81, 83, 84, 132, 133, 136, 137, 138, 139, 141, 142, 153, 181

arson, 34, 67, 73, 133
assault, x, 34, 42, 58, 59, 62, 65, 66, 70, 71, 73, 74, 75, 76, 77, 78, 79, 122, 127, 133, 136, 138, 142
assaults, 62, 64, 146
assessment, 6, 16, 17, 22, 28, 30, 149, 150, 153, 186
assignment, 4, 22
asthma, 11
attitudes, 84, 151
Attorney General, 92, 93, 96, 105, 107, 108, 115
auditory hallucinations, 161
authority, 34, 90, 92, 96, 99, 114, 115, 118, 119, 145
auto theft, 34
autopsy, 24
availability, 187
awareness, 93, 134, 135

B

back, 28, 92, 132
background information, 89
bail, xii, 130
barriers, 100, 188
base rate, 158, 167
base rates, 158, 167
battery, 34
benchmarks, 110
benefits, 137, 147
Best Practice, 187
bias, 122, 152
birth, vii, 1, 83, 188, 191
bonding, 16, 30
boot camps, 6, 123
borderline, 15
borderline personality disorder, 15
boys, 16
brain, 149
burglary, 34, 66, 67, 71, 73, 133, 136, 137, 142, 143
Burglary, 62, 65, 71, 75, 76

C

campaigns, 135, 150
capital punishment, 150
cardiopulmonary, 4, 23, 24
cardiopulmonary resuscitation (CPR), 24
care model, 150
caretaker, 168, 173, 175, 178, 180
cell, 170
census, 6, 31, 32, 34, 68, 70, 72, 74, 77, 80, 81, 189, 190
Census Bureau, 68, 70, 72, 74, 77, 80, 81
Centers for Disease Control, 2
certification, xi, 19, 24, 129
chain of command, 24
child abuse, 100, 101, 113, 121, 122, 128
child protective services, 124
child welfare, 92, 124, 184
childhood, 30, 185
children, 62, 63, 83, 91, 92, 93, 96, 182, 185, 186, 187, 188, 189, 191
citizens, 84, 91
civil rights, 145
cocaine, viii, 10, 37, 180
cohort, 188, 190
communication, 22, 26, 155
communities, 59, 101, 113, 184
community, 5, 6, 7, 12, 15, 91, 92, 99, 106, 107, 111, 115, 117, 119, 121, 122, 125, 137, 138, 139, 142, 143, 145, 148, 160, 176, 184
community service, 92, 121, 122
comorbidity, 158, 162, 169, 176, 181, 182, 184, 185, 189, 190
comparative advantage, 150
compensation, 115
competency, 149
compilation, ix, 57
compliance, 21, 100, 104, 119, 121, 123, 124
components, x, 4, 19, 21, 22, 26, 84, 87, 95, 98, 99, 114
composition, 76, 121, 158, 181
concentration, 118
conception, x, xi, 87, 88

conduct disorder, 10, 145, 159, 162, 165, 166, 167, 168, 172, 173, 174, 177, 179, 180, 186, 191
confidence, 50
confidentiality, 90
confinement, vii, viii, 1, 2, 3, 4, 5, 6, 7, 8, 10, 14, 15, 16, 17, 19, 22, 27, 28, 34, 101, 110, 120, 121, 123
consensus, 94, 95
consolidation, 101, 139
constraints, 98, 181
construction, 153
consulting, 33
contracts, 117
control, 90, 91, 94, 103, 110, 116, 126, 127, 134, 138
controlled substance, 34
conviction, 136, 145
correlation, 128
costs, 102, 107, 108, 128, 135
counsel, 93
counseling, 99, 111, 122, 123, 124, 146
counterfeiting, 34, 62
courts, vii, ix, x, xi, 6, 51, 52, 53, 87, 89, 92, 93, 100, 106, 129, 130, 131, 133, 137, 144, 149, 153
CPR, 19, 23, 24
credentials, 17
crime, ix, 29, 58, 59, 60, 64, 67, 69, 76, 84, 90, 91, 92, 94, 101, 102, 107, 126, 127, 131, 133, 134, 135, 136, 137, 141, 142, 149, 151, 152
crimes, ix, x, xii, 8, 57, 58, 59, 60, 61, 64, 65, 67, 69, 76, 87, 88, 89, 90, 102, 105, 108, 117, 118, 119, 127, 130, 131, 134, 135, 136, 141, 145, 147, 182
criminal activity, 153
criminal behavior, 135, 146
criminal gangs, 102
criminal justice, 39, 67, 90, 91, 92, 117, 133, 134, 144, 148, 149
criminal justice system, 67, 90, 91, 92, 117, 133, 134, 144, 146, 148, 149
criminality, 149, 186
criminals, 147
critical period, 181
CRS, 127, 128
culture, 147
cynicism, 146

D

danger, 160
data analysis, 6
data collection, 32, 160
death, 2, 5, 8, 10, 14, 16, 17, 18, 19, 24, 25, 26, 27, 60, 150, 182, 188, 190
death penalty, 150
deaths, 5, 8, 11, 12, 25, 27, 28
debates, 108
decision making, 96, 115, 153
decisions, 38, 131, 138, 150, 151
defendants, 92
deficiency, 2
deficit, 10, 159, 165, 168, 169, 171, 172, 173, 175, 177, 178, 179, 180
definition, 6, 17, 67, 81, 91
deinstitutionalization, 117
delinquency, ix, 51, 53, 59, 90, 91, 93, 97, 100, 103, 104, 110, 113, 115, 116, 117, 123, 124, 128, 136, 150, 153, 154, 181, 190
delinquent adolescents, 29
delinquent behavior, 113, 117, 162
delinquents, x, 30, 87, 89, 93, 117, 186, 188, 189, 190
delivery, 112, 117
delusions, 161
demographic characteristics, vii, viii, 2, 3
demographics, 142
denial, 22
Department of Agriculture, 113
Department of Education, 113
Department of Health and Human Services, vii, 1, 29, 32, 113, 187
Department of Justice (DOJ), 30, 31, 32, 33, 34, 50, 85, 90, 95, 101, 103, 105, 114, 123, 125, 126, 127, 153, 155, 187, 190, 192, 193
depression, 10, 16, 30, 176, 186, 188, 189

depressive disorder, 165, 187
Depressive disorders, 176
detainees, xii, 157, 158, 159, 160, 173, 175, 176, 180, 181, 184, 186, 190
deterrence, 130, 132, 136, 137, 152, 153, 154
Diagnostic and Statistical Manual of Mental Disorders, 29, 161, 165, 184
diagnostic criteria, 159, 162, 173
dichotomy, 150
disabilities, 100, 102
discipline, 123
discretionary, 103, 107, 117, 119, 120, 121, 131
disorder, 10, 159, 161, 162, 165, 166, 167, 168, 169, 170, 171, 172, 173, 174, 175, 177, 178, 179, 180, 182, 183, 185, 188, 189, 190, 191
disposition, 6, 53, 141
disproportionate growth, 75
distress, 30
distribution, viii, 2, 3, 27, 34, 103
dominance, 94
draft, 32, 33
drinking, viii, ix, 37, 38, 39, 40, 41, 43, 44, 45, 46, 47, 49, 150
drug abuse, 73, 75, 79, 100, 112
drug dealing, 136
drug offense, ix, xi, 7, 34, 51, 52, 53, 54, 130, 140, 142, 144
drug use, 29, 49, 106, 167, 168, 173, 175, 178, 180
drugs, viii, ix, 14, 37, 38, 39, 40, 41, 42, 44, 45, 46, 47, 48, 49, 122, 136, 161, 182
DSM, 29, 34, 161, 165, 168, 172, 174, 177, 179, 181, 184, 185, 188
DSM-IV, 29
due process, 92
duplication, 113
duration, 161
duties, 185
dysthymia, 159, 176, 187, 192

E

economic activity, 84
education, 89, 93, 94, 96, 113, 115, 126
educational programs, 103, 124
educational services, 146
embezzlement, 34, 63
emotional, 10, 12, 29, 182, 185, 186, 187
emotional abuse, 10, 12
emotional disorder, 29, 182, 185, 186
employees, 97, 111, 121
employment, 119, 145
environment, 6, 12, 13, 100, 186
ethnic groups, 45, 160
ethnicity, vii, viii, 37, 38, 39, 43, 44, 46, 48, 55, 76, 142, 158, 159, 160, 166, 170, 178, 181, 182, 188
evidence-based practices, 106
evolution, 89
exclusion, 67
execution, 147
exercise, 96, 115
expenditures, 99, 108
eye, 149, 151

F

failure, 14, 27, 34
fairness, 145
false positive, 161
familial, 188
family, 10, 16, 22, 27, 63, 122, 139, 144, 182
family environment, 182
family members, 22
family support, 144
farms, viii, 2, 3, 6
fax, 33, 155
FBI, ix, 57, 58, 59, 60, 65, 67, 68, 70, 72, 74, 77, 80, 81, 84
fear, 141
fears, ix, 57
Federal Bureau of Investigation, 61, 64, 66, 84

federal government, x, 87, 88, 89, 90, 92, 94, 95, 96, 97, 105, 109, 110, 112, 113, 114, 115, 116
federal law, 92, 93
feedback, 33, 155
feelings, 146
feet, 62
felony, 131, 133, 139, 145, 150, 151
females, x, 16, 43, 44, 45, 47, 49, 53, 58, 64, 73, 74, 75, 78, 159, 160, 162, 166, 167, 168, 169, 170, 171, 180, 181, 182, 183, 184, 192
financial aid, 90
fines, 52
firearm, 62
first aid, 23
first-time, 136, 142, 148
flexibility, 107, 127
flow, 59
fluctuations, 40
focusing, 49, 109, 130, 132
forgery, 34
freedom, 175, 178, 180
funds, 50, 85, 89, 94, 97, 98, 99, 107, 108, 111, 117
futures, 141

G

gangs, 106, 120, 121, 122
gender, vii, viii, 34, 37, 38, 39, 44, 46, 49, 74, 99, 122, 137, 138, 139, 142, 152, 158, 159, 160, 162, 170, 181, 182, 190
gender differences, 49
generalized anxiety disorder, 167
girls, 16
goals, 99, 130
government expenditure, 108
government policy, 97
grants, 88, 89, 93, 94, 96, 98, 101, 102, 103, 104, 105, 106, 108, 117, 119, 120, 121, 122, 123, 124, 128
grass, viii, 37
groups, x, 40, 41, 42, 45, 58, 59, 61, 74, 77, 79, 133, 143, 160, 167
growth, 67, 69, 75, 79, 90
guardian, 7
guidance, 35
guidelines, 60

H

hallucinations, 161
handling, 96
hands, 62
hanging, 13
harm, 12, 15, 28, 183
health, 17, 22, 103, 128, 158, 183, 184, 185, 191
Health and Human Services, vii, 1, 29, 32, 96, 113, 187
health care, 185, 188
health care professionals, 185
health problems, 183
health services, 24, 99, 100, 102, 112, 123, 158, 183, 184, 187, 188
healthcare, 3, 12, 28
heart disease, vii, 1
heroin, viii, 37
high-risk, 22, 176
high-risk populations, 176
hip, 136
hiring, 105, 106
homeless, 186
homicide, 133, 147
homicide rate, 147
homicide rates, 147
hospitalization, 24
house, 94, 97, 121, 126
household composition, 39
housing, 4, 13, 19, 22, 23, 25, 26, 28
Housing and Urban Development, 96, 115
human, 154, 182
human immunodeficiency virus, 182
human nature, 154
hyperactivity, 10, 159, 165, 168, 169, 171, 172, 173, 175, 177, 178, 179, 180
hypothesis, 151

I

identification, 20, 22, 26, 28
Immigration and Customs Enforcement, 97
impairments, 176, 182
implementation, viii, 2, 96, 99, 107, 110
imprisonment, 141
impulsivity, 16
incarceration, 99, 138, 141, 142, 143, 146, 147, 150, 183
incentive, 124, 128
incidence, 11, 189
independence, 118
indices, 139
ineffectiveness, 110, 147
inefficiency, 94
influenza, vii, 1
information sharing, 106
injustice, 144, 145
inmates, 101, 146
innovation, 117
instability, 16
institutionalization, 93, 117
institutions, x, 15, 87, 91, 95, 114, 117, 120, 121, 141, 146, 147
instruction, 21, 24, 26
instruments, 4, 5, 13, 32, 62, 159, 183
insurance, 188
interactions, 146
Interagency Forum on Child and Family Statistics, 125
internalizing, 176
intervention, 23, 26, 104, 121, 153
interview, 40, 49
interviews, 40, 134, 140, 161
intoxication, 4, 34
investment, 111
irrationality, 149
isolation, 14, 27

J

jails, 101, 118, 119
job skills, 123, 141
joining, 120
judges, 92, 105, 106, 137, 147, 151, 155
judgment, 154
jurisdiction, xi, 12, 13, 67, 84, 98, 99, 107, 108, 118, 126, 129, 132, 133, 137, 138, 142, 143, 151
jurisdictions, 84, 143
jury trial, 91
juvenile crime, ix, xi, 57, 58, 68, 88, 90, 93, 109, 129, 130, 132, 133, 134, 135, 136, 149, 151, 152, 153, 154
juvenile delinquency, x, 87, 90, 92, 94, 95, 96, 97, 99, 100, 101, 102, 103, 104, 112, 113, 114, 115, 116, 117, 118, 119, 124, 126, 127, 128
juvenile delinquents, 30, 93, 186, 190
juvenile detention facilities, 13
Juvenile Justice and Delinquency Prevention Act, x, 87, 88, 90, 95, 114, 120, 128
juvenile victims, 62, 121, 188

K

kidnapping, 34, 133

L

labeling, 144, 154
labor, 39
labor force, 39
language, 95, 100, 110, 111, 112, 118, 120
language barrier, 100
large-scale, 132, 137, 139, 143
law, ix, 17, 34, 39, 57, 59, 60, 61, 64, 65, 66, 67, 68, 75, 78, 81, 84, 94, 112, 126, 133, 134, 136, 137, 153, 154, 155, 187
law enforcement, ix, 57, 59, 60, 61, 64, 65, 67, 81, 84, 94, 126
laws, vii, xi, 63, 76, 88, 90, 91, 92, 93, 107, 109, 118, 129, 130, 131, 132, 133, 134, 135, 143, 145, 148, 149, 151, 152, 154, 155
leadership, 104, 123

learning, 100, 102, 144, 146
learning difficulties, 102
learning disabilities, 100
legal protection, 93, 183
legislation, vii, x, 87, 89, 90, 93, 94, 111, 127, 128
licensing, 5
lifetime, 38
likelihood, 38, 102, 132, 135, 136, 137, 142, 168, 181
limitations, 59, 159, 181
liquor, 34
literacy, 102
litigation, 123
living arrangements, 7
local educational agencies, 122
local government, 3, 89, 93, 94, 99, 103, 104, 105, 106, 107, 108, 111, 116, 117, 123, 126
location, 4, 104, 134, 139
lockups, 101, 118, 119
long period, 67
longitudinal study, 190, 191
low-income, 102
LSD, viii, 37
lung, vii, 1
lung disease, vii, 1

M

machine-readable, 80, 84
Madison, 33
magnetic, iv
Maine, 83
major depression, 188
major depressive disorder, 165, 187
majority leader, 97, 121
males, x, 16, 43, 44, 45, 47, 49, 53, 58, 74, 78, 159, 160, 162, 166, 167, 168, 169, 170, 171, 180, 181, 182, 183, 192
maltreatment, 128
management, 20, 28, 30, 116, 146, 161
mandates, x, 87, 88, 89, 95, 97, 98, 99, 100, 110, 114, 117, 123, 124, 126, 127
mania, 166
manic, 159, 162, 169, 170
manic episode, 159, 169, 170
manslaughter, 34, 62, 65, 127
mask, 23
mass media, 150
measurement, 159
measures, x, 23, 88, 90, 93, 95, 105, 109, 121, 140, 142, 143
media, 133, 150
median, 176
mediation, 121
medication, 10, 161
medications, 183
men, 152
mental disorder, 10, 159, 169, 170, 171, 174, 181, 183, 184, 192
mental health, xii, 4, 13, 17, 22, 24, 26, 29, 30, 99, 100, 102, 103, 106, 110, 112, 123, 128, 138, 157, 158, 175, 183, 184, 185, 186, 187, 188, 190
mental illness, 10, 12, 34, 187
mentoring, 99, 102, 111, 112, 121, 122, 146
mentoring program, 102, 122
meta-analysis, 152
metropolitan area, 142
military, 123
minorities, 101, 110, 160, 179
minority, 58, 101, 110, 120, 121, 123, 127, 141, 184
minors, 96, 97
models, 146, 150
moderators, 30
momentum, 95
money, 117, 127, 128
moratorium, 149
morbidity, 179, 182
mortality, 4, 19, 24, 25, 26, 27, 188
motion, 131
motor vehicle theft, 66, 67, 73
mouth, 23
movement, 14, 90, 105
multidisciplinary, 24, 25
murder, x, 34, 58, 60, 61, 62, 64, 65, 66, 69, 70, 77, 127, 131, 133, 134, 154
myopia, 151

N

narcotic, 34
nation, 160
National Research Council, 183, 188
natural, 143
negative relation, 136
neglect, 10, 100, 101, 122, 182
nicotine, 189
NOS, 165
nurses, 17

O

observations, 39
obsessive-compulsive, 159, 162, 166
obsessive-compulsive disorder, 159, 166
odds ratio, 162, 168, 170
Office for Victims of Crime, 34, 50, 55, 85, 155, 192
Office of Justice Programs, 1, 30, 31, 32, 34, 50, 55, 85, 126, 153, 155, 186, 187, 190, 192, 193
Office of Justice Programs (OJP), 126
Office of Juvenile Justice and Delinquency Prevention (OJJDP), 33, 50, 85, 88, 96, 114, 155
Office of National Drug Control Policy, 97
ownership, 4

P

pain, 141
paints, 146
panic disorder, 162, 166
paradox, 178
parenting, 122
parents, 7, 16, 91
parole, 34
partnership, 122, 128
pathways, 181
patients, 17
PbS, 29
peer, 27
peers, 14, 27, 28, 34
penalty, 136, 150
pendulum, 109
perception, 90, 145
perceptions, 134, 145
periodic, 21
permit, 24, 102, 135, 155
personal communication, 155
personality, 159, 165, 186
personality disorder, 159, 165, 186
philosophy, xi, 88
physical abuse, 10, 12, 14, 34
planning, 94, 97, 116, 126
play, x, 87, 88, 89
pneumonia, vii, 1
police, ix, 57, 67, 91, 107
policymakers, 39
poor, 16, 91, 182
population size, 77
positive correlation, 136
posttraumatic stress, 166
post-traumatic stress, 10
posttraumatic stress disorder, 166
poverty, 102, 182
power, 116
powers, 114
predictors, 152
predisposing factors, 22
pre-existing, 101
pregnancy, 182
preventive, 181
prisons, xi, 130, 141, 143, 146, 147, 148, 149, 150, 151
privacy, 27
private, 3, 4, 5, 6, 16, 93, 99, 103, 104, 115, 116, 117, 120, 121, 122
private sector, 104, 115, 116
probation, 7, 8, 13, 34, 53, 91, 100, 102, 105, 106, 107, 112, 121, 124, 125, 134, 137, 141, 143, 191
probation officers, 91, 102, 105, 106, 112, 125
problem behavior, 38, 42, 182, 183
problem-solving, 30
procedural rule, 91

processing variables, 139
program administration, 94
programming, viii, 2, 6, 12, 13, 19, 26, 28
property, iv, ix, xi, 7, 8, 34, 42, 58, 63, 67, 76, 130, 137, 138, 139, 140, 142, 143, 144
property crimes, ix, 58, 67
proportionality, 151
proposition, 92
prosecutor, 138
prostitution, 34, 63
protection, 12, 91, 93, 143, 160
protective factors, 39, 182
protocol, 14, 25
psychiatric disorder, vii, xii, 10, 157, 158, 159, 173, 175, 179, 180, 182, 184, 186, 187, 189, 190, 191
psychiatric disorders, vii, xii, 10, 157, 158, 159, 173, 175, 179, 180, 182, 184, 186, 187, 189, 190, 191
psychiatric morbidity, 179, 182
psychiatrist, 161
psychiatrists, 17
psychological problems, 29
psychologist, 161
psychopathology, 181, 182, 185, 187, 188, 189
psychosis, 158, 159, 161, 169, 170, 183
psychotic, 10, 161, 162, 166, 167
PTSD, 165, 186
public, vii, viii, xi, 1, 2, 3, 7, 8, 34, 90, 93, 95, 99, 107, 117, 120, 121, 122, 124, 127, 130, 131, 134, 135, 155
public awareness, 93, 134, 135
public health, vii, viii, 1, 2
Public Health Service, 29, 128
public safety, 107, 127
public schools, 155
punishment, x, 10, 87, 89, 91, 93, 109, 133, 134, 135, 136, 150, 151, 152
punitive, xi, 88, 90, 109, 132, 133, 149

Q

quotas, 101, 110, 124

R

race, vii, viii, 4, 34, 37, 38, 39, 43, 44, 46, 48, 53, 55, 81, 137, 138, 139, 158, 159, 160, 166, 170, 178, 181, 182
racial groups, 77, 79
random, 158, 159
range, 42, 83, 92, 96, 114, 115, 122
rape, 34, 62, 63, 65, 69, 70, 76, 127, 133
rearrest, 137, 138, 142, 182
reception, viii, 2, 3, 16, 19, 25, 34
recidivate, 138, 150
recidivism, xii, 110, 130, 131, 132, 136, 137, 138, 139, 140, 142, 143, 144, 145, 146, 147, 148, 149, 150, 151, 152, 154, 157, 158
recidivism rate, 110, 130, 132, 137, 138, 140, 142, 143, 144
reconciliation, 119
recreation, 123
recreational, 103
recurrence, 182
reflection, 93
reforms, xi, 129
regional, 84, 121
regular, 117, 119
regulations, 119
rehabilitate, x, 87, 90, 93, 148
rehabilitation, x, xi, 87, 88, 89, 93, 96, 109, 112, 115, 118, 144, 146
reimbursement, 123
relationship, 27, 30, 100, 109, 113, 136, 145, 151
relationships, 6, 29, 147, 152, 182, 184, 186
reliability, 186
remission, 182
resentment, 144
residential, viii, xii, 2, 3, 5, 6, 14, 16, 19, 25, 34, 141, 157, 190
resources, xii, 12, 24, 105, 112, 118, 128, 157
restitution, 52, 119, 121
resuscitation, 4, 24
rewards, 135
risk behaviors, 182

risk factors, 5, 15, 182, 188
risks, 135, 155, 182
robberies, 64
robbery, 34, 59, 65, 66, 69, 70, 74, 77, 78, 127, 133, 134, 136, 137, 138, 142
rods, 13
runaway, 116, 176, 186
rural, 99, 101, 139
rural areas, 99

S

safety, 3, 12, 106, 148
sample, viii, 37, 40, 137, 138, 139, 142, 143, 158, 159, 160, 175, 176, 189
sampling, 160
sanctions, x, 53, 88, 95, 105, 106, 107, 109, 118, 121, 127, 130, 132, 133, 134, 136, 141, 144, 147, 148, 150, 151, 154, 155
scholarship, 102
school, viii, 2, 3, 6, 7, 8, 9, 16, 19, 21, 24, 25, 34, 42, 99, 101, 102, 106, 111, 117, 119, 122, 139, 150, 155
Secretary of Agriculture, 128
Secretary of Defense, 128
security, 3, 136, 145
segregation, 14
self, 10, 15, 29
self-concept, 145
self-destructive behavior, 23
self-incrimination, 93
self-mutilation, 10
self-report, viii, 5, 15, 16, 37, 38, 136, 161, 168, 173, 175, 178, 180, 181
self-report data, 38
self-reports, viii, 37
sentences, xii, 90, 130, 134, 135, 141, 142, 144, 149, 155
sentencing, xi, 90, 118, 129, 130, 132, 136, 141, 144, 149, 150, 151, 152, 153, 155
separation, 91, 159, 162, 166
series, 59, 90, 93, 114, 117, 118, 124, 132, 133, 155
severity, 133, 135, 136, 137, 142, 145, 154
sex, 4, 34, 46, 48, 185, 190
sexual abuse, 4, 10, 12, 16, 146, 182
sexual activity, 182
sexual assault, 34, 122
shape, x, 87
shares, 142
sharing, 106
short period, 6, 23
short-term, 6, 12, 135, 137
signs, 22
skewness, 152
skills, 104, 123, 141
skills training, 104
SMA, 32
social responsibility, 122
social work, 17
social workers, 17
socialization, 152
socioeconomic, 137
Speaker of the House, 97, 121
Special Action Office for Drug Abuse Prevention, 115
spectrum, 109
stability, 67
stages, 141
standards, 17, 19, 20, 22, 25, 26, 35, 101, 110, 124
statistics, 59, 60, 67, 71, 73, 116
statutes, xi, 129, 131
statutory, 67, 131
stigmatization, 144
strategies, xii, 96, 104, 157, 158
streams, 90, 112
stress, 10, 24, 166, 185, 190
stroke, vii, 1
students, 117
subgroups, 158, 159, 167
subsidy, 93, 104
substance abuse, 4, 10, 12, 103, 106, 110, 122, 123, 166, 182, 183, 184, 185, 188
suffering, 10
suicidal, 4, 10, 12, 15, 16, 20, 22, 23, 25, 30, 31, 182
suicidal behavior, 4, 10, 12, 15, 16, 22, 30, 31
suicidal ideation, 10, 15, 16, 22, 23

suicide attempts, 15, 16, 189
suicide rate, vii, 1
summer, 153
supervision, 12, 23, 26, 52, 91, 92, 121, 123
supply, 116
support services, 102
Supreme Court, 93, 126
Surgeon General, vii, 1, 29, 32, 128
survival, 147
symptom, 161
symptoms, 22, 161, 162, 168, 170, 173, 175, 176, 178, 180, 181, 190

T

teaching, 146
technical assistance, 90, 102, 120
teenagers, vii, 1
television, 13, 23, 25
tension, 109
term plans, 96
territory, 98
testimony, 29
theft, 34, 42, 62, 63, 66, 67, 71, 73, 75, 76, 136
thinking, 136
threat, 10, 14, 27, 34, 148
threatening, 23
time periods, 133
timing, 185
tobacco, 189
traffic, 34, 63
training programs, 26, 99, 111
trajectory, 189
transition, 102
translation, 185
trauma, 32
treatment programs, 100, 102, 119, 120, 124
trial, xi, xii, 91, 92, 127, 129, 130, 149
tribal, 105
tribes, 126
truancy, 34, 126
tutoring, 123

U

UCR, ix, 57, 59, 67
uncertainty, 27
urban areas, 101

V

vacation, 84
validity, 143, 189
vandalism, 34, 102
variables, 133, 137, 138, 139, 142, 182
variance, 8
variation, 39
verbal abuse, 10, 14
violence, xi, 88, 101, 102, 106, 109, 110, 113, 122, 128, 147, 152, 188
violent behavior, 128
violent crime, ix, 57, 58, 64, 65, 67, 69, 76, 90, 97, 108, 132, 133, 136, 147, 182
violent crimes, ix, 58, 64, 65, 69, 76, 90, 108, 182
violent offenders, 140, 149
virus, 182
voice, 191
voluntary organizations, 115
vulnerability, 181, 182

W

waking, 12, 14, 28
water, 105
weapons, xii, 59, 62, 66, 78, 130, 139
welfare, 67, 91, 92, 124, 184
whites, 43, 78, 79, 160, 166, 167, 170, 179
witnesses, 93
women, 190

Y

young adults, 141, 188